Training the Counsell

These are exciting times for counsellor training. There has been a dramatic increase in courses in Britain and throughout the world, but until now there has been no comprehensive book available on all the issues involved. *Training the Counsellor*, based on a decade of practice and research in counselling training, provides a sound theoretical framework and a wealth of shared experience which will be invaluable to all counsellor trainers.

Mary Connor gives the reader the opportunity to reflect upon live issues in counsellor training, beginning with a personal perspective on developments over the last thirty years and on the transitions which counsellors have to make when they become trainers. The focal point of the book is an integrative four-stage model for training competent and reflective counsellors. The four stages are: the development of attitudes and values; knowledge and skills; client work and supervision; reflection and evaluation. The author explores the training relationship from both trainer and trainee perspectives and she examines the role of the trainer as facilitator, educator and assessor. She also discusses ethical issues and professional development.

Training the Counsellor is above all a resource book which the reader can consult on topics ranging from course design, through to ideas about assessment, group dynamics and ethical issues. Together with its companion volume *Supervising the Counsellor*, it will be essential reading for counsellor trainers and for people involved in training other helping professionals.

Mary Connor is Director of the Counselling and Consultancy Unit, University College of Ripon and York St John.

Training the Counsellor

An integrative model

Mary Connor

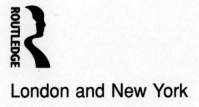

London and New York

First published 1994
by Routledge
11 New Fetter Lane, London EC4P 4EE

Simultaneously published in the USA and Canada
by Routledge
29 West 35th Street, New York, NY 10001

© 1994 Mary Connor

Typeset in Times by
Florencetype Limited, Stoodleigh, Devon
Printed and bound in Great Britain by
Mackays of Chatham PLC, Chatham, Kent

British Library Cataloguing in Publication Data
A catalogue record for this book is available from the British Library.

Library of Congress Cataloging in Publication Data
A catalog record for this book has been requested.

ISBN 0-415-10218-9 (hbk)
ISBN 0-415-10219-7 (pbk)

To my mother, father and brother.
In memory of their wisdom.

Contents

Illustrations

Preface

My intention in writing this book has been to share my experience of a decade of counselling training and to provide a resource for counsellor trainers. I hope that you, the reader, will feel that it is the sort of book to which you can return whenever the need arises – whether it be for help in course design; for guidance when dealing with a difficult situation with a trainee; to reflect upon an ethical issue; to get ideas about assessment; or to read some of the research findings about counsellor training.

The book combines theory and practice and the focal point is the model for training competent and reflective counsellors. This is a model which has evolved from my own training experiences, and from my research into counselling training. I have included trainee as well as trainer perspectives and I have used extracts from learning journals where appropriate. The examples are mostly based upon real training experiences.

Chapters vary in length and weight. They can be thought of in pairs. The first two chapters are fairly light. Chapter One sets the scene with personal reflections on developments in counselling training during the past thirty years. Chapter Two focuses on the transition which is experienced by counsellors who become trainers. Experiences of trainers from different theoretical orientations are included.

The next two chapters are rather more heavy. A model for training competent and reflective counsellors is presented in Chapter Three and in Chapter Four the model is discussed in practice, with reference to one counselling diploma course. This model is the result of personal involvement in counsellor training and examining, at a university college, at colleges and universities throughout Britain in the capacity of external examiner and consultant, and from lecture tours in the Far East. The model is integrative and cyclical and it is based upon an approach to training which emphasises intentionality as a basis for professional development. Chapter Four is full of practical information. The course which is discussed in this chapter is the Advanced Diploma in Counselling at the University College of Ripon and York St John. The core theoretical model for that course is the Skilled Helper Model (Egan 1993).

The next two chapters explore the training relationship and I hope that the reader will find that these give much food for thought. The dynamics of the training relationship are discussed in Chapter Five and much of this chapter is informed by psychodynamic theory and practice. Group dynamics and group process are considered. This chapter gives several examples of issues from both trainer and trainee perspectives. Chapter Six moves on to look at the trainer as a facilitator and two guiding principles are put forward in relation to the empowerment of trainees and in relation to the development of learning opportunities.

Chapters Seven and Eight are more theoretical and address the roles of the trainer as educator and as assessor. Chapter Seven includes theories of learning, learning styles, personality and motivation of the learner, and relevant research into aspects of counselling training. Chapter Eight addresses issues concerned with validity and reliability in assessment as well as looking at practical examples of self and peer assessment, and of the assessment of attitudes, knowledge, skills and competence.

In the final two chapters of the book the focus is upon ethical issues and professional development. Chapter Nine is a practical exploration of ethical issues from the standpoint of three ethical values: integrity, impartiality and respect. Guidelines are put forward for the way in which courses may be designed and organised if they are trying to operate from these ethical values. Several practical examples are described showing the complexities of ethical dilemmas in training. The last chapter gives twelve aspects of professional development for consideration by the trainer including training supervision, networking, and collaborative partnerships with other courses.

The book finishes with the experience of one trainee, Joanna Holt. I came into contact with Joanna in my role as external examiner of her counselling course. I am most grateful to Joanna and to her tutor for sharing this learning with us. I have chosen to finish the book with an extract from her learning journal as a reminder that when we engage in counsellor training we are involved in helping to bring about change which can be quite profound.

I have endeavoured to include as many practical examples as possible and to draw from the real experiences of both trainers and trainees. Hilary Cowling and Rod Walsh are two trainees who have been particularly generous in allowing me to use their learning journals and supervised practice files from the two-year Advanced Diploma course at York. Both were trainees with an outstanding ability to be honestly self-reflective and it was for this reason that I asked if they would be prepared to share their learning with you, the reader. Some of the examples in the book are from their experiences and some are from other sources, including the experiences of my colleagues.

This book is being published alongside *Supervising the Counsellor* by Steve Page and Val Wosket. The two books complement one another and the reader will find useful accompanying material in the other book, which has also been developed from work in the Counselling and Consultancy Unit at York.

Mary Connor

Acknowledgements

I would like to thank all those who have helped me to write this book. Professor Gordon McGregor and Tony Bolger were instrumental in getting me started. Professor Gerard Egan has been most generous in sharing his ideas and he has had a profound influence upon my work. John Bennett has been my colleague for several years and I have learned a tremendous amount from him. I gained much from my friends Michael Wash and Graham Dexter when we worked together on an earlier publication. For the past ten years at the York Summer Schools I have worked closely with Jay Adams, Val Davies, Tony Ford, Justin Price and Graham Higgins, and I have learned something different from each of them.

Alan Dunnett, Val Wosket and Steve Page from the Counselling and Consultancy Unit have contributed most generously with knowledge, experience, honest feedback and much support. Other colleagues who have helped are Christine Kennett, Chris Marshall and Jane Wilson. Liana Warbrick unstintingly helped with word processing and Sandi Harja and Pete Smith came to the rescue when there was the threat of computer failure. Judy Donovan shared her expertise about groups. Steve Reilly advised on psychodynamic perspectives. John Young read drafts with the eye of an experienced proofreader and was a mainstay throughout. Marian Orchard gave the support of a real friend and helped with the bibliography. Helen Jones counselled me against inertia and procrastination. Friends and colleagues who ferreted out pertinent references include Christine Connolly, John Bushell, Sheila Cross, David McAndrew and Tamsin Prout.

This book would be diminished if it were not for the trainee perspective and I am indebted to Hilary Cowling, Joanna Holt and Rod Walsh for so generously providing access to learning journals and supervised practice files so that they could be mined for illustrative material. I would also like to thank Andy Betts and Julian Allisstone for their contributions, and the staff of the Exeter University counselling courses for their collaboration. To all those trainers and trainees with whom I have worked, I thank you for what you have enabled me to learn.

My family has given me both the support and the space that I needed in order to complete the book. I offer special thanks to Tina, and to Polly, Terry, Roz, Pat, Rosaleen, John, Nuala and Geoffrey. Finally, I thank two friends, Chris and Phil, who have shared for many years my struggles and celebrations as a counsellor trainer.

The British Association for Counselling has kindly given permission for extracts from their Codes of Ethics and Practice to be quoted. These Codes change from time to time and readers are advised to refer to the Association in order to keep themselves informed of such changes.

Chapter 1

Developments in counselling training
A personal perspective

This chapter begins with my own training as a counsellor in 1969 and traces counselling developments in Britain over the past thirty years. In the early 1970s the first batch of trained counsellors were taking up posts as trainers and they searched for useful models. These initially came from the United States, and the influence of Rogers, Carkhuff, Egan, Gilmore, Kagan and Ivey is highlighted. In the mid-1980s a significant impact came from the British Association for Counselling when it set up the BAC Course Recognition Group and in 1988 produced a scheme for the recognition of counsellor training courses. This raised issues such as eclecticism or integration, supervision, standardisation, and training for trainers, and these are discussed against the backcloth of current professional and educational developments. This leads to the conclusion that counselling training will come of age when there are properly recognised courses for counsellor trainers world-wide.

These are exciting times. Counselling training is in its infancy and the infant is lively and energetic, exploring new territory, getting into scrapes and growing so fast it is hard to keep up. The demand for new counselling courses is increasing daily in every corner of our society.

THE BEGINNINGS

It seems a far cry from the year of 1969, when I was seconded from my job as a geography teacher to do a one-year full-time advanced diploma in counselling at Keele University. The first diploma courses in Britain were located in universities: Keele and Reading, then Birmingham and Exeter. They began in the mid-1960s. As they were based in universities they had to have a strong academic flavour, and people like myself were able to use that opportunity to move on to a Masters degree if successful. At that time the emphasis in training was on the client-centred approach, with Rogers to the fore. It was quite a shock to the large number of teachers and educators who populated my course because we had expected something much more structured and directive. I well remember going back to my school only to receive horrified looks from the rest of the staff when I tried to explain what was meant by being non-judgemental. I had to lie low with my ideas for a good few years until the culture was ready to accept them.

The British training scene was heavily influenced by visiting American professors as well as by American training films. In 1969 I was introduced not only to Carl Rogers on film, but also to Fritz Perls and Albert Ellis as they each counselled the famous 'Gloria'. We learned about theories mainly from books, lectures and discussions. Our lecturers had not been counsellors themselves, but came from the fields of education, psychology, social work and careers guidance.

We were very fortunate to have access to video equipment and an interviewing room with a one-way screen. I remember a few sessions where one person would counsel and the whole group would observe through the one-way screen. There was an emphasis on the use of tests in counselling to aid assessment and to 'diagnose' the problem, and when I finished the course and became a school counsellor I remember requisitioning a whole battery of tests including Cattell's 16PF, Eysenck's Junior Personality Inventory, the Minnesota Counseling Inventory, the Rothwell Miller Interest Blank and Stott's Social Adjustment Guide. These would not only be used with individuals who came for counselling, but also with a whole cohort of pupils to assess where there might be developmental needs. It was as if the profession of counselling had to establish itself by using tried and tested forms of assessment, emulating the psychologists who had already achieved respectability.

The notion of the self-development of the counsellor was being grasped and I well remember the T-group where we sat for an hour each week with a lecturer and wondered what on earth we were doing there. We each had a counselling placement too, for one term of the course. Above all we had plenty of essays, written examinations and a dissertation to complete. No one seemed to have heard about supervision at that stage and I don't remember ever doing any structured exercises to practise counselling approaches. Strange as it may seem now, the word 'skill' was not in the vocabulary at that time. Carkhuff's work on Rogers' core conditions was only just percolating through in Britain at this stage and so we knew about congruence, respect and empathy but we did not know much about the specifics of communicating these qualities. We knew that the research showed that these core conditions needed to be experienced by the client in order to be therapeutic, but we weren't introduced to the mechanics of it all. Ideas about experiential learning had not really taken on in universities and so almost every session was a lecture, where we took copious notes, followed by discussion. Occasionally there would be student-led seminars, but very little in the way of active workshops. So in 1969 counselling training was still quite formal and yet I had a wonderful year at Keele because the course staff (Jim Gill, Tony Bolger, Peter Daws and Una Maguire) were really committed to the development of counselling, and to us. I had a sound grounding in counselling theory, I was given some excellent training in research methodology, some useful frameworks for doing case-studies, plenty of practice in the administration of tests and an opportunity to counsel. The rest came later.

Meanwhile, there was another kind of training being offered through helping agencies and voluntary organisations. Such training courses were either heavily influenced by the psychoanalytic tradition or, at the other extreme, were keen to disclaim the notion of counselling in favour of terms such as guidance, helping or befriending. In areas such as social work, health and education, the behavioural approach was often favoured because it promised quick results.

In the late 1960s counsellors who had been trained on the one-year full-time or two-year part-time diploma courses were now emerging from the universities and were having to make the case for employment as counsellors. Arguments had to be put forward in terms of cost effectiveness as well as in terms of therapeutic effectiveness. There was much suspicion around. Halmos was a sociologist who questioned what he referred to as 'the faith' of the counsellor. He asserted that counsellors did not have a clear idea about where they were coming from. At a later date he says:

> The counsellor's influence on his society is in a process of rapid growth. . . . This is what mainly explains my sociological interest in the contemporary counselling philosophy. In studying this philosophy one observes that the counsellor is reticent about his

first principles. He is wont to deny that he asserts anything non-deterministic and non-mechanical about the nature of his help or indeed that he asserts these qualities about the nature of man. As a rule, he wants us to believe that a psychological theory is all that is needed to explain, account for, and justify his practice.

(Halmos 1982: 49–50)

Counselling was also receiving criticism because it was seen to be a means of social control. Cicourel and Kitsuse (1963) pinpointed the dangers in a study of some American high schools where it was evident that counsellors were trying to fit pupils into the system rather than helping them to determine their own goals.

COUNSELLORS BECOME TRAINERS

During the 1970s the counsellors who were trained on the first courses were growing in number and strength and Thorne writes about their impact on counselling training:

Many of the students from these pioneering courses subsequently gained posts of influence, particularly in educational institutions, and it was not long before many of them found themselves taking a training role in addition to their clinical work. The emergence of the British practitioner/trainer had a significant effect on training provision, for it was now increasingly possible to design courses that drew on the actual experience of practising British counsellors, as well as on the well established tradition from across the Atlantic. Gradually, too, trainers from other disciplines lost their primary role; courses became more clearly focused as they passed into the hands of those who were proud to call themselves counsellors and did not owe their principal allegiance to another profession.

(Thorne 1991: 2)

During the 1970s I noticed that counselling was beginning to be accepted and people were starting to apply the Rogerian principles of congruence, respect and empathy in other forms of helping relationships, such as nursing and teaching. This acceptance of the validity of basic counselling principles, and the acknowledgement that counselling skills could be effective in producing change and development, helped to boost the need for training across a wide field of paraprofessionals as well as amongst the growing body of professional counsellors.

Those of us who were now being asked to start training others had to look around to find the current state of the art. Brigid Proctor talks about how, on returning from work in the USA, she was asked to take over a course at a time when she had not even been a counsellor. She had a social work background and had worked as a probation officer. She was asked to take over a course which she describes as a 'scissors and paste job, with a little bit of everything and no formal counselling theory and practice' (Proctor 1991: 50). Under the leadership of Brigid Proctor, this course became well known for its radical attempts to be trainee-centred in all aspects of course organisation:

> The ideology was one of student-centred co-operative learning. Our ideas and values derived from Carl Rogers, from radical psychiatry and from the principles on which therapeutic communities were based. We believed that counselling students should experience in training the kind of empathy, genuineness and respect for their own personal directions which we wanted them to be offering to clients. We also believed that this necessarily entailed becoming purposeful and confident in working with others. The learning community would be possible only to the extent that they experienced themselves as 'owning' the responsibility that truly lay with them.
>
> (Proctor 1991: 52)

I envied this course for its ability to take the risks of being truly student-centred. I knew that I would need to work in a more structured way and I have reflected whether my background in education makes me more orthodox in my approach, and whether Brigid Proctor's social work and probation background helped her to be more radical in hers. This leaves me pondering the effect of the professional background upon the counsellor trainer and the fact that the course will reflect that background, for good or ill.

Another early course developed under the leadership of Francesca Inskipp, later joined by Hazel Johns, Peter Cook and Ian Horton. This was based at North East London Polytechnic and there are two characteristics of this course which impacted upon my own development. One was their use of the Egan Skilled Helper Model in training. The other was their carefully thought out procedure for assessing counselling skills, which I later emulated and which was based on the work of Egan, Kagan and Ivey as discussed below.

A MODEL FOR TRAINING: THE SKILLED HELPER

When I was appointed as a full-time lecturer in counselling in 1979 I had run brief skills training courses in the evenings or for a couple of days at a time. Now I was expected to develop one-term or one-year courses. I looked around for some material that would help and I was told of Gerard Egan's work. His first edition of *The Skilled Helper* was published in 1975. The British Association of Counselling (BAC) held a Northern Conference at which Gerard Egan was a visiting speaker. This was the early 1980s and by now there was an awareness that training must involve not only theoretical knowledge about counselling but also training in specific skills – a basis for which trainers found in the Egan model. He also offered a methodology – the triad of counsellor, client and observer which to this day most counselling courses use as a basis for the 'laboratory' or 'counselling practicum' experience as it was then called. Egan has always stated that his model is a model of the counselling process. But, sadly, many people did not hear that, and in Britain it is still often referred to mistakenly as the 'Egan skills model'. Despite this misunderstanding, the Skilled Helper model has been successfully used because it has provided a clear framework for understanding the skills required at different stages of the counselling process. Egan calls it a problem management model.

DEVELOPING COUNSELLING SKILLS: MICROCOUNSELLING AND INTERPERSONAL PROCESS RECALL (IPR)

There were two other important influences from the USA at that time in counselling training. One was the influence of Susan Gilmore (1973) who had looked at the importance of developmental groups being used as a basis for skill development on counselling courses. Some courses still refer to the experiential group element of the course as 'the Gilmore groups'. The other influence was that of Norman Kagan (1967) who developed the method of Interpersonal Process Recall which provided a helpful model for analysing counselling practice sessions. The method involved the counsellor, client and an inquirer debriefing a session together, either as it was actually happening, or immediately afterwards, preferably using a video recording of the session.

Carkhuff (1969) had isolated specific therapeutic skills and later developed useful scales for discriminating levels of effectiveness. Ivey had been trying to use the microteaching model from education and by 1971 Ivey and Authier had produced a large volume with the title *Microcounseling* in which they quoted numerous examples of the effectiveness of this as a training approach. It offered to trainers a systematic framework for skill development. The task appeared straightforward: to teach one skill at a time and so to build up a repertoire of responses. This was an analytic approach to the development of counselling skills and it helped to move counselling training away from the mystique which, to date, had often surrounded therapeutic effectiveness. Trainees would be given a written definition of the skill to be practised; they would see a demonstration of the skill either live or on video tape, and they would videotape their own performance and evaluate it against the written definition and against the modelled performance. This methodology was influenced by Bandura's (1969) work on behavioural principles and by Strong's (1968) work on social influence theory.

Throughout the 1980s and up to the present time the influence of Carkhuff, Kagan, Ivey and Egan can be seen in most counselling training courses where trainers have taken on, and adapted, the basic principles: isolating specific skills for development; having clear definitions of these; demonstrating them; giving the opportunity to practise within small groups where trainees rotate roles of counsellor, client and observer; and using video or audio recordings as a basis of debriefing and analysis. Baker and Daniels (1989) conducted a meta-analysis of eighty-one courses where the microcounselling approach was used. They concluded that it had made a significant impact on counselling training effectiveness, particularly as an effective approach for teaching simple, clearly defined skills. However, two points which emerged from their research need further consideration. The first concerns the problem of maintenance of skill over time and more research is needed to test out how well trainees sustain and develop skills. Research is also needed to identify factors which prevent trainees from being able to maintain proficiency acquired during training. The second point concerns the capacity of the microcounselling approach when training people in 'higher order skills in more complex combinations' (Baker and Daniels 1989: 219). There is a need for evidence about the appropriateness of this approach when training counsellors who need more than the basic skills.

The microcounselling approach lost a certain amount of favour in the late 1980s because it was feared that it would result in a mechanistic approach to counsellor training and might produce responses in trainees which were specific to the practice situation but which did not become integrated into a total style of counselling. The issue is about developing counselling competence and an individual counselling style, rather than just the performance of counselling skills. One way in which trainers have addressed this question is to design a course developmentally. This is what I have done. In the first year of the course trainees are expected to gain a working knowledge of the core theoretical model and to be able to demonstrate the specific skills which are required at each stage of the model (such as paraphrasing, summarising, goal-setting). In the second year of the course, it can be assumed that there is a satisfactory standard of basic skill development and the focus then turns to the higher-order skills (such as immediacy and self-disclosure) and to qualities such as support and resourcefulness.

DISTINGUISHING BETWEEN COUNSELLING AND COUNSELLING SKILLS

In 1985 the British Association for Counselling set up a working group to look at the recognition of counsellor training courses and by 1988 a scheme had been developed and agreed by representatives of the main training sectors: universities, polytechnics, voluntary agencies and private counselling organisations. There had been an ongoing debate in counselling circles about the difference between using counselling skills and counselling. The publication of the BAC Scheme for the Recognition of Counsellor Training Courses was a most significant development for counselling training in Britain. The codes of ethics and practice for counselling (as distinct from those for counselling skills) had helped to focus the minds of those who were designing courses at different levels. But the Course Recognition Scheme left no one in any doubt about where the BAC drew the line between counsellor training and training in counselling skills. Counsellor training needed to be substantial (with a minimum of 400 hours contact time), coherent, intentional and comprehensive.

The BAC scheme for course recognition has had a profound effect on shaping good practice in counsellor training. Those wishing to apply for recognition have to take a good, hard look at their course and trainers usually embark on significant course developments once they know the criteria for recognition. The process becomes a learning experience which does not end with gaining recognition. Built into the recognition system is a requirement that each course becomes partnered with another recognised course to provide ongoing collaboration, monitoring and peer evaluation.

BRINGING IT ALL TOGETHER

The BAC scheme has been successful in allowing for the diversity of different counselling specialisms whilst at the same time providing a common framework for course design and delivery. At the time of writing, recognised courses include approaches as diverse as the psychodynamic, the person-centred, the integrative, and psychosynthesis. What do they have in common? They must all provide detailed information on eight basic elements of training (BAC 1990): admission; self-development; client work; supervision; skills training; theory; professional development; assessment and evaluation. Whatever the course orientation there must be evidence of extended understanding and working knowledge of a core theoretical model.

ECLECTICISM OR INTEGRATION?

During the 1970s and 1980s there was a growing number of courses which preferred to introduce trainees to a variety of counselling approaches in the belief that every client is different and will require an approach which respects individual need. Such courses described their approach as 'eclectic'. Critics referred to 'wild eclecticism' in which trainees would be offered a 'pick and mix' approach, with the danger that clients would then be at the mercy of whatever approach the trainee felt like trying out at the time. However, Herr asserts that we have been mistaken in thinking that there is 'a single answer to a single question: Does counselling work?' A more appropriate question is 'What treatment, by whom, is most effective for this individual with that specific problem and under which set of circumstances?' (Paul 1967 in Herr 1978: 107). Assuming that there are as many answers as there are individual clients, then counsellors will need to have a broad generic training and it could be argued that specialisation is not for basic training, but for those who already possess a basic counselling qualification.

In 1993 the BAC recognition scheme drew up guidelines for counsellor training courses which described themselves as either eclectic or integrative. There was emphasis on being clear about a core theoretical model, whether this be eclectic or integrative. It was made clear that the eclectic or integrative model must inform all aspects of the course including theory, practice, and supervised work with clients. The move is towards coherence, with trainees being clear about the philosophical and theoretical foundations for their practice.

SUPERVISION

One of the most exciting developments in the late 1980s and early 1990s in Britain has been the development of training courses in supervision. At the time of writing there is still only a handful of such courses. New models are being developed (Page and Wosket 1994) and this is an area of counselling where we do not seem to be so far behind our American colleagues. However, although we are seeing a rapid increase in understanding about counselling supervision, there is a great need to develop the field of training supervision.

STANDARDISATION

Certain minimum standards are now laid down with regard to the inclusion in a counselling course of personal development work, counselling practice, work on a core theoretical model, client work and supervision. It is expected that a BAC-recognised course will provide in excess of 400 contact hours with the assumption that many more hours are covered by the trainee in unstructured learning time. Work with clients must be logged and the course must insist on a minimum of 100 hours for this with adequate supervision. A minimum of one hour of supervision for every eight counselling hours is the usual guidance for trainees.

The next step will be to bring standardisation into the assessment of counselling competence. When we use the term competence we are referring to the ability to perform to recognised standards. In Britain there is as yet no clear consensus within the counselling profession about recognised standards of trainee performance, although as can be seen from the discussion above, we are gaining greater clarity about standards in the design of counselling training courses. A lead body has been set up in the UK to draft standards in the sector of 'advice, guidance and counselling' and this development is with a view to setting up a national system of NVQs, or National Vocational Qualifications. Some would argue that performance criteria will be at a basic level of counselling and helping skills and that higher-order counselling skills cannot be measured in this way. However, the thinking that has already gone into clarifying what is meant by certain skills and competencies is a first step towards some sort of standardisation in the field of counselling.

Two other developments will hasten the move towards standardisation in counsellor training. Credit Accumulation Transfer Systems (CATS) are being developed to allow students on further and higher education courses, including counselling certificates, diplomas and Masters degrees, to follow modular programmes which are standardised so that they award credit points at well-defined levels of achievement. It is then possible to know (theoretically) that what has been achieved on one course at a particular level is comparable with that of another course at the same level. This is to allow for greater flexibility of movement between courses. Counsellor trainers have some problems with the idea of modular courses if they do not allow for the developmental learning which is at the heart of counsellor training. Coupled with the development of CATS schemes is the Accreditation of Prior Learning (APL) which can allow greater access on to courses, as well as ease of movement between courses. Once more, for such a system to work effectively there has to be agreement about the standard of competence which is required and which can be achieved.

TRAINING AND ACCREDITATION OF TRAINERS

Counselling training will come of age when there are recognised courses for training trainers. There is, to my knowledge, only one award-bearing course in Britain for counsellor trainers and it is a Masters programme. There is a great need for a professional training and development course for counsellor trainers which would cover the following important areas: education; teaching and learning strategies; experiential training workshops; counselling research; codes of ethics and standards for trainers; dynamics of training relationships; group process and group dynamics;

managing the tutorial; assessment policies procedures and practices; development of training materials; development of resource bases; facilitation skills; training placement; work shadowing; mentoring; training supervision. There is a move towards an accreditation scheme for counsellor trainers and when this is in operation, together with qualifications for counsellor trainers, the infant that is counsellor training will truly come of age.

WORLD PARTNERS

Counselling in Britain has been strongly influenced by developments in the USA. There has also been a steady stream of influence from Australia and New Zealand. There are exciting training developments going on in other less well publicised areas, for example Malaysia where significant work is being carried out in training young people as peer counsellors. We have so much to learn from one another. My hope is that when counselling training comes of age we will find ways of tapping into this knowledge in a world forum of counsellor trainers and that courses will be set up around the world where trainers may learn and share together.

Chapter 2

From counsellor to trainer

The chapter begins by looking at some of the assumptions, values and beliefs which counsellors from different orientations bring to training. Trainers from person-centred, gestalt, psychodynamic and cognitive-behavioural backgrounds speak about their experiences. Differences between being a counsellor and a trainer are highlighted in relation to role, client group, task, process and outcome. The idea of the 'good enough' counsellor trainer is explored alongside such aspects as the trainer as model; the living reality of being professional and being human; the reflective practitioner; and person-centred competence. Finally there is an attempt to define an effective counsellor trainer, together with consideration of some of the pathways to training.

Counsellors are trained. Counsellor trainers often have to teach themselves. Those who train will need to ask: who is my client? Is it the trainee, or the client who will be counselled by that trainee? Is it the trainee or the organisation who hires the trainer? Is it the trainee or the person sponsoring the trainee? The answers to these questions will affect the ways in which training is delivered.

ASSUMPTIONS, VALUES AND BELIEFS

A counsellor who becomes a trainer will bring assumptions and beliefs about people. A person-centred counsellor will be strongly influenced by Rogers' three core conditions for effective helping relationships: genuine concern, warm respect, empathic understanding. A training model which is high on facilitation and empowerment and negotiation and non-directiveness would be appropriate for such a trainer. The advantages of the person-centred approach to training have been outlined in *Freedom to Learn in the 80s* (Rogers 1983). Some of the disadvantages arise from trainers who understand empowerment of the individual as separate from empowerment of the group and the result can vary between anarchy and chaos! Alan speaks as a trainer who embraces a person-centred philosophy of counselling:

Alan

There is probably a healthy tension between the trainer's need to remain person-centred and the organisational and managerial needs relating to the facilitation of a group of counsellors in training. The notion of 'following the flow' is only tenable so long as it is given the respect it deserves alongside other notions: the notion of responsibility to the trainee's client group, of maintaining ethical standards, of extending and broadening as fully as may be the professional competence of the trainees. Just as forest or moorland or meadow needs to be appropriately tended and managed to maximise the growth and development of appropriate flora and fauna, so the training group demands consistent and careful management if the growth is not to be uneven, rank, unprofitable.

A counsellor trainer who is humanistic but grounded in gestalt, or one of the therapies which emphasise catharsis, may wish to train in a way which encourages strong emotional expression. It is likely that this would result in a higher proportion of time being spent in intensive experiential group work and in highly charged one-to-one sessions. The advantages are that trainees will become very self-aware and, one hopes, more confident in allowing the expression of strong feeling in their clients. The disadvantages may be that some trainees are not able to use powerful therapeutic interventions appropriately with one another during training. Christine is a trainer with a gestalt background. She discusses the importance of matching her approach to the developmental needs of her trainees:

Christine

Contact-orientated approaches such as gestalt demand a willingness on the part of the counsellor or therapist to develop and use the self as instrument. Developmentally speaking, this is an advanced skill and one which directly challenges the need for safety and acceptance in the trainee counsellor, as in the client. It is as unrealistic to expect counsellors in the early stages of training to risk the levels of immediacy modelled by the trainer as it is to expect trainees in the client role to lower their defences and explore their innermost feelings, whether in a gently or vigorously cathartic way.

Catharsis, it must be remembered, is not an end in itself, but part of the process (in gestalt terms) of need emergence and completion. Removed from this context, or facilitated in isolation from the particular theory that underpins and supports its use as a therapeutic intervention, it is of little value. The result is that trainees may go through the motions in order to comply, or confuse catharsis with aggression, or engage in forms of histrionic behaviour which are devoid of contact. At the other extreme, trainees may simply go round in circles, unable to recognise the appropriate and timely leverage into facilitation of full and healthy expression of suppressed or retroflected emotion. Both of these outcomes are likely to produce eventual feelings of frustration and inadequacy in the trainee along with experience of being deskilled.

In respect of the above, an important learning for me as a trainer has been to make fewer and fewer assumptions about what is in fact possible to circumscribe and contain in the training situation, in terms of my own expression of self and facilitation of the same in my trainees. The boundary between being real and being appropriate in disclosing here and now feelings and experiences must be respected by trainees and trainers alike. This is particularly true in the early stages when trust and safety are the foremost concerns of trainees. On those occasions where I have overestimated an individual's capacity to engage, or, out of awareness, overstepped this boundary allowing my process to dominate, the resultant learning, whilst powerful, has not been without short-term damaging effects which have necessitated much working through in a rebuilding of the relationship.

The psychodynamic trainer will want to use developmental theory as a basis for understanding people and will focus on the ways in which the past impacts on the present during training. The ability to offer containment during training by being clear about boundaries would be an important feature for this trainer. Steve is a counsellor from a psychodynamic orientation and he talks about how as a trainer he finds himself slipping back into counselling mode:

Steve

The difference between the needs of the trainee and the needs of the client is the area in which as a trainer I feel most tested. When I feel under pressure I am still aware of the temptation to slide into counsellor mode. I believe this stems both from my own desire to retreat to where I feel most sure of my footing and the desire of trainees to have their personal therapeutic needs met.

Those counsellor trainers who favour the cognitive-behavioural, behavioural and rational-emotive approaches will want to train from clear objectives, using contracting, goal-setting, action planning and evaluation as a basis for learning and teaching. Whilst such strategies will produce an intentional learning environment, the disadvantage may be a reluctance to spend sufficient time on feelings. Val shares her experience of the tension which can occur between the cognitive behavioural structuring of the learning situation and the need to take into account the feelings of the trainees:

Val

I have found from experience that most students respond favourably to clear structures and objectives, for example detailed and explicit course programmes, notice of submission dates for assignments well in advance and early indications of what is expected of them in terms of assessed components. As this is the way I prefer to work myself I have to be careful to make allowances for the student who naturally operates in a less structured, organised and cognitive manner. I recall one student who characteristically went through a process of acute anxiety and self-doubt, followed by a period of despair and confusion before producing any piece of written work on his course. This process normally came to a head in a tutorial where the panic-stricken student bewailed ever embarking on the course and stated his intention of immediate withdrawal. Eventually I learned that if I simply gave time, support and gentle encouragement to this student and allowed him to express his 'performance' fears fully, he then became receptive to considering strategies for approaching his work in a more systematic and constructive fashion, and invariably to good effect as he consistently produced work of a very high standard.

PURIST, ECLECTIC OR INTEGRATIVE?

Trainers will range between those who have a clear orientation towards one approach, those who are integrative, and those who are eclectic. There is much debate currently about the relative values of being integrative and eclectic (Wolfe and Goldfried 1988). Trainers who are integrative use a core theoretical approach or model as a basis for training and all other theories and approaches are introduced within the framework of this model. Eclectic trainers draw from theories and approaches as appropriate to the course, but without reference to a core model or theory. The eclectic approach has been referred to derogatorily as 'wild eclecticism' (Patterson 1985) and it could be viewed in this way if a trainer were just to dip into theories and techniques at whim. It is not unknown for trainers to follow such whims, with the excuse that they are allowing the course 'to unfold naturally, according to the wishes of the students'. It seems that there is some middle ground in this debate. An example is Egan (1990) who refers to 'integrative or systematic eclecticism' and quotes Held (1984) who talks of 'strategic eclecticism'. Whatever position is taken, any counsellor who is becoming a trainer needs to ask: Am I purist, integrative or eclectic in my counselling and in my training?

FROM COUNSELLOR TO COUNSELLOR TRAINER

Table 2.1 on p. 18 shows the shift in emphasis between counselling and training along five dimensions: professional role, client, task, helping and learning medium and desired outcome.

The main difference between counselling and training is the difference in focus between personal change and development in counselling and professional development and competence in training. If I am a good counsellor will I be a good counsellor trainer? One could argue that one does not necessarily follow from the other. In fact, there is some evidence to suggest that the very reasons why some people become counsellors would militate against them being good trainers.

If you prefer to work with one client, rather than with groups; if you have opted out of working with a team of others and prefer to work on your own; if you do not fit easily into organisations – then you should consider seriously whether you could be a good

Table 2.1   From counsellor to counsellor trainer

	The counsellor	The counsellor trainer
Role	Counsellor	Trainer
Client	Client	Learner
Task	Personal Growth	Professional Development
Medium	Relationship	Learning Situation
Outcome	Personal Competence	Professional Competence

trainer. If your counselling orientation is very much with the individual client as a separate entity from the context in which he or she lives and works, then you may not be fulfilled as a trainer. If you do not like to be accountable to others, particularly to those in authority or positions of power, then you may not be happy as a trainer in that you will be answerable and accountable yourself, but also you will have authority invested in you which may give rise to disquiet. A trainer works primarily with groups of learners; a trainer usually works with a team of others; a trainer usually works for or within a training organisation; a trainer is accountable to several stakeholders including the learners, the employer, the employing authority, academic award-bearing organisations and professional counselling organisations.

Counsellor training demands much in the way of personal resources in the trainer. It is a complex job, not to be embarked upon lightly. It demands all the skills of an educator, but more than this. The counsellor trainer will be experienced by trainees as a model. In other words, there will be expectations that the trainer will behave in ways which are congruent with the counselling approach which is being put forward. The counsellor trainer is also a target for transferential material and cannot hide behind professional expertise or superior wisdom. In counselling training there is nowhere to hide, and therefore those contemplating this work who are not prepared to 'bring themselves' into the training equation need to think again about whether they will survive the exposure. For those who have the confidence, courage and ability to be transparently open and real in the training relationship the rewards are great. It is exciting and invigorating to be part of someone's learning journey and to share the agonies as well as the ecstasies along the way.

THE GOOD ENOUGH COUNSELLOR TRAINER

It may be helpful to think in terms of the good enough counsellor and the good enough counsellor trainer. What does the good enough counsellor trainer look like? She or he will be an experienced counsellor in current practice and in regular supervision, including training supervision. The good enough trainer is not perfect but is constantly engaged in the search for knowledge and competence and this personal and professional engagement will be one of the most valuable sources of shared learning with trainees. For this reason, the ongoing experience of being a client in counselling will also be important for the trainer.

Professional qualifications in counselling are important for the counsellor who wishes to train. Credibility is gained by those who ensure that their own qualifications are at least at the level of the course on which they are teaching. It is then important to keep updating by short courses, conferences, workshops, research or writing. Membership of professional counselling organisations and links with other trainers through course moderation are valuable ways of keeping up to date. The good enough counsellor trainer models:

1 a way of being;
2 the living reality of being professional and being human;
3 the reflective practitioner;
4 person-centred competence.

A way of being

The BAC *Code of Ethics and Practice for Trainers* (1985) gives some guidelines about the way in which a counsellor trainer manages his or her responsibility to learners and to their clients through the ethical values of integrity, impartiality and respect. The Rogerian (1961) core conditions of congruence, respect and empathy are as important for the counsellor trainer as they are for the counsellor. The trainer who lives these qualities of relating with colleagues and with learners is giving a powerful example to trainee counsellors. Moreover, the complexities of these qualities in everyday interactions and relationships are then open to scrutiny and can be observed, discussed and evaluated by learners as well as by the counsellor trainer.

The living reality of being professional and being human

Each counsellor trainer is aware of the interface between being professional and being human. Some theoretical orientations – for example the psychodynamic – suggest that it may be positively unhelpful to share aspects of self with clients and learners because it can move the focus away from the client and because it can be a source of inappropriate fantasy about the counsellor or trainer. Those from a cognitive or behavioural orientation would not see much necessity in self-sharing. Some humanistic therapies, however, stress the value of using self as a therapeutic tool and some humanistic trainers see great value in sharing aspects of their personal life with learners as an important learning resource. Whatever the orientation, it is important that the trainer remains professional without being too aloof, and is human without leaking unnecessary material on to unwitting learners.

Being professional involves not only the Rogerian core qualities, but also clarity, objectivity, fairness and competence. In psychodynamic terms, the professional trainer will 'hold' learners through safety and support. This will be a loose holding which allows flexibility within clear boundaries and parameters. Being human involves the shadow side of ourselves and others: vulnerability, exposure and the possibility of getting things wrong. Owning and valuing human frailty can be a great source of strength for both trainer and learner. The learner who experiences the humility which is born of humanity in a really professional trainer is being exposed to learning which may be genuinely profound.

The reflective practitioner

The concept of the internal supervisor can be carried over into the training arena. Counsellor trainers need to be training reflective practitioners, and what better way to do this than constantly to engage learners in ongoing reflection upon the learning process. The counsellor trainer will also use regular supervision of training in order that his or her own internal supervisor may be at work during training sessions. This will be particularly important when dealing with difficult group dynamics involving projection, transference or countertransference. This will be discussed in more detail in the chapter which deals with dynamics in the training relationship.

Person-centred competence

Person-centredness is not confined to work with clients. It is also important in relationships between trainers and learners. By using negotiation and facilitation the trainer empowers learners to take responsibility for their own learning. Person-centred competence implies that in doing this the trainer does not abdicate his or her appropriate responsibility. This responsibility includes the development of a learning climate, management of the learning group, management of resources for learning (whether these be books, articles, people, video or audio tapes) and management of assessment criteria and methodology. There is a constant challenge for counsellor trainers to use their own competence and to be person-centred in a way which will empower learners rather than disable them.

TOWARDS A DEFINITION OF AN EFFECTIVE COUNSELLOR TRAINER

Criteria for effectiveness will involve outcomes and results. An effective counsellor trainer is one who produces knowledgeable, competent, confident, resourceful, sensitive, flexible and caring counsellors able to work in whatever counselling setting and with whatever clients and issues are appropriate. Specific orientations will demand additional criteria – behaviourists, for example, will want to produce intentional counsellors. Therefore the meaning behind the word 'competent' will vary according to orientation.

There has been a strong argument for a process orientation in counsellor training in the UK, rather than an outcome orientation. Whilst the process of counselling and of counsellor training is of paramount importance it must not become the excuse for a sloppiness in thinking. There is still too much uncertainty about the effectiveness of psychotherapy and counselling, and counsellor trainers need constantly to update the training process with current debate, from research and practice, about outcome.

It can, however, be argued that unless the learning process is effective, the outcome of learning will not be effective. The effective counsellor trainer will develop a community of learners each contributing uniquely to her or his own learning and to the learning of others. As the therapeutic relationship is central to the counselling process, so the quality of relating between trainer and trainee and between trainees themselves will be an important indicator of effectiveness. It is disappointing when this core aspect of counsellor training is overlooked and when courses do not use the sometimes difficult tension in trainer/trainee relationships as material for first-hand experiential learning. It takes the sort of openness, humility and courage that is the hallmark of the effective counsellor trainer to be able to grasp such opportunities as they present themselves.

Learning takes place within individuals and within groups. The effective counsellor trainer will provide a variety of structured and unstructured learning experiences, realising that each learner has a preferred learning style (Honey and Mumford 1984) and that flexibility is the key that will open different doors in different ways for different learners. It follows that learners should not become clones. On the contrary, the learning experience should be about each person becoming clear about his or her own best way of being a counsellor. This way may be completely opposite from the way of their trainer. The effective trainer will be encouraging individuality, but never at the expense of the needs of the client, or indeed of others. Interdependence rather than independence will be the aim.

Resources for learning include course members and trainers, but the effective trainer will also familiarise learners with the vast array of counselling theory as presented in books, journals and tapes. Access to up-to-date and well-stocked libraries is important. The effective counsellor trainer will not only be well informed about such resources but will also encourage and support learners to use them confidently.

Counselling training is increasingly becoming competency focused. The effective trainer will have a clear understanding of the major competencies; will be able to explain these clearly and demonstrate them live to learners; will offer systematic skills practice opportunities with the use of video, peer and tutor feedback; and will prepare students fully for assessment.

Preparation for assessment begins with the communication of clear objectives and criteria. Ongoing monitoring of student apprehension and fear provides the opportunity for support and tutorial help. The way in which students are prepared for assessment will be a crucial aspect of trainer effectiveness. It will call upon skills of support, challenge, honesty, consistency and clarity. Ongoing feedback is going to be essential so that assessment is encouraged to be self-assessment as well as tutor and peer assessment and so that it is formative as well as summative.

BECOMING A COUNSELLOR TRAINER: PATHWAYS TO TRAINING

This book is written for those who will be engaged in the training of counsellors. It is not aimed at those involved primarily in the teaching of counselling skills.

Counselling training in the UK is still in its infancy, despite the fact that the first university diploma courses were started here in 1965, almost thirty years ago. There has been steady development in the USA and in Australia and New Zealand. Recent developments in Malaysia, particularly relating to the training of school counsellors, are significant. Only in the past few years has there been a scheme in the UK for the recognition of counsellor training – that set up by the BAC. If counsellor training has been slow to develop, the training of counsellor trainers has hardly begun! At the time of writing there is only a handful of short courses for trainers in the UK. However, as the demand for counsellor training is at present increasing rapidly, it might be supposed that courses for the training of counsellor trainers will be the next phase in the recognition process.

To become a counsellor trainer one will normally have come through one of two routes. The first is the route of obtaining formal counselling qualifications to at least certificate level, but preferably to diploma or advanced diploma level. This counsellor will have built up counselling experience whilst doing training. The second is the route of years of practical experience, possibly with a voluntary counselling organisation which has offered its own training, an organisation such as Relate, Catholic Marriage Advisory Council or the Samaritans. Some counsellors have the richness of a training experience which combines formally validated qualifications from a higher education institution such as a university, with those offered by an independent counselling organisation. Some seek higher academic qualifications in counselling and study to Masters or doctoral level. It should not be assumed that those with higher degrees will be the best counsellor trainers. Unfortunately, it is possible in the UK for some to gain Masters degrees in counselling with little counselling experience. An outstanding diploma student may well be a much better applicant for a post as counsellor trainer. The writer speaks from the experience of teaching and externally examining on both types of course and is in no doubt that the quality of the course followed by the student is a far better indicator of its appropriateness for a would-be trainer than the title given to the award obtained. It is well known that in teaching situations teachers revert to their own experiences of being taught far more often than they realise or intend. If this is the case, the counselling training received by the potential trainer will find its way into the training situation, for better or for worse. The message for those who would be counsellor trainers is: choose your own counselling training course carefully.

Any counsellor who is contemplating becoming a trainer would be advised to start by getting involved in short training workshops. If you have no teaching or training background it would be useful to take a course in adult learning so that you become familiar with learning and teaching processes. You will also need to become familiar with the management of groups and with the management of the learning situation. Such skills as using flip charts and OHPs, writing handouts, drawing up assessment criteria, liaising with other professionals such as supervisors, and interviewing and marking, are skills which will need development for those embarking on counselling training.

Conferences are arranged annually by the Standing Conference for the Advancement of Training and Supervision (SCATS) and by such organisations as the York Summer School. It is now possible to do a certificate and diploma course in counselling training. Those who take seriously the training of counsellors will consider such courses carefully. Such courses and conferences provide training, contacts and very valuable possibilities for networking. BAC produces directories of training courses in the UK. If you are contemplating becoming a trainer it would be useful to find out which counselling training courses are recognised by BAC and arrange to visit such courses which, it is hoped will be exemplars of good training.

The BAC has a Code of Ethics and Practice which reminds trainers of their responsibility to 'consistently seek ways of increasing their professional development and self-awareness' (BAC 1985: 2.1). It is best to start as we mean to go on, and to prepare carefully for becoming a trainer, rather than that which often happens which is that trainers have little or no preparation. We would not accept such standards in our counsellors. Why do we accept them in our counsellor trainers?

Chapter 3

An integrative model for counsellor training

In this chapter a rationale is put forward for the use of an integrative model, and the development of the model is linked to ten assumptions about counselling training. The model for training competent and reflective counsellors is presented and discussed stage by stage. Trainee and client are at the core of the model. Interpersonal and intrapersonal development are central and are embedded within a four-stage learning cycle. Learning objectives are listed at the beginning of each stage. Stage 1 focuses on the development of attitudes and values. Stage 2 concentrates on the development of knowledge and skills. Stage 3 moves on to client work and supervision. Stage 4 is the opportunity for reflection and evaluation.

A model offers a framework for the training process within which a variety of approaches and skills may be located. Models have the advantage of being easily understood and are therefore likely to be used. The Egan counselling model (1990) is a good example of this and is now used in places as different as Australia, China, Malaysia, South Africa, USA and Argentina because it speaks to counsellors and helpers whatever their cultural background. However, models may be criticised because they can appear to over-simplify complex processes (McLeod 1992b), and because, if they focus in counselling training upon skills apart from counsellor attitudes and beliefs, they may produce mechanistic counsellors. The microcounselling model of training (Ivey and Authier 1971) is now seen to have limitations in this respect although it has contributed significantly to the field of counselling skills training.

The integrative model of training which is discussed in this chapter is the result of my experience during a decade of training, examining and research in this field (Connor 1986). The British

Association for Counselling helped counsellor trainers to be clear about the core elements of counselling training whatever their preferred core theoretical model. The guidelines produced by BAC for course recognition (1988) list eight key elements in counselling training, including such areas as personal development, theory, skill development and supervision. Whilst an external examiner for several counselling courses throughout the UK I have become increasingly aware that trainers need to know not only the key elements which should be in any counsellor training programme, but also the way in which these key elements may be related to one another within the programme, in order to provide a coherent and developmental framework for training. Additionally, counsellor trainers need to understand how learning theory may contribute to their understanding of the way in which learners learn. The model presented in this book is developed from counselling theory and from learning theory. Kolb's (1984) theory about the experiential learning cycle has particular significance. He proposed a four-stage learning cycle which begins with concrete experience, reflection upon the experience, then the formulation of hypotheses and finally the testing out of these in new situations. My model takes from Kolb the importance of learning from and through experience and the notion that learning does not take place until there has been reflection upon experience. However, the model is not dependent solely upon experiential learning. There is a belief that didactic as well as experiential learning has its place within a total counsellor training programme which is aimed at producing professional practitioners.

The model is designed to develop competent and reflective

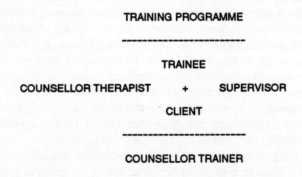

Figure 3.1 Significant influences upon the counsellor in training

counsellors and is therefore a model for professional development. It includes all aspects of professional development and integrates learning stages, resources, theory, process, practice, outcome, assessment and evaluation. All aspects of training are interrelated and the integration will be experienced in different ways and at different times by individual learners. This chapter sets out the model and describes the elements at each stage of the model. The next chapter illustrates the model in practice as it is used in one counsellor training course.

TEN UNDERLYING ASSUMPTIONS ABOUT COUNSELLOR TRAINING

1 Counsellor training is a professional training and counsellors are accountable for the quality of their work.
2 Work with the client is at the heart of all training.
3 Counsellor training is about learning rather than teaching.
4 The trainee is learning about self, client, and self with client.
5 The counsellor trainer has the responsibility for providing the necessary conditions and resources for learning to take place.
6 The trainee is able to take responsibility for learning.
7 A counselling course is a collaborative learning community.
8 Trainees and trainers are both robust and vulnerable.
9 Trainees respond positively to affirmation and high expectation and they are capable of achieving results beyond the ordinary.
10 Learning is a lifelong process.

THE MODEL FOR TRAINING COMPETENT AND REFLECTIVE COUNSELLORS

There is no purpose in training a counsellor unless there are clients to be counselled, and as one of the most significant characteristics of counselling is the relationship between helper and helped, so the core of the model is trainee and client as separate persons in relationship. With trainee and client firmly at the centre of a four-stage learning cycle, all stages feed into the intrapersonal and inter-personal development of the trainee. In addition, significant people have an impact: the trainer, the trainee's counsellor or therapist, the supervisor and the personal development group facilitator.

The model is intended to be cyclical, but at any one time a course or an individual learner may need to focus upon and highlight

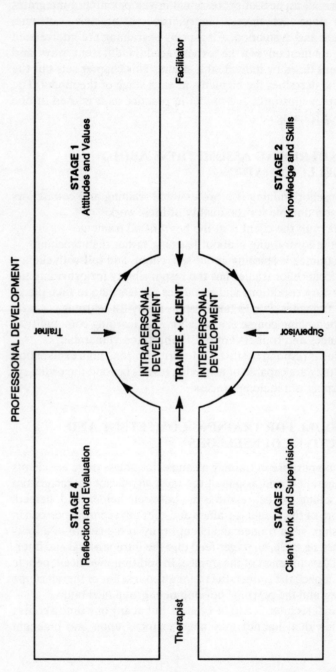

Figure 3.2 The model

one aspect of training, but always in the context of the whole framework. It can be used in a diagnostic way by trainers wishing to assess whether each element of training is being given sufficient attention. It may also be used as a diagnostic tool by learners wishing to assess themselves on areas of strength and areas which they may be overlooking or which need further development.

THE CORE OF THE MODEL: INTRAPERSONAL DEVELOPMENT

Learning objectives

1 To develop understanding and appreciation of self.
2 To become aware of and utilise personal strengths and assets.
3 To become aware of blind-spots, blocks and vulnerabilities.
4 To identify areas to work on in personal counselling.
5 To appreciate experientially the significance of developmental stages in personal development.

Central to effective counselling is the counsellor's way of being which includes personal growth and the ability to form therapeutic relationships. All aspects of the training model are designed to feed into the sort of intrapersonal and interpersonal development that will make a difference to the ability to form and sustain therapeutic relationships and the therapeutic alliance (Garfield and Bergin 1986). The training process is therefore designed to maximise opportunities for personal growth, but always at the service of clients. When personal growth 'takes over' and becomes an excuse for narcissistic absorption in self, it has ceased to be of value in professional training. It is, however, almost inevitable that for trainees there will be periods of introspection resulting from their increased self-awareness and this is part of a developmental process.

Intrapersonal development is self-development through self-awareness and self-acceptance. It focuses upon the process of self-exploration which identifies personal strengths and personal weaknesses, blocks, resistances and vulnerabilities. Such self-exploration will uncover hidden assets as well as damaging unfinished business and lurking inner conflicts. Intrapersonal development helps the trainee to get in touch with all the different facets of self and indeed to befriend their different selves, including their shadow side (Jung 1968).

The work of Freud (1949) and of Erikson (1965, 1982) provides a good starting point for exploring the development of self through critical life stages and the way that the past is present. Erikson talks of eight critical stages and the tasks associated with each, and Corey and Corey (1989: 118) add questions for the trainee helper. Developmental issues arising from these stages of development are shown in Table 3.1.

Self-exploration which is based upon developmental and psychodynamic approaches will help the trainee not only with self-development but also in the understanding of the development of their clients. Additionally, it helps trainees to recognise in themselves the basis of transference, countertransference, resistance and projection. See also a useful chapter on counselling and the life cycle by Woolfe and Sugarman (1989).

Courses will vary in the amount of emphasis which is given explicitly to this core area of training. Some trainers see intrapersonal development mainly as a by-product of all the other aspects of training; another view is that intrapersonal development

Table 3.1 Life stages and development issues

Life stage	Task		Developmental issues
1 Infancy	Trust	vs Mistrust	Trust, fear
2 Early childhood	Autonomy	vs Shame and doubt	Confidence, expressing feeling
3 Preschool age	Initiative	vs Guilt	Sexual identity, sexual expression
4 Middle childhood	Industry	vs Inferiority	Competence as a learner
5 Adolescence	Identity	vs Role confusion	Identity, self-esteem, meaning
6 Early adulthood	Intimacy	vs Isolation	Closeness, dependence
7 Middle adulthood	Generativity	vs Stagnation	Creativity, closing options
8 Late adulthood	Integrity	vs Despair	Wholeness, fragmentation

Source: adapted from Erikson (1965)

is central and the curriculum must evolve around the personal development needs of the group. A humanistically oriented, person-centred course may well do this. A psychodynamic course will emphasise the importance of personal therapy as the main vehicle for intrapersonal development and indeed for the whole training process. Integrative courses will vary in emphasis – some will require trainees to have counselling or therapy as a condition of participation on the course, while others will make it a recommendation rather than a requirement.

In addition to undergoing counselling or therapy during training, there will be explicit provision for intrapersonal development through developmental workshops; experiential, encounter or personal development groups; and through the continual reflections made in a learning journal or log. Personal growth is a lifelong process which progresses in fits and starts because we are both human and fallible. Self-development may be exciting and affirming, but it is also often distressing and confusing. In this important area of trainee development the course and the staff will need to offer a sensitive mix of support and challenge. Commitment by staff to their own ongoing personal development will be a powerful example for trainees. Trainers are able to demonstrate this by modelling the process of continual searching, by openness in experiential group work and by appropriate self-disclosure regarding their own continuing development.

THE CORE OF THE MODEL: INTERPERSONAL DEVELOPMENT

Learning objectives

1   To understand areas of strength and areas for development in a range of interactions: with peers, staff, clients and in personal and professional relationships.
2   To gain confidence in appropriate self-sharing.
3   To develop skills of giving and receiving feedback.
4   To facilitate growth in self and others through active participation in personal development groups.
5   To develop helping relationships with clients.
6   To continuously reflect upon successes and setbacks and to use such reflection as the basis for setting realistic objectives for development.

7   To develop the internal supervisor, active not only during sessions with clients but also in other interactions whether group or individual.

The essence of counselling is that personal change and growth is facilitated through a helping relationship and therefore the ability to form therapeutic relationships is at the heart of effective counselling. The ability of the trainee to form helping relationships will be enhanced through intrapersonal development but will be communicated largely through interpersonal development.

On a counsellor training course opportunities need to be maximised for the trainee to develop effective relationships, not just with clients but in all the course interactions with staff and peers. The explicit provision for interpersonal development is through experiential, encounter or personal development groups. Such groups provide a safe forum for giving and receiving feedback about self, and also provide the trainee with the possibility of facilitating personal growth in other members of the group (Gilmore 1973; Small and Manthei 1988). On some counsellor training courses such groups are facilitated by an outside facilitator, on others by an internal staff member or self-managed by the group of trainees.

If the aim is to provide a safe environment in which to self-challenge, to challenge others and to be challenged, then it is my opinion that a developmental model of facilitation is best. This means that a facilitator is appointed and that gradually as the group gain in confidence and skill they share in the facilitation, with the facilitator eventually becoming more of a consultant to the group. There is another issue – the question of whether the facilitator of personal development should be a core staff member. There are compelling reasons why this should not be so. Trainees will only be able to engage in meaningful personal development when they feel free from judgement, assessment and evaluation. Too many boundaries become blurred with regard to assessment and with regard to confidentiality if a core staff member facilitates such a group. It is well known, however, that trainees take to such groups current training issues and it is important that whoever facilitates the group is in accord with the values espoused by the course and is held in trust by both staff and trainees alike. Clear contracting is essential. Trainees need to be clear about the objectives of the group, about the role of the facilitator and about the way in which the work of the individual in the group may need to be communicated to course staff.

The use of a learning journal or learning log is a means of ongoing personal reflection which encourages the setting of objectives with regard to personal and interpersonal development. Regular community or course meetings offer the opportunity to practise relating in a more structured group than the experiential group so that skills of assertiveness, negotiation and facilitation may be developed. The use of a learning partner for regular review is another opportunity for personal growth and for facilitating that growth in another.

Whether the way of relating on a course (to both tutors and peers) should be assessed has long been a subject for debate. It has been felt that work in an experiential group should not be assessed because such assessment would inhibit the free expression of thoughts and feelings. In this model it is appreciated that personal development work needs to take place without the scrutiny of assessment. Yet, what about trainees who do not contribute effectively in a group? Can they be effective counsellors other than in a limited way? And what if such trainees are very good at all assessed parts of the course and yet cannot themselves engage in personal development or help others to do this in a group? These are difficult questions with no easy answers. This model is based on professional development and therefore suggests that some sort of feedback into the assessment process needs to be made in the area of personal development and relating to others on the course.

Rogers (1961: 56) reminds us that:

> The degree to which I can create relationships which facilitate the growth of others as separate persons is a measure of the growth I have achieved in myself. In some respects this is a disturbing thought, but it is also a promising or challenging one. It would indicate that if I am interested in creating helping relationships I have a fascinating lifetime job ahead of me, stretching and developing my potentialities in the direction of growth.

If we believe, as Rogers does, that the ability to know oneself and to engage continuously in personal growth will be a measure of the ability to help others, then trainers have a serious responsibility not only to provide opportunities for growth, but also to remind trainees of their responsibilities. This is the core of the training process. If these responsibilities are not acknowledged and acted upon, the training process is adversely affected, not only for the individual but also, possibly, for other trainees within the group.

THE FOUR-STAGE LEARNING CYCLE

The learning cycle is experiential and cyclical. The experiential element requires that learning involves the active participation of the learner and that learning is through the experience of doing and reflecting upon doing. The essence of learning is not action, but reflection upon action. The cycle operates continuously throughout training at both a macro level of major course elements and at a micro level of specific learning tasks and activities.

The model has learner and client at the centre with the learner engaged in intrapersonal and interpersonal development. All four stages of the model contribute to this development. Stage 1 provides the groundwork for the development of the core therapeutic qualities in the counsellor through exploration of attitudes, values and beliefs. Stage 2 builds upon that, with counselling theory and the development of counselling skills and strategies. Stage 3 is the point at which the learning from the previous two stages is put into practice with clients and under supervision. Stage 4 is the stage of reflection upon learning, researching counselling activity and assessing and monitoring progress.

Whenever a trainee is engaged with a client it is expected that she/he will be drawing upon the development of core qualities and values that have been explored in Stage 1 and the knowledge, understanding and skills of Stage 2. After work in Stage 3 there would be the evaluation and reflection of Stage 4. The whole cycle is at work continuously. Throughout all stages of the learning cycle there are significant people who contribute to the development of the trainee, notably the trainer, the group facilitator, the trainee's supervisor and the trainee's therapist or counsellor. All of these contribute to counsellor competence and their contribution needs to be fully integrated into the trainee's reflections upon learning through the learning journal, learning portfolio and counselling practice file.

LEARNING CYCLE STAGE 1: ATTITUDES AND VALUES

Learning objectives

1   To become aware of personal assumptions and beliefs.
2   To explore and clarify values and attitudes.
3   To develop core therapeutic qualities.

4   To be aware of ethical and professional issues and expectations
    in counselling.
5   To develop a personal code of professional ethics.

Stage 1 underpins the rest of the training cycle. Attitudes, values
and beliefs will come into play consciously and unconsciously
throughout all of the stages of the model. They need to be highlighted. McLeod and McLeod (1993) studied the relationship
between personal philosophy and counsellor effectiveness. They
concluded that a 'person-centred' perceptual organisation or belief
system was an important factor in counsellor effectiveness, but
they also noted that a review of the research literature over the
past thirty years revealed very little in this important area of how
counsellors make sense of the world. A study by Whiteley *et
al.* (1967) is quoted as a study which investigated personal construct systems and which concluded that counsellors who have
flexible construct systems were more effective than those who had
rigid construct systems. This stage of the model aims to increase
flexibility through greater awareness.

Philosophical assumptions and beliefs

The model starts with where the learners are, rather than where
other thinkers, writers and counsellors are. It starts with learners'
assumptions and beliefs: about self, about people, about helping
and counselling. It is desirable that trainees have the opportunity
to define their own philosophical positions, addressing such statements as: human beings are inherently good; everyone is intrinsi-
cally free; all human beings are equal; power corrupts; the past
determines the present and future.

Two things will be noted in this list: assumptions and beliefs about
self, others, helping and counselling merge. Once basic philosophical beliefs have been explored it is then possible to move into
the major schools of thought about counselling. Lively debate
would be encouraged in such areas as deterministic beliefs about
people being victims of their childhood and upbringing; about
whether it is really possible for equality to exist in the counselling
relationship; whether freedom is an illusion because we are all
conditioned by forces in society beyond our control; whether there
is such a thing as altruism; and what are the sources of motivation
in counsellors. This debate is the groundwork of counselling, the
hinge upon which a philosophy of counselling will turn. Training

needs to make unconscious and subconscious assumptions conscious, so that counsellors can unambiguously know what are the things they believe with certainty, what they half believe and what they are needing to explore further during training. Counsellors will differ in their beliefs. Trainers will differ in their beliefs. Clients will differ in their beliefs. This is the richness of the human experience. Discussion will highlight differences but it will also highlight areas of broad agreement amongst those involved in helping and counselling.

Counselling training needs to be an opportunity to broaden horizons so that there is greater understanding of the counsellor's own beliefs, but also the opportunity, through debate with others, to understand and accept *their* beliefs. This is important for the development of empathy. It is crucial that training courses make clear their own philosophical stance in course leaflets so that intending applicants may make a realistic assessment about whether this course is compatible with their own beliefs.

> Both of these – knowing both yourself and others in caring, reflective, unvarnished ways – will help you develop the wisdom that enables you to move beyond the technology of helping, the helping alliance, and even the 'real relationship' to the kind of authenticity celebrated by Rogers in 'A Way of Being'.
>
> (Egan 1986: 362)

Useful texts for learners wishing to grapple with underlying philosophies in counselling include Corey (1986) who summarises the basic philosophical concepts behind the major counselling theories, and Yalom (1980) who explores the existential perspective on issues such as freedom, responsibility, meaning, being and identity. A text which offers a strong challenge to some of the philosophical assumptions in counselling is Masson (1990). Techniques such as Helping Relationship Incident stories (Combs and Soper 1963) can be used in order to explore personal philosophy and perceptual organisation. Trainees write stories about helping experiences and these are assessed along twelve dimensions (in McLeod and McLeod 1993).

Values and attitudes

Values usually denote worth, desirability, prizing. People act upon values and are sometimes surprised to find that their actions indicate preferences of which they had been unaware. Egan (1990) stresses that values are a set of criteria for making decisions and he distinguishes between 'espoused values' and 'values in use'. He discusses five major sets of values that are involved in the helping relationship: pragmatism, competence, respect, genuineness and client self-responsibility. It is a worthwhile exercise to be honest with ourselves about the values which we ostensibly espouse and those upon which we actually act and by which we live.

An attitude is a settled way of thinking. A belief implies acceptance of something as true or existing. Attitudes, values and beliefs affect the qualities which are to be found in the counsellor and which may be defined as characteristics, traits or attributes. We are characterised by what we believe, value and think.

Attitudes can change, but because they are by definition settled modes of thinking, they may not be easily amenable to change. Selection for counselling training needs to take this fact into account and criteria for selection should include flexibility and openness to learning. It has been found that short courses may well develop technical skills, but longer courses allowing for developmental change are necessary for change in attitudes. Which of us can say that we do not need to change some of our attitudes? Certainly, good training courses have been evaluated by trainees as producing 'profound' change. Profound means deep rather than extensive, and it is more likely to mean permanent rather than temporary. Such profound change is encouraged in this training model through the interrelation of all the elements. Attitudes are not changed just by talking about them, or indeed by getting tutor feedback. Qualities are not developed by just practising skills or writing essays. They develop through the sum total of the learning experience and they are more likely to develop if there is intentionality in the learning process through ongoing structured experiences for reflection, reviewing and objective setting. In this model this would be through regular entries in a learning journal and regular review with a learning partner. This would include reflections upon taught sessions, practice, work with clients, supervision, experiential groupwork and reflections upon reading.

It is sometimes difficult to talk to trainees about the way in which their attitudes and qualities are perceived because it can seem to be judgemental. For this reason counsellor trainers may miss important opportunities for enabling growth in the learner. In this model, the attitudes and qualities shown in the relationship between learner and trainer are viewed as an important indicator of the way in which their attitudes and qualities will be perceived by the learners' clients. One of the assumptions of the training model is that learners are robust and vulnerable. Dealing with difficult relationships on the course shows that there is this assumption, and the way in which the trainer handles the situation will be a test of his or her true appreciation of this robustness and vulnerability.

Another assumption is that learners respond positively to affirmation and high expectation and that they are capable of achieving results beyond the ordinary. Every opportunity should be taken to offer encouragement to learners to stretch themselves in setting their own personal goals and in the personal and lifelong search for their attitudes, values and beliefs. No better form of encouragement exists, than the example of a trainer who is seen to be engaged in this endeavour.

Core therapeutic qualities

Rogers' (1961) 'necessary and sufficient conditions' of genuineness, respect and empathy are agreed by most to be necessary, if not sufficient, for effective helping relationships that will produce valued change in the client. Garfield and Bergin (1986: 171) note:

> virtually all schools of therapy accept the notion that these or related therapist relationship variables are important for significant progress in psychotherapy and, in fact, fundamental in the formation of a working alliance.

Truax and Carkhuff (1967) researched these core conditions and stated that in order to be therapeutic they must be perceived by clients to be present in the helper. The helper must be able to communicate these qualities. These authors also asserted that the order in which they were communicated seemed to be important: clients needed to know firstly that the counsellor was congruent (genuineness), secondly the client needed to experience positive regard (respect), and finally they needed to know that they had been understood (accurate empathy). Later research challenged some of these findings placing more emphasis on the significance of client variables (Strupp 1980). However, most are agreed that these core conditions are at the heart of effective counselling.

At Stage 1 the focus is upon the assumptions, beliefs, values and attitudes which comprise these core conditions of genuineness, warmth and empathy. Most agree that these core conditions are the expressions of attitudes towards others and that the ability to express these attitudes is affected by perceptual factors, sensitivity, and the ability to respond affectively, cognitively and behaviourally. There has been much debate about whether, for example, empathy is a quality or a skill. The writer believes it is both. There are important skills of empathic responding which include the ability to paraphrase and to reflect feelings accurately. However, prior to any response is the qualitative capacity, sensitivity, imagination and willingness to 'be with'.

Campbell, Kagan and Krathwohl (1971) distinguish between the ability of an individual to identify accurately the feelings of another and the ability to use this knowledge or understanding effectively to promote positive client growth in a counselling relationship. They point out that a person may be highly sensitive but unable to use this aptitude.

> Individuals high in affective sensitivity may not have the communication skills to either convey their empathy or to effectively explore the world of the client. ... Counsellors who are high in affective sensitivity and have within their repertoire the appropriate communication skills may, nevertheless, still not be effective if they lack role-taking ability and are, consequently, unable to respond to the client at an emotional level.
> (Campbell *et al.*, cited in Arbeitman 1984: 40)

Arbeitman identified four components in the development of empathy and these included affective sensitivity (experiencing the experience of the other), role-taking (acts of imagination), emotional responsiveness and empathic communication. At Stage 1 of this model the trainee would be developing the first three components in particular. Trainers would be providing the sort of stimulus material through live experiences, audio tapes, video tapes, films and stories which would increase understanding and sensitivity of self and other, and which would provide opportunities for checking understanding against the understanding and perceptions of others in a variety of group activities.

I researched the use of videotaped material as a means of increasing empathic sensitivity and of developing skills. This was with a group of trainee nurse teachers (Connor 1986). A video tape of a nurse–patient interaction was used to assess the ability

to identify patient feelings, values and concerns and to identify
skills used by the nurse. A pre-test, post-test design was used and
the trainees were tested on the same video example, with the same
questions, before and after a ten-week training course. The results
showed that although there was a significant difference in the ability to identify empathic responding skills before and after training,
there was no significant difference in the ability to identify the
concerns, values and feelings of the patient and scores were low
both before and after training. This matches results in research by
LaMonica *et al.* (1976) and indicates the importance of immersing
trainees in learning experiences which will develop perceptual
understanding, cognitive flexibility and emotional responsiveness
before concentrating on specific behavioural skills.

Rogers (1961) formulates ten questions for those engaged in
therapeutic relationships. These are a useful way of helping learners
to examine their own ideas about the qualities for effective helping.
They are asked in a way which encourages questioning, searching
and exploring. They also raise questions about how such qualities
are communicated in practice. Texts such as this are useful resources
at the initial stage of counsellor training. In order that they may be
used effectively, trainers need to allow course time for reading and
private reflection preceding discussion. A residential, early in the
course, is the ideal opportunity. These are some of the questions:

1 Can I be in some way which will be perceived by the other
   person as trustworthy, as dependable or consistent in some
   deep sense?
2 Can I be expressive enough as a person that what I am will
   be communicated unambiguously?
3 Can I let myself experience positive attitudes toward this
   other person – attitudes of warmth, caring, liking, interest,
   respect?
4 Can I be strong enough as a person to be separate from the
   other?
5 Am I secure enough within myself to permit him his sep-
   arateness. Can I permit him to be what he is?
6 Can I let myself enter fully into the world of his feelings and
   personal meanings and see these as he does? ...
10 Can I meet this other individual as a person who is in the
   process of becoming, or will I be bound by his past and by
   my past?

(Rogers 1961: 50–5)

Ethical and professional practice

Counselling courses train people to be more than well-intentioned helpers. They train helpers for a profession. This is not an appendage to training, something which needs to be considered once the course is almost over. It needs to be at the forefront of trainer and trainee awareness and that is why the context of professional and ethical considerations is prior to learning about theories and skills at the next stage of the model. When the trainee starts training, he or she is entering the professional body of counselling and needs to know the standards, values and regulations of that body. In the UK the BAC represents the profession of counselling and safeguards professional standards through accreditation procedures, recognition of counselling training courses, publication of codes of ethics and practice, and through complaints procedures.

Exploration of ethical and professional practice can be informed from a variety of sources. For example, the thorny question of confidentiality needs to be viewed from legal, medical, social service and religious perspectives, as well as from counselling perspectives, because of the overlap between different helping professions. At the time of writing there is much professional interest in the whole area of sex and touch within therapeutic relationships and Russell (1993) highlights examples of sexual abuse by counsellors. The BAC Annual Conference in 1993 debated the point at which, if ever, a sexual relationship could take place between counsellor and client after the termination of therapy. The issue of physical touch within therapy is one that is less easily amenable to strict codes of practice and one which needs much discussion during training.

At this stage in the training model codes of ethics and practice would be discussed and this would be the opportunity for learners to test their own personal codes with those produced by professional counselling organisations. Case-study and case-example from learners' experience can be a useful way to start such discussion and may lead to exercises where the individual and the group draw up their own codes before being introduced to the official ones. It is useful to look, not only at a code produced in your own country, but also to find those from other countries. In the UK, the British Association for Counselling has produced a *Code of Ethics and Practice for Counsellors* (1992); in the USA the American Association of Counseling and Development has produced a Paper on Ethical Standards (1988) and the National Board of Certified

Counsellors has produced a Code of Ethics (1987) reproduced in Corey and Corey (1989: 228). A useful chapter on professional issues in counselling is included in the *Handbook of Counselling in Britain* (Dryden *et al.* (eds) 1989).

LEARNING CYCLE STAGE 2: KNOWLEDGE AND SKILLS

Learning objectives

1 To become familiar with major counselling theories and approaches.
2 To develop a thorough working knowledge of a core theoretical model.
3 To focus upon the therapeutic process in relation to change.
4 To understand the major causes and manifestations of client problems, including developmental psychology and an understanding of mental health and mental illness.
5 To understand family and social systems, organisations and contexts.
6 To appreciate the work of helping agencies.
7 To practise the counselling skills necessary for competence in the core theoretical model.
8 To learn, and to apply, a variety of helping strategies and interventions.
9 To identify and own personal strengths and limitations in relation to skills and strategies.
10 To develop an integrated counselling style.

In terms of course time it could be argued that Stage 2 of the model takes the lion's share. The danger is that trainers overemphasise the content of this stage, forgetting that unless the work of Stage 2 is grounded in the insights of Stage 1, and unless it is transferable to the actual practice of Stage 3, then it is of little use.

The first six learning objectives are concerned with knowledge and understanding about counselling, about people, about other helping agencies, about client problems, about concepts of change and about the settings and systems in which we live. Courses will vary significantly in their focus and yet all of these aspects will need to be addressed. The next three learning objectives concern skills and strategies. The final objective is the one that brings everything together for the trainee.

1 Familiarity with major counselling theories and approaches

Whatever the orientation of the course there is a responsibility to inform trainees about theories and approaches, noting historical development, major influences and relevant research findings. There are some excellent overviews, particularly in Corey (1986: 6). He presents a table which is an overview of contemporary counselling models and, later in the book, another showing goals of therapy across the major theories. In these tables he summarises the following approaches: psychoanalytic, Adlerian, existential, person-centred, gestalt, transactional analysis, behaviour therapy, rational-emotive therapy and reality therapy. The rest of the book is devoted to chapters on each of these, including key concepts, therapeutic process, application, contributions of the theory, limitations and questions for reflection and discussion.

Trainees appreciate seeing examplars of these theories and approaches and there is no better way of understanding counselling in practice than to see Rogers, Perls and Ellis with Gloria, or Lazarus with Cathy, or Meichenbaum and Strupp with Richard on the much celebrated series on film and video tapes now available through Concord Films (UK) and entitled 'Three Approaches to Psychotherapy'. The idea behind this series was to get three well-known exponents of a theory to interview the same client and then have the client evaluate the contribution of each. Books such as Proctor's *Counselling Shop* (1978) may be useful also because it contains interviews with well-known counsellors from a variety of theoretical backgrounds.

2 Developing a thorough knowledge of a core theoretical model

A model is a framework within which theory may be coherently located and which provides a basis for practice. The BAC guidelines for the Recognition of Counsellor Training Courses (1990: 6) states that there should be enough counselling theory to enable students to make explicit:

The explanations, predictions and underlying assumptions of the core theoretical model.

The therapeutic process and basis of change as conceived in the core theoretical model.

The document goes on to say that:

The Core Theoretical Model of a course may be Behavioural, Psychodynamic, Gestalt, Person Centred, etc. It is important that the course really does focus in depth on this theoretical model, taking students towards the limits of theory, practice and research. It is not simply a matter of, for instance, expecting students to take a 'broadly person centred' approach with clients. If 'person centred' is the core theoretical model of the course then that has to gain considerable emphasis in all the course elements.

The issue of eclectic and integrative models is then addressed:

This emphasis on a core theoretical model does not mitigate against eclectic or integrative courses, but it does demand that courses taking an eclectic or integrative approach regard that eclectic or integrative nature as their core theoretical model, exploring fully the philosophical, theoretical and practical implications of the eclectic or integrative rationale.

(BAC 1990: 22)

The next chapter gives an example of the way in which one Advanced Diploma in Counselling course uses the Skilled Helper Model (Egan 1993) as the core theoretical model of the course.

3 Focusing upon the therapeutic process in relation to change

At the heart of the client's concerns is the desire for change. Therefore, this must be at the heart of the counsellor's concern also. Trainees need a good grounding in change theory, both personal change and group and organisational change. Whatever the core theoretical model, trainees need to know how this particular therapeutic process brings about change in the client. Research findings as well as personal experiences are important. A deep understanding of the psychology of change and resistance to change is essential. There has, perhaps, been too much attention paid to research on counsellor variables in relation to change, and not enough to the vulnerability, powerlessness and self-defeating patterns of thinking, feeling and behaving in clients. The contributions of Beck (1976), Ellis (1985), Meichenbaum (1977) and others in the cognitive-behavioural schools have been particularly valuable in helping us to understand the complexities of change. Berne (1972) and those involved in transactional analysis, together with those from the behavioural schools, help us to understand the pay-offs for resisting change.

4 Understanding of the major causes and manifestations of client problems, including developmental psychology and an understanding of mental health and mental illness

The area of training which is concerned with understanding client problems, their causes and manifestations, is often done through optional workshops where trainees choose certain topics of particular interest to them. This raises an important issue about professional training as against a 'pick and mix' approach. If there were rigorous standards of training and if these were consistent, we should be assured that all trainees knew about the most common problems with which they could have to deal. Clients have a right to expect this of a trained counsellor. It does not seem good enough that trainees can do all their course assignments, seminars and workshops around one or two client problems. This is just as bad as not being introduced to the major theories of counselling. We must then ask ourselves what the client problems are that all trainees should know about. Are there basic themes which permeate several problems and is the theme approach the best?

If we start with developmental psychology, themes arising from life stages emerge: attachment and loss; identity; self-worth; addiction and obsession; trust; sexuality; competence. Most of the problems which clients bring will emerge from such themes. The group itself provides a rich learning resource on these problems – from the experiences of group members in their own life and development and from their experiences of helping and counselling. At this point in the training programme it is very beneficial to involve other helping professionals or volunteer workers who have specialised experience. I remember clearly a fascinating session where a member of the course who worked in a secure unit with sex offenders gave an alternative perspective from the one that would have been put forward by a counsellor. The approach could be described as 'tough love'. It was a different way of caring. But it challenged strongly held views and trainees really began to think about treatment for abusers in a different way. Similarly, a counsellor working in a drug centre who is continually subjected to violent outbursts from clients can give first-hand insight into the alternative expressions of unconditional positive regard. A counsellor from a marriage counselling organisation can talk about what it feels like when trying to offer equal attention to two non-communicating people in couple counselling.

Perhaps the most important area in which to involve outside expertise is in the area of mental health and mental illness. There is a strong case for this being a crucial part of counsellor training. Trainees need to be able to recognise signs and symptoms which might indicate serious disorder or imminent breakdown. They also need to be aware of the major classifications of mental illness and of the treatments given, including medication. Counsellors are being appointed to GP surgeries and there may be increasing overlap between such a counsellor and the community psychiatric nurse. They need to know and understand the same language when it comes to patient or client care.

5   Understanding family and social systems, organisations and contexts

Because the client usually comes for counselling on his or her own, there is a danger that the counsellor does not appreciate the settings and context in which the client lives. Training must provide an appreciation of factors which will inhibit, disable and disempower clients. An understanding of basic processes in systems, particularly the family as a system, is essential. The literature on family therapy is particularly useful in apreciating family dynamics and conflicts (Minuchin and Fishman 1981). Processes in political and social systems also need to be understood. Issues such as poverty, disability, unemployment and homelessness need to be explored alongside issues of equality in gender and race. Dryden *et al.* write about issues for the counsellor when working with those who are oppressed. They ask:

> Do counsellors working with clients from oppressed groups have an adequate understanding of what it is like to be a member of those groups on a day-today basis, quite apart from living with what is often a painful collective as well as individual history? Second, have such counsellors worked experientially as clients or trainees, on their own conscious and unconscious culturally specific conditioning that may make them feel superior to people from other groups?

(Dryden *et al.* (eds) 1989: 415)

These writers emphasise that work on these issues may produce a heavy burden of guilt on the part of the trainee and this needs to be recognised and worked through. They include a useful table which lists kinds of oppression: the oppressive role (e.g. 'white', male, rich), the oppressed role (e.g. 'black', female, unemployed) and the nature of primary oppression (e.g. racism, sexism, ageism). No doubt most of us fit into both categories of oppressive role and oppressed role and this will provide much useful material for experiential work on these issues. However, it will also be important for trainees to meet people who experience the sort of multiple oppression that is encapsulated in the term which is so trivially bandied about and yet which has such profound meaning: 'down and out'. Such people will be found not only on the streets but also, less visibly, in distress in all our schools, hospitals, housing estates, churches and voluntary and public sector agencies.

6 Appreciation of the work of helping agencies

This area has already been mentioned in relation to the study of client problems. Once more, a coherent approach is necessary to ensure that trainees are familiar with all the relevant agencies. We automatically think of psychiatrists, psychologists and social workers. Who else might be included from the voluntary sector? And shouldn't GPs and nurses be on the list of those most likely to be involved with our clients?

7 Practising the counselling skills necessary for competence in the core theoretical model

Evidence abounds in the research literature about the efficacy of skills training in counselling (Carkhuff 1969; Ivey and Authier 1971; Kurtz *et al.* 1985; Hargie 1988; Gallagher 1993). Their findings are discussed in Chapter Seven on the trainer as educator. Thompson (1976), however, found that the literature needs closer examination. When doing my own research I noted that there were very few experimental designs which included follow-up studies and therefore it is not certain whether skills which appear to be well developed on a counselling course are transferred into the real counselling situation, and whether such development is maintained over time. My research showed differential results over time in trainee self-perception and this raises interesting research questions.

At the post-test stage of the Self Perception of Skills Schedule (SPSS) there was a significant increase in the perceived ability

to paraphrase in a tentative manner, but this declined markedly
at the follow-up stage. However, the perceived ability to reflect
feelings, which increased at the post-test stage, maintained a
marked increase at the follow-up stage, with one-third of the
group using a high rating whereas only five per cent had done so
at the beginning of the course.

(Connor 1986: 245)

The skills should be taught within the framework of the core
theoretical model and within the framework of Stages 1 and 2 of
the learning cycle so that they are embedded within counselling
values and core conditions, rather than being developed as
mechanical skills. If this embedding does not occur, then there is
the danger that counselling will be harmful rather than helpful. It
is rarely neutral.

A systematic approach to skills training is important so that
skills can be learned one at a time and built upon sequentially until
there is a coherent set of skills which have been learned and practised and which reflect the competencies of the core model. An
issue for training is whether trainees use their own material when
they are in the client role, or whether they role-play. There may be
room for both, but my experience is that the best learning can take
place when the practice session is experienced as real and when
trainees are asked to always be themselves in the client role and
to bring medium-weight concerns which are appropriate to time-
limited practice sessions.

Skills training is usually done in small groups of three or four and
is best done with regular and frequent supervision. Trainees need
to observe one another, give feedback, practise skills, and receive
feedback. Training groups usually consist of three trainees in the
rotating roles of client, counsellor and observer. Where video
equipment is available it constitutes an additional form of feedback. The best provided courses have video feedback available
for every training group at every skills practice session and in
this case a fourth member of the group may act as the facilitator
of feedback. The following chapter gives an example of this in
practice.

Experience as an external examiner has highlighted for me that
there is still little agreement about the way in which this area of
training should be assessed. Trainees need to be clear about the
objectives of skills training and the criteria against which they will

be assessed. Some courses do not assess performance, but assess reflection upon that performance. It is my belief that there should be agreed and explicit baseline standards of performance which are assessed and that, additionally, the ability to reflect upon performance is also assessed. There are stages in skill development and courses need to be sure which stages must be successfully passed at which points on the course.

8 Learning and applying a variety of helping strategies and interventions

The training situation should be the ideal place to experiment with new ideas, techniques and interventions within the safety of a supportive environment and where no damage will be done to clients. The best counsellors are surely the most flexible and resourceful counsellors who have a fund of strategies from which to find those which are appropriate for each individual client. A limited repertoire of techniques suggests a limited counsellor.

Wild eclecticism is not the aim, but reflective and creative practice is. We do not want trainees to use techniques without understanding the power of them and the best way to understand the power is to experience the technique oneself, both as client and as counsellor. Visualisation is useful in a variety of counselling situations. Trainees must not see it simply in terms of relaxation, but need to know the depths that can be reached very quickly using visualisation exercises. Empty chair work needs careful timing, structuring, pacing and debriefing. Trainees need plenty of practice with such a technique. Sculpting, art work, role play and brainstorming are other useful techniques which can be used in a variety of counselling approaches and settings, but which also require plenty of practice.

9 Identifying and owning personal strengths and limitations in relation to skills and strategies

Trainees will gradually get a sense of their own counselling style and it is to be hoped that all the above areas of knowledge and skill will be integrated into a holistic counselling approach. As the way of being is distinctive and individual it is acceptable to not be good at everything. It is a strength for a trainee to know her or his own limitations of effectiveness and to know what feels true and what feels false in the use of counselling skills and strategies. Of paramount importance is the welfare and safety of clients.

10   Developing an integrated counselling style

The final objective of Stage 2 takes us full circle back to Stage 1 because an integrated style will be the sum total of attitudes, values, beliefs and qualities as well as knowledge, skills and strategies. The aim of the first two stages of the learning cycle is to prepare the trainee for the supervised counselling practice of the next stage. To this we now turn.

LEARNING CYCLE STAGE 3: CLIENT WORK AND SUPERVISION

Learning objectives

1   To distinguish between counselling and other helping activities.
2   To set up counselling contracts with real clients.
3   To practise counselling competencies in real counselling situations outside of the course.
4   To regularly reflect upon counselling practice through use of a counselling log, case-notes and learning journal.
5   To experience regular supervision, both individual and group.
6   To develop the internal supervisor.
7   To develop confidence as a counsellor.

The third stage of the learning cycle involves work with clients. The BAC Course Recognition document (1990) states that this work needs to be with real clients and that although it must occur during training, it does not have to start at the beginning of training. Several trainees have difficulty getting client work simply because they do not have the credentials that training will give. Courses often specify that a certain number of hours must be completed before an award can be given to the trainee, even if the completion date for counselling hours logged is later than the end of the taught part of the course. It is essential that this aspect of training is highlighted at the point of application and selection for the course, so that trainees and trainers lose no time in ensuring that regular client work is taking place. The ideal situation is that all arrangements for work with clients are in full operation before commencement of the course.

Clarification is needed about the question: who is a real client? There have been problems at assessment where this issue has been fudged and where trainees have colluded to be clients for one another. Whilst such peer counselling is to be encouraged as an element of practice in the second stage, it does not fulfil the objectives of Stage 3. Logged work with clients should be with clients outside the course and where there is a clear counselling contract. Several training courses have networks between courses so that someone on, for example, a certificate course may be counselled on a regular basis by someone from a diploma course. This is just one way of overcoming the problem of finding real clients at the early stages of training.

This leads on to another issue which trainees often raise at the beginning of training. It is the distinction between counselling within a professional contract (however short) and using counselling skills as part of a helping role as, for example, nurse or teacher. At the commencement of training it is important to explore the helping spectrum including advice, guidance, support, befriending, counselling and therapy. The BAC codes of practice for counselling skills and for counselling are useful documents at this stage of exploration.

Preparation for client work involves consideration of all the managerial and administrative aspects of work with clients and course time will need to be devoted to practical matters such as location, frequency of sessions, length of sessions, contracting and boundaries.

There are three main ways in which client work can be recorded. The counselling log just lists sessions; case-notes are the opportunity for in-depth reflection and they may be accompanied by transcripts and recordings of sessions; and, finally, the learning journal is the place where reflections on practice in specific sessions can be incorporated into general reflections about developing counselling competence.

It is suggested (BAC 1990) that 100 hours of client work needs to take place during training and this work needs to be carefully supervised by a minimum of one supervision session to every eight counselling sessions. Should supervision take place on the course, or by external supervisors who can have a quite separate relationship with trainees? Is group supervision on the course sufficient or is individual supervision also necessary? These are questions for all courses, and courses differ markedly in their answers! The criteria for arriving at the answers must be criteria concerned with the welfare of clients and the safety of trainees, rather than criteria which are concerned with the economic staffing of courses. The ideal training experience would seem to involve the experience of group supervision within the course in addition to individual supervision by an external supervisor who has been appointed because of appropriate qualifications, experience and ability to work facilitatively with trainees.

The task of supervision with trainees involves support, training and aspects of managing the counselling relationship. It needs to be made clear to trainees that supervisors should not be in a line-management relationship to them in the practice setting. All supervisors should be issued with a code of practice for supervisors and regular meetings between the supervisor group and the course staff need to be arranged to provide a forum for discussion and an opportunity for professional development.

There is an issue about confidentiality. Trainees will rightly expect that work taken to the supervisor is confidential. The course staff will rightly expect to know how much use the trainee is making of supervision. Courses need to develop explicit guidelines which are agreed by trainees and their supervisors (see the following chapter for an example). Joint learning statements written by trainee and supervisor together at the end of a training period are one way of bridging the supervision with the rest of the course. If there is serious concern about the way a trainee is working with clients, then there must be a clear route for transmitting such concern from the supervisor to course staff without breaching confidentiality with the trainee.

The supervisor assesses trainee counsellor competence in a formative way and the trainee counsellor assesses his or her own competence every time he or she prepares for supervision and every time case-notes and supervision notes are written. This then leads into the final stage of the learning cycle: reflection, assessment, research.

LEARNING CYCLE STAGE 4: REFLECTION AND EVALUATION

Learning objectives

1 To reflect continuously upon learning both in the course and in work with real clients.

2 To engage in, and learn from, the process of assessment: self, peer and tutor assessment.
3 To become familiar with research processes which are appropriate in the field of counselling.
4 To become actively engaged in counselling research.

Reflection

It has been said that there is no learning without action and that there is no action which promotes learning other than that which is subject to reflection. The first two stages of the learning cycle prepare the trainee for counselling in action and the final stage allows learning to take place as a result of reflecting upon that action. The reflections from this stage highlight issues and areas for further learning and so the learning cycle begins over again.

These reflective processes may be built into the structure of the course to ensure that they are regular, continuous and systematic. Counselling supervision is in itself enforced professional reflection on a regular basis. Trainees need to take that a step further and reflect upon the supervision. There will be many opportunities for verbal reflection during groupwork, action learning sets, seminars, workshops, tutorials and with learning review partners. However, the tangible evidence is mainly in written assignments, several of which will be assessed. These will include the learning journal, case-notes of counselling, notes from supervision, joint learning statements between trainee and supervisor, and personal and professional development profiles. At the heart of the reflective process in this model is the learner who is being asked to set her or his own specific learning objectives session by session and to use the journal to reflect upon these session by session, noting what has been achieved, what has not been achieved, what factors in self and others are helping learning to take place and what is sabotaging learning.

Assessment

In this training model one of the basic assumptions is that learners can take responsibility for their own learning. In addition to assessing their own learning they are given the opportunity to help with the assessment of others on the course. The processes of reflection outlined above are the basis for self-assessment and for the ownership of personal and professional learning objectives.

There is no better way to understand what is expected in a written assignment than to have access to examples of work from other members of the group. A three-stage process of assessment is recommended, starting with a written self-assessment, then written feedback from peers, and finally tutor assessment. Courses need to be clear about what they expect in the way of self and peer assessment and some courses distinguish between self and peer feedback and tutor assessment. This may be the most honest way to address the issue of final marks, grades and decisions about pass or fail when these in reality rest with the course director and the awarding body for certificates and diplomas. Chapter Eight explores these and other issues with regard to assessment in counsellor training.

Research

When the word research is mentioned on counsellor training courses many trainees get very apprehensive, thinking that they will be inundated with a barrage of statistics. Yet all professionals who monitor, reflect upon, and ask questions about their own work are engaged at some level in action research. What is important at this stage in the learning cycle is to develop a questioning frame of mind, a research mentality.

Responsibility lies very much with the trainers themselves to exemplify good research practice by continuously researching their own counselling work. They may then be able to communicate an enthusiasm for asking research questions and they will have gained the credibility which comes from having engaged successfully in small-scale or large-scale research themselves.

Training courses often expect a small-scale research project, critical study or dissertation as a major assignment. This, well done with good tutorial support, can give trainees confidence and can whet their appetites so that, once qualified, they can take knowledge of research methodology and research processes into their professional life and, one hopes, they will continually investigate their own counselling work. At this final stage in the learning cycle, research questions which are raised will be explored by work done in the next cycle of Stages 1, 2 and 3.

Evaluation in this model is formative as well as summative.

Trainees are engaged in ongoing evaluation of self, others and the course itself. Processes for such evaluation will include learning partners, learning journals, community and course meetings with ongoing negotiation and contracting of course content. Evaluation does not just happen at the end of the course, but starts at the beginning when trainees are encouraged to set their own learning objectives and continuously to evaluate the course and themselves against these objectives. If objectives are framed as behavioural outcomes then evaluating against desired outcomes is fairly straightforward. Monitoring and evaluation which is built into the very dynamic of the course gives the impetus for constant incremental change.

In this chapter a model of training has been discussed and several areas of the model are given further discussion in specific chapters later in the book. The next chapter focuses upon the experience of using this model as a basis for one counselling training course: a diploma in counselling.

Chapter 4

The model in practice

The focus of this chapter is the way that the model informs the design and delivery of a diploma in counselling which has been developing over several years. The course objectives are listed and the selection process is explained. Details are given of a typical course session showing how it relates to the four stages of the learning cycle. Groupings of learners for different activities are explained and then details are given of each stage of the model in practice.

In order that the reader may get some insight into the way in which the model works in practice an example is given of one diploma course. This Advanced Diploma in Counselling is a two-year part-time course of 424 hours. It is recognised by the British Association for Counselling. The course sessions are for six hours weekly with an additional residential weekend at the beginning of the course and several non-residential weekend workshops throughout the two years.

The aim of the course is to develop competent and reflective counsellors by providing a theoretical foundation and practical training in an integrative model of counselling. The core theoretical model of the course is the Egan 'Skilled Helper' model. It is intended that students would be prepared to work as counsellors in such fields as health and medicine, careers guidance, education, social work, youth and community work, voluntary and pastoral work, staff care and counselling at work, as well as in practice as independent counsellors. The course emphasises that counselling is concerned with change, both personal and organisational, and therefore it helps students to understand about counselling in organisations as well as with individual clients.

PROFESSIONAL DEVELOPMENT

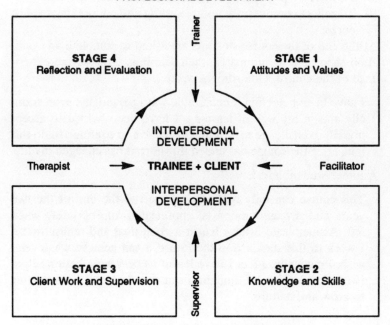

Figure 4.1 The model

STATED COURSE OBJECTIVES

1 To examine, historically and philosophically, the contributions
   of various theoretical approaches to counselling.
2 To study concepts of self in relation to the development of
   human relationships.
3 To explore the provision of counselling and guidance in the
   context of organisational systems.
4 To develop a working knowledge of the Egan model.
5 To increase awareness of personal strengths and limitations
   through experiential group processes.
6 To develop the skills of working with individuals and groups.
7 To explore the application of counselling skills to human
   resource management in organisations.
8 To plan, implement and evaluate specific counselling strategies, appropriate to a range of client problems and settings.

9   To increase awareness of ethical and professional issues.
10 To reflect continuously upon learning and counselling experiences.

At the end of the course students are asked to complete an evaluation sheet and to summarise their learning, interest and experience of the course. One student wrote:

> I have been helped in innumerable ways personally, professionally and in my way of learning. I have been helped to accept myself, to challenge myself and to resolve to continue to do this long after the course has ended. In short, it has changed my life.

Another student adds:

> This course can only be fairly assessed at the end of the two years and my assumption is, appreciated appropriately when left. Academically I have learnt a great deal and realise that if I work to this standard in the future, I can achieve whatever I wish. Practically, I feel I have learnt to become a better helper (with skills). Where I thought, I can now feel, and I am starting to grow and mature.

The selection process

The course refers to its members as students, which is appropriate to a course which is embedded in a university college. Throughout this chapter the word student will be used, rather than trainee. Selection is taken seriously by course staff because the place offered is for two years and the course is demanding. Selectors need to be assured that successful applicants will make full use of the place that is offered not only in terms of personal commitment but also in terms of commitment to others on the course as a member of a learning community. The selection process takes place over one full day and is divided into two parts. Between the two parts there is the opportunity for applicants to meet current or former members of the course informally.

The first part of the process entails the giving of course information followed by a group interaction exercise. This provides an opportunity for detailed exchange and clarification of information about course content, assessment and participation. The group exercise provides an opportunity for selectors to observe how individual applicants relate to and interact with each other in a group situation in order to ascertain existing counselling skills and attitudes as well as the potential for developing these. Such skills and attitudes include awareness of self and others, the core conditions of genuineness, warmth and empathy, and specific communication and interpersonal skills as employed within the counselling process.

The second part of the process involves individual interviews. The aim is to provide, through the individual interview, an opportunity for further detailed information exchange including clarification of the primary motivation or incentive for seeking entry to the course and how this meets with the course aims and objectives, particularly with regard to the interface and interrelationship between the educational, professional training and personal development components of the course.

Additionally the aim is to assess against identified selection criteria the capacity to:

- cope with the emotional, intellectual and academic requirements of the course;
- make use of, and reflect upon, significant life experiences;
- apply counselling skills and knowledge appropriately in specific helping situations;
- be self-critical and be able to make use of feedback, both positive and negative, generated through participation in the group exercise;
- be aware of the social and cultural context in which they live and work and in particular the nature of prejudice and oppression of minority groups.

The selection process is designed to assess capacity, potential, openness and commitment.

Comments from a selector:

We explain that the selection process is two-way and that applicants need to decide whether they wish to select this course as well as us selecting them. We have become more and more aware that clear information is vital so that applicants know what they are letting themselves in for in terms of course philosophy and demands. We want to be as open as possible about selection criteria, including that for the group exercise, so we tell them beforehand what we are looking for. Some might disagree with this but we believe it is only fair that people know what to expect.

We have also become more challenging during the individual interviews because it gives the opportunity to observe how a trainee is going to respond to the many challenges on the course. Non-traditional applicants are increasingly coming forward and we have gained confidence in selecting those who do not fit normal entry requirements because we have found that motivation and openness to learning are the two most important factors and non-traditional applicants often do very well if they can just get past the selection process.

Course structure

Each course group consists of sixteen students with a course leader, course tutor and experiential group facilitator. The group facilitator has no role in the assessment of students. Outside the taught course, each student has an appointed supervisor for individual supervision. Client work takes place outside the taught part of the course.

The course is structured to reflect and address the three aspects of the core model, namely, a problem management process, the application of specific skills, and a relationship offering the core conditions for effective helping relationships.

Thus the daily organisation of the course comprises a beginning session of theory and discussion to increase understanding, followed by a period of counselling practice in training groups to develop skills and competencies. The final sessions of the day are consultation with a learning review partner and (alternately) group supervision or experiential groupwork to address personal and professional development and for the development of interpersonal relationships.

The balance between intrapersonal and interpersonal development, theory and skills practice, consistent with the core theoretical model, is created through both the course structure and course content.

Teaching style

It is hoped that the quality of teaching on the course reflects the core model in that it is both trainee-centred and challenging. In parallel with the Skilled Helper model's emphasis on client responsibility, resource development and collaboration, students are encouraged to take responsibility for their own learning while the course tutors act as facilitators (see Chapter Six). The emphasis is upon experiential learning, and resources for learning include the valuable knowledge, skills and experience of the course members.

Tutors endeavour to develop an atmosphere of enthusiasm, openness and trust where each person feels secure enough to engage in learning experiences which are both personally and professionally challenging and meaningful. Negotiation of course content is viewed as a group responsibility and students are routinely involved in the programme planning for each term. Immediacy and self-disclosure are modelled and encouraged by course tutors, as is openness to feedback.

In order to maximise the opportunities for experiential learning and for learning with others, the course is divided into several groupings. These groupings are explained below.

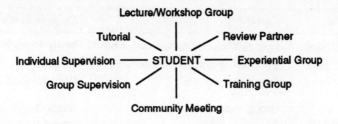

Figure 4.2 Course groupings

Lecture/Workshop Group: The whole course group of sixteen.

Review Partners: Each student chooses one review partner for the year and they meet every session to reflect on their learning journals, to share progress and to set learning objectives.

Experiential Group: Eight students meet fortnightly with a facilitator. This alternates with the group supervision group.

Training Group: This is a group of four students who remain together for a whole year to practise counselling skills and interventions. They rotate roles of counsellor, client, observer and facilitator and each group has video recording and playback equipment. They obtain specific and immediate feedback from self, peers and trainers.

Community Meeting: The whole group of sixteen meet together with the trainers each week for ongoing monitoring and evaluation of the course.

Group Supervision: This is a group of four who remain together for the year. They are joined by a group supervisor who is one of the two core staff of the course.

Individual Supervision: Each student has an individual supervisor who is appointed by the course leader. The supervisor is separate from the course and the student sees the supervisor between course sessions.

Tutorial: Each student will have an individual tutorial twice each term with a core member of staff to discuss progress and to get help with written assignments.

Table 4.1 A typical course session of six hours

Time	Activity	Stage of model
110 mins	Lecture/Discussion/Demonstration	Stage 1 and 2
100 mins	Counselling practice in groups	Stage 2
90 mins	Experiential group	Core of model
	or	
	Group supervision	Stage 3
30 mins	Review partner	Stage 4
30 mins	Community meeting	Stage 4

THE CORE OF THE MODEL: INTRAPERSONAL AND INTERPERSONAL DEVELOPMENT

One of the course documents states that the personal development of the student is emphasised and encouraged as an important dimension of training within the structure and content of the course, within the course assessment and extending where appropriate beyond the parameters of the course into the personal and professional life of the student. Explicit provision within the course is made in three ways.

1 The experiential group

Students participate in a group of eight members with a facilitator who is not involved in the core teaching or any assessment on the course.

Guidelines on the experiential group process are given to students at the beginning of the course to take the mystique out of personal development and to enable them to set personal objectives within a framework for personal growth. Information from these guidelines follows:

It is hoped that the experiential groups will develop their own aims and objectives and become self-directing and self-monitoring. In this setting the group members have the opportunity to engage in personal growth and development through facilitator and peer-led experiential group processes. The experiential group provides a forum for the observation and practice of group counselling skills and approaches and the exploration of interpersonal relationships. Ground rules governing issues such as confidentiality and self-disclosure will be established at the beginning of the group and will also evolve as the group progresses. These will be negotiated within the group by the group members and the facilitator.

The group provides the opportunity for participants to continue to explore in an experiential way aspects of theory presented in workshops throughout the course (e.g. if there has just been a session on TA a group member may wish to explore his or her lifescripts within the group). The experiential group also provides a forum for exploration of issues arising from other components of the course such as:

1 Objectives formulated in the learning journal.
2 Relationships with course members and tutors.
3 Personal issues, for example, those arising from the Personal Development Profile.
4 Links between the experience of being a group member and the experience of being the client in a counselling relationship.
5 Connections between personal learning in the group and the professional development of the counsellor.
6 Awareness of the skills and values of the counsellor as they inform ways of being in the group in relation to self and others.

In the first year of the course it is envisaged that the experience of participants will centre around awareness of being in the group and aspects of group process such as:

Trust building	Boundaries and contracts	Immediacy
Self perception	Appropriate self-disclosure	Creativity
Risk taking	Interpersonal relationships	Resistance
Power and control	Giving and receiving feedback	Authority
Dependency and autonomy	Conflict management	Intimacy
Defensive processes	Interpersonal style	Experimentation

The style of facilitation will combine appropriate challenge with support and is likely to include: modelling behaviours which help to create a climate of trust, risk-taking and safety amongst members; focusing awareness on aspects of individual and group process in the 'here and now'; exploring creative ways of working with issues as they arise; introducing structures which invite members to reflect on significant issues at different stages of the group's life.

Members will be expected to take responsibility for their own participation in the group and to take shared responsibility (along with the facilitator) for the precise nature and development of the group experience. In the second year of the course it is expected that the group will become increasingly self-directing with group members taking the opportunity to practise their own group facilitation skills.

At the end of each year of the course students will compile Joint Learning Statements combining self and peer assessment with feedback from the group facilitator. The focus will be on the student's way of being in the group with the emphasis on participation and involvement. The content of the Joint Learning Statement will constitute part of the ongoing work of the group and is likely to include observations on relevant themes and issues listed in these guidelines in addition to future objectives arising out of the overall learning experience. Although not assessed, the Joint Learning Statement is a course requirement, to be submitted at the end of each year.

(Wosket and Kennett 1993)

At the end of the course students reflect upon the experience of being in the experiential group. One says: 'I've had to take a long, hard look at aspects of myself I thought I'd handled long ago.' Another adds: 'In many ways I would like to start again, but from where I am now.' These comments highlight the developmental nature of personal work in groups, and the feelings of frustration that can result from the growing awareness of self. Because work in the experiential group may touch difficult and painful areas for the student it is essential that there is sensitivity and consistency in the group facilitator so that one student, for example, is able to say that she has benefited enormously in terms of both professional and personal development and that: 'The supportive climate has been a rare and valuable experience.'

2 Opportunities for being in the client role

The experiential group provides learning experiences which are linked directly with the experience of being the client in a counselling relationship. In the processing and debriefing of such experiences, group members are encouraged to make these links explicit through identification with the client in counselling alongside their immediate here-and-now experience. This is an extension of being in the client role as practised in skills training groups and in brief exercises including role play which often form an integral part of theory sessions.

It is strongly recommended that students engage in properly contracted personal counselling or therapy whilst on the course, particularly where there appear to be unresolved personal issues and for those who have not previously experienced an ongoing counselling relationship. Hilary is a second-year student who reflects in her learning journal about a recent experience of some counselling which took place over the summer break between the first and second year of the course.

Hilary

The short-sharp-shock treatment was the feel of my counselling which took place intensively over three weeks. This was how we had contracted it to be and at that time it was right. It entailed a month of sleepless nights, mind in a spin, pain and discomfort but oh, what learning, what insights and how enthusiastic I feel about the future. I taped the sessions not only for me as a client to re-hear, but for me as a counsellor to learn about the technique. And I have learned. As a lot of my problems were centred around irrational beliefs we worked with a lot of RET. This I have backed up with reading about RET. It is hard to put into words what has happened for me but I have come out of the counselling having travelled far in my self-knowledge and belief in myself. I have spent time finding out what I really believe in, what I value, what I really want out of life, as well as who I really am. I have explored my parenting role, my sexuality, my work. I realised how hard it is for a client to talk about things that feel so deep or uncomfortable, like sexuality, yet the feeling of being heard, respected and not judged is powerful.

The power of the client/counsellor relationship has provided much food for thought both as client and counsellor. It is a wonderful experience to be held in regard, to be listened to, to be understood. For me this was a powerful tool in moving me on to understanding myself, to be able to trust the counsellor with my very being. Yet in my vulnerable state, I began to experience the power of maybe becoming too close, dependent even? This opened up so many questions for me as a counsellor who likes to work in a client-centred way with bereaved people that I have taken it to supervision and would like to discuss it on the course. Awareness is the key and boundaries which are clear-cut.

Although tutors will facilitate arrangements for counselling to be set up between members of different courses (for example students on introductory courses receiving counselling from those on the diploma course), the responsibility for the counselling contract lies with the student. Review partners provide opportunities for on-going peer counselling relationships, one in each year of the course. In addition, personal development days during both years provide opportunities for working through personal issues in a more extended way.

3 The learning journal

Aspects of personal learning from both within and outside the course are recorded in the journal. Relevant entries may include reflection upon significant experiences in terms of thoughts, feelings and behaviours, exploration and re-evaluation of attitudes and personal values, and exploration of ideas and opportunities for making personal changes. Evaluation of self-development is encouraged by means of the setting and reviewing of specific learning objectives which may also be reflected upon with the review partner. Termly summaries of learning are required in order to review and assess personal progress and development during the preceding period and to set objectives for the immediate future. These summaries form the basis of the Personal Development Profile which serves as a self-assessment device to evaluate personal growth and development over each year of the course and to identify future self-development objectives. The following extract is from the same student, Hilary, who summarises in her learning journal themes from the autumn term in her second year of the course.

Hilary

This term began with me being keen to see whether my experience of being counselled over the summer was really going to make an impact on my life. I feel that many themes in this term's journal have been ongoing throughout the course. It feels like a journey with two steps forward and then one back. Forward moving but with learning situations to ensure I don't get too complacent. Generally I see a growth in awareness within the group dynamic and in skills training and giving feedback. This is true in my counselling where I find I am able to pick up on most of the issues my supervisor has pinpointed.

My counselling has grown this term too, with more referrals and the opportunity for the experience of longer term clients. In terms of skills my aim has been to be 'with' my clients this term, being relaxed enough to allow them their pace and confident enough in my abilities not to have to 'prove' my skills.

In relation to personal growth an awareness of a lack of personal space and relaxation has been a theme during the term. As I have felt stressed with the research project and course work on top of my other work and being a mum I have acknowledged a need for 'Me'. I have not fully met this although I have met a very immediate need to have some longer term therapy. These feelings have been bubbling up all term, refusing to be submerged and I've finally got the message!

LEARNING CYCLE STAGE 1: ATTITUDES AND VALUES

On the selection day students begin the exploration of their assumptions and beliefs and this then continues throughout the course. They are asked to read extracts from Carl Rogers' work (1961) and to comment on his beliefs about the person in relation to their own beliefs. In the group exercise on selection day they are asked to discuss their own views on the most important qualities in those who wish to be counsellors, and their assumptions, values and attitudes begin to be expressed.

One of the first exercises on the course is the one mentioned in the previous chapter, where all students are given Rogers (1961) ten questions about helping relationships. This happens at the induction weekend with plenty of time for reading, assimilating, reflecting and discussing. Another early exercise in the course is that of looking at the philosophical assumptions behind the major theories of counselling. Yet another is called the philosophy of counselling exercise, which invites students to answer questions about their own motivation, values, beliefs and moral and ethical concerns.

Students are given copies of codes of ethics and practice for counselling skills, for counselling and for supervision. The course group discusses these and it is a useful exercise to draw up a code of practice for those on this particular course. Such discussions do not have to be carried out separately from the work on theories and on client problems. Indeed, some of the most useful ethical discussions occur when using real client problems within the current experience of the students.

Although we view this work as foundation work, it needs to happen in an ongoing way throughout the course, rather than just at the beginning. For this reason there are regular sessions throughout the two years of the course on ethical and professional issues. Students are encouraged to lead the sessions and to bring issues which have either arisen from their work with specific clients, or because the issue is of general interest. Course staff would want to ensure that amongst the issues discussed are: power, responsibility, freedom, accountability, competence, confidentiality, prejudice, equality, oppression, justice, exploitation.

LEARNING CYCLE STAGE 2: KNOWLEDGE AND SKILLS

Between 150 and 200 hours of the course are devoted to learning counselling theory, including the theories of personality, learning and human development assumed within the core model and within individual theories of counselling, and pertinent to the study of specific client problems and issues.

The core theoretical model of the course: the Egan model

A coherent grounding for learners is provided by Egan's Skilled Helper Model (Egan 1993). This core theoretical model is integrative. It provides a framework for the counselling process which draws upon psychodynamic, humanistic and behavioural theory as appropriate for different stages of the counselling process. It is an intentional model of counselling based upon the assumption that action leading to valued outcomes is what the client wants and that effective action is preceded by awareness, insight and clarification. The counsellor provides a balance between support and challenge in order that the client may be able to take responsibility for his or her own development within a relationship of trust. The model assumes that human beings are both sensitive and robust; that they can learn the model and use it for themselves; that there is always a wealth of untapped potential which can be released and mobilised; that there is a shadow side in human beings which produces self-defeating behaviour; that thinking and feeling affect action; that affirmation is very powerful but not always enough to produce change in human beings; that change can be very difficult because of inertia and entropy.

One of the main features of this model is the way that it moves from a person-centred approach in the here and now, to the future-centred focus of brainstorming the preferred scenario and finally through to the behavioural stages of goal setting and action planning. It uses a loosening and tightening pattern of creatively exploring and then focusing down. This is because of the belief that human beings often have problems because they feel stuck or trapped. This counselling process provides the opportunity to explore wants rather than oughts and to engage in creative brainstorming in order to broaden options in relation to thoughts, feelings and behaviours.

Within the model is the appreciation of human fallibility. Early in the process there is the awareness of blind-spots and counsellors are taught to challenge blind-spots empathically rather than reinforce them by just listening to them.

It is essential that counsellors using this model remain person-centred throughout. This is difficult for trainees, once they are introduced to some of the active and behavioural interventions. The distinction is drawn between being directive, and drawing from behavioural strategies in a person-centred way that involves influencing the process but not the content.

Egan stresses that the model is for the client. The client is not there for the model. Trainees are taught the complete model but are reminded that clients may only need one part of it, and that it can be accessed at any point which is appropriate for the needs of the client. Egan states that he gives principles, not formulae, and he also points out that pragmatism drives the model. Learners are encouraged to use the model in the way Egan intended, as a flexible framework which will provide a map for the counselling process.

Theoretical context

During the first term of the first year the focus is on those aspects of counselling theory which underpin the Egan model. These include:

- concepts of the person as viewed from both humanistic and behavioural perspectives and emphasised at each stage of the 'Skilled Helper' model;
- the role of the environment in facilitating growth, learning and change, for example the importance of the core facilitating conditions emphasised in the person-centred approach;
- the nature of eclecticism, including areas of convergence and divergence;
- applied developmental and cognitive-behavioural psychology;
- applied personality theory as assumed within the different stages and processes of the core theoretical model and manifest in the counselling process;
- an understanding of social psychology as underpinning a people-in-systems (Egan and Cowan, 1979) approach to counselling and helping, for example the ways in which social systems affect personal growth and development.

Students are also introduced to relevant theoretical concepts underpinning the therapeutic process and basis of change as conceived in the Egan model. These include the assumptions and explanations underlying a problem management process, underpinned by a therapeutic relationship which provides the essential core conditions for growth and change. This is through the development of the client's personal and environmental resources and the setting and attaining of appropriate and realistic goals. Relevant theoretical concepts relating to the identification and management of resistance, disincentives, inertia and entropy, on the one hand, and the use of rewards, on the other, are included as part of the process.

Theories of counselling

The introduction of the core theoretical model early in the first term is preceded by an overview of the common theories of counselling and therapy and their roots in the main schools or traditions of psychoanalysis, humanism and behaviourism. During the second term, students are given a more detailed introduction to other theoretical approaches, for example, psychodynamic, gestalt, cognitive-behavioural, transactional analysis, existential, neuro-linguistic programming. The person-centred approach is the focus for the induction weekend. Comparisons between aspects and stages of the Egan model and other theories are made explicit as are opportunities for combining and integrating various relevant theoretical perspectives and their practical applications at different stages of the Egan model. Examples are: the application of psycho-dynamic principles at stage 1a, 'telling the story'; gestalt or rational-emotive perspectives at stage 1b, 'challenging blind-spots' at stage 1c, 'finding leverage'; transpersonal approaches at stage 11a, 'the preferred scenario' (Egan, 1993). Opportunities for exploring other theories are provided in year two of the course when students become familiar with, for example, personal construct theory and psychosynthesis.

Social psychology

In addition to counselling theory students are introduced to some of the theories pertaining to social psychology, in particular the theoretical explanations underlying the social systems in which we live and how these affect both client development and counsel-ling practice. This would normally include a basic apprecia-tion of general and family systems theory, the psychological processes of separation and indviduation, theories associated with gender differentiation and gender role stereotyping, and the sexual development of the individual including the dynamics of gender and sexuality in human object-relationships. The theories and underlying assumptions associated with individual differences based on race, culture, religious, political and ethical beliefs are similarly introduced during the first year including the theories underpinning transcultural counselling, feminist approaches to counselling and therapy, and relevant social and historical perspectives on the development of individuals and human groups.

People in organisations

During the second year of the course students are introduced to relevant theoretical concepts underpinning the management and development of human resources including learning and motivation, group and team dynamics, people management and an appreciation of equal opportunities and its application to organisational procedures and practices.

Client issues and problems

An ongoing element throughout both years of the course is the study of specific client problems and issues such as:

- bereavement and loss
- anxiety and depression
- physical, sexual and psychological abuse
- eating disorders
- dependency on drugs and alcohol
- marital breakdown
- intimate relationships
- sexual orientation and identity

Developing counselling skills

This course has developed a systematic approach to skills training, heavily influenced by the work of Kagan (1967), Carkhuff (1969), Ivey (1978) and Egan (1993). The intention is to provide regular opportunities for skills training within the course and for practice and reflection outside the course. The course provides video-recording and playback equipment in small microteaching rooms where training groups of four students rotate the roles of facilitator, counsellor, client and observer with supervision provided by a course tutor. Two rooms are fitted with fixed equipment and two rooms use manpack equipment. When a student is in the role of facilitator the responsibility includes timekeeping, operation of the video equipment and organisation of the peer feedback session immediately following counselling practice. When a student is in the role of client he or she is asked to bring real issues or concerns for the counsellor to work on, rather than role playing the problems of another person. This is an essential feature for the success of the training groups because they become real, with students really trying to help one another in an authentic way.

The 'client' is asked to consider carefully, and to take responsibility for, the issue brought to such a session which will be time-limited and which will be focused upon the learning of the person who is the 'counsellor'. When in the role of counsellor students are reminded that this is an opportunity for practice of specific skills or strategies related to a task which has been agreed and it is not in any sense a complete counselling session. The 'observer' is asked to write notes and to give very specific feedback on both verbal and non-verbal behaviour, but only after feedback has been given by the counsellor first focusing on his or her own performance, then by the client and finally by the observer. This feedback sequence keeps responsibility with the student who is practising the skills, the counsellor, by focusing first upon that person and, in effect, asking that person to then ask the client and observer for their feedback. As the course progresses, students are asked to tell one another their learning objectives at the beginning of a practice session so that the whole group is able to focus on feedback which has been requested rather than imposed. This leads to intentionality and openness rather than lack of direction and then defensiveness in the face of unsolicited feedback. It has been the experience of the course tutors that these training groups can become the most powerful learning experience on the course. They give students the opportunity to offer genuine support and challenge to one another whilst also giving them the chance to disclose important things about themselves in a small group setting which has constant membership for one year.

Although these groups are not intended to be for personal development, students have reported that they have sometimes felt safer to explore personal issues in a task-oriented group such as this, rather than in the larger experiential group set up for that purpose. Could it be that the training group allows students to disclose as and when they wish, and that a group which is specially for the purpose of personal development can actually inhibit self-disclosure because the expectation is too great that at a certain preordained time everyone will gaze upon their navels? This is an ongoing issue for the course.

The organisation of training groups

Students rotate the roles of counsellor, client, observer and facilitator and hopefully each student has the opportunity to be in each role during each practice session, or at least over the space of two sessions. Tutors have a rota for visiting the groups. The order in which roles are rotated is significant. It is helpful if the counsellor moves to observer, observer to client, client to facilitator and facilitator to counsellor so that direct experience is alternated with observation and facilitation. Table 4.2 shows how these roles are rotated in the groups.

Table 4.2 Arrangements for training groups

Group A Room 1 Video facilities	Group B Room 2 Video facilities	Group C Room 3 Video facilities	Group D Room 4 Video facilities
Facilitator	Client	Observer	Counsellor
Counsellor	Facilitator	Client	Observer
Observer	Counsellor	Facilitator	Client
Client	Observer	Counsellor	Facilitator
Visiting Tutor	Visiting Tutor	Visiting Tutor	Visiting Tutor

The work in training groups is supplemented by additional skills practice in theory workshops and at the residential weekend. The experiential group also provides opportunities for more fluid and spontaneous practice and feedback on counselling and interpersonal skills used in group interventions.

During the first year of the course the skills practice in training groups is closely linked to the microskills and process of the Egan model. In the second year students are encouraged to integrate techniques and ways of working from a variety of models and approaches covered on the course. This development is reflected in the assessment requirements at the end of each year of the course: at the end of the first year students are required to identify, demonstrate and evaluate specific skills and competencies and to identify the three stages of the Egan model in their counselling presentation. They are also asked to demonstrate an awareness of dynamics in the relationship. In the second year they are required to demonstrate and evaluate counselling competence, incorporating skills and approaches from other theoretical orientations in one video-recorded session through the five aspects of support, challenge, resourcefulness, flow and immediacy.

LEARNING CYCLE STAGE 3: CLIENT WORK AND SUPERVISION

Client work

It has already been suggested that the trainee and client are at the heart of the training model and that the core area of personal development together with the first two stages of the model are in preparation for this third stage of work with clients. It is the most important activity of the course and yet it is the one which of necessity lies outside the course. Therefore, the course tutors have to devise ways of bringing the experience of counselling work and supervision back into the course.

There are a number of professional and ethical issues when students start to work with clients, which this course has addressed. One issue is that of completing a requisite number of hours of counselling before being allowed to qualify; another is about drawing the distinction between counselling, supporting, befriending or using counselling skills; another concerns the expectations of agencies which allow the trainee to counsel, particularly if they see this as parallel to the sort of placement offered to students on other types of courses and if a question of payment (on either side) arises. The point at which a trainee is expected to start work with clients is another difficult issue which requires clarification. Taping and transcribing sessions for assessment requires the consent of the client and this course has introduced permission slips which have to be signed by both client and counsellor before client sessions can be presented for assessment.

On this course students are required to complete a minimum of 100 hours of counselling practice over the two years of the course, or if necessary this can continue after the taught part of the course but must be completed satisfactorily before the award of Diploma is made. All counselling sessions undertaken, which must be with someone who is not a member of the course, are logged in a supervised practice file. In addition, five hours of counselling work each term is analysed in detail and written up as case-notes. Students are encouraged to experiment by using different frameworks for writing case-notes and they are reminded that confidentiality must be maintained by, for example, using symbols or codes and not including any specific information which could lead to a client being identified.

Case-notes will provide the following evidence: intentional counselling in terms of objectives, process, outcome and evaluation both from the client and the counsellor perspective; use of a variety of frameworks for reflecting on practice; reflections upon the counsellor, the client and the relationship between the two; work with a range of clients.

Several safeguards exist to ensure that the client work is counselling rather than befriending or supporting and this is an area which is covered at interview. Students are normally only selected for the course if they have arrangements in place for contracted counselling work to take place. At the induction residential weekend full discussion of definitions and terms takes place, in the context of the BAC codes of ethics and practice for counselling and for counselling skills. This is usually found to be very helpful by students.

Supervision

There are three functions of supervision for the trainee: the training function, the supportive function and the managerial function. In order to provide this there is provision of both individual and group supervision on the course.

Each student has an individual supervisor from outside the course, appointed by the course director. A minimum of two individual supervision sessions each term is required and these are written up in the supervised practice file. The BAC requirement is for one supervision session for every eight counselling sessions for a counsellor in training. If more sessions are wanted by students then they are encouraged to make an additional arrangement for these either with their supervisor, or if that is not physically or financially possible, with another supervisor. The course tutors are able to tap into a network of supervisors through the courses which are offered in supervision. Group supervision is also provided on the course, in groups of four and with a course tutor. Students are reminded that they should not normally bring the same material to individual and group supervision but, if they do, this must be made explicit at the start of a session with reasons why more work is needed on the material in question.

All the course methodology emphasises that the student takes responsibility for his or her own learning and this starts with the setting of learning objectives. In group supervision, the student will bring material to the group and will set the agenda for the supervision session, thus becoming proactive rather than reactive.

Individual supervisors are selected not only because of their own experience and knowledge as counsellors, but also because of their suitability to work with trainees. They are only selected if they have an appreciation of the core values and objectives of the course even though they may operate from a different theoretical model in their own counselling.

Supervisors are required to complete a Supervisor Registration Form at the time of appointment to a student or students on the course, giving details of their supervision training and experience and the arrangements for their own supervision. It is the intention of the course to use, where possible, supervisors who have a qualification in supervision or those who are working towards this goal. This indicates the high value placed by course tutors on the work of the supervisor. Close links are fostered between the course and the supervisors who are normally expected to attend twice yearly meetings with students and tutors together. These meetings combine student and supervisor support, administrative clarification and professional development. Half of the meeting will be taken up by a lecture or discussion with the whole course and the supervisors on some current counselling issue or approach, the latter half of the meeting consisting of tutors and supervisors talking through the practicalities of their relationship and the task of supervision with trainees. Issues which supervisors raise are, for example, the nature of the contract when it is between three parties – student, course tutor and supervisor; confidentiality; what to do if a student does not attend for supervision; what to do if the counselling work of a student is giving the supervisor cause for concern; how much time to allow for discussion of the student's experience of the course as against their work specifically with clients; what to do if the student obviously requires extra supervision over and above that which has been paid for by the course; how to draw up the joint learning statement with the student at the end of the year; whether to ask to see the student's case-notes and notes on supervision in the supervised practice file; whether to ask students to bring audio or video recordings to supervision.

The course stresses the importance of the relationship between the student and the supervisor and expects confidentiality to be maintained. However, because supervision is provided as part of professional, rather than personal, development there are professional requirements to safeguard the welfare of clients. If a supervisor has any serious concern about a student it is therefore clearly expected that the concern will be conveyed to the course tutor, but only after discussion with the student. Moreover it is preferable that the communication is from student and supervisor together. Similarly, if course tutors are concerned about a student they will need to contact the supervisor, but in the first instance this will normally be via the student.

At the end of each year the student and supervisor draw up a joint learning statement and this is placed in the supervised practice file as a summary of the learning from counselling work done that year. The course tutors find it best if both supervisor and student write something and then discuss what they have written as part of the final supervision session for that year.

LEARNING CYCLE STAGE 4: REFLECTION AND EVALUATION

The course is designed to encourage ongoing reflection upon all aspects of the learning process. A course document (Wosket and Kennett 1993) states that students are helped to develop as reflective practitioners and to monitor their own work and personal development in the following ways:

1   The Learning Journal which encourages reflection upon all aspects of the course, on counselling work undertaken in the work setting, and on relationships with peers and tutors.

Students are required to set, monitor and evaluate specific learning objectives and goals. A reflective summary is required at the end of each term.

2 The Personal Development Profile which is compiled at the end of each year to pull together the threads of personal and professional development and to set future short-term and long-term goals.

3 The Supervised Practice File where students are required to write critical evaluations of five counselling sessions per term and all meetings with their supervisor.

4 Through regular workshops on ethical and professional issues which encourage students to recognise and address issues and dilemmas in their own counselling practice.

5 Through the procedures for ongoing constructive feedback. Feedback includes: self, tutor and peer assessment of written assignments, practical work in training groups, personal development in the experiential group, professional development in group and individual supervision, weekly review with a learning partner.

The advantage of continuous reflection and feedback is that learning opportunities are fully exploited by constantly bringing them into awareness. The mind is sharpened by continually focusing and so the cycle of setting objectives, acting upon them and reflecting upon the action is constantly moving forward. The disadvantage, from the student point of view, is that it seems relentless. The learning journal is the main vehicle for reflection and it either becomes a constant companion and friend, or an albatross forever hanging round the neck. For most students it is probably a bit of both. As one student said in the course evaluation: 'It was hard work, and lots of it. I hadn't quite appreciated how much.' What did constant reflection do for this student? 'I have changed for the better. I am now happier with me and with my clients, can make better use of models and theories, have insight into my faults and how I can improve them, have shared learning with others both on and off the course, hopefully I am a better counsellor and I can truly say that I am one now.' For this student learning and reflection helped to bring about a sense of wholeness and integration.

Reflection upon the course itself is encouraged, as well as reflection upon personal learning. For this reason a community meeting takes place on each day of the course so that students and staff evaluate progress collaboratively, reflecting on the experience of the course and its design and administration. They negotiate the course timetable, plan future events and clarify course requirements together. This experience helps to turn reflection into evaluation so that course evaluation becomes an ongoing process rather than just something that happens at the end of the course. It is the experience of tutors and students alike that although the community meeting is valued by most, it is also disliked by some and thought to be a waste of time by others. Students take turns to facilitate the meeting and this successfully shifts the power base away from the tutor who then has to request time to discuss business items. It has been found to be useful to have a formal agenda for the first part of the meetings so that trivial detail does not take over. It has also been found to be useful to distinguish clearly the purpose of the community meeting from that of a personal development group, otherwise some members try to use it for therapy rather than for community issues.

Competent and reflective practitioners will continually engage in research into counselling and into their own counselling work. The course prepares students for this by having a module on research in the second year of the course. This is a practically based module with the objective of helping students to design a small project on some aspect of their own counselling work. It gives them an introduction to the whole field of counselling research, to appropriate methodology and to ways of collecting, analysing, reporting and evaluating data. The important part of this exercise is to convey the message that everyone can be a researcher and to help each student to develop a research mentality. For those who have little in the way of academic background this can be daunting, and yet what a feeling of achievement there is when a student says at the end of the course:

I think that this course has pushed me to my limits at present. In achieving what I have done I have gained confidence and produced work that I never imagined I was capable of. I do not intend to stop there though because what it has given me is the incentive to go on. So I may in the future embark on another course. Although I say I hate the academic work I have greatly improved and notice the difference in the way I now write notes at work. I can actually enjoy reading now and feel that I have the right to be in a library instead of feeling like a fish out of water.

Chapter 5

Dynamics of the training relationship

In this chapter dynamics are explored through three themes in the training relationship: trust and dependency; authority and control; competition and rivalry. Unconscious processes are discussed: projection, transference, countertransference and resistance. Examples are given from several training situations and from both trainer and trainee experience. When focusing upon the theme of authority and control different perspectives are discussed: loose holding; group dynamics and group processes; archetypal roles; transactions and games.

This chapter is intended to be a practical exploration of some of the issues which arise when trainers and trainees relate to one another in the training relationship. This relationship is one in which power, authority and responsibility are initially invested in the trainer as provider of the course although the trainer will be trying to collaborate with the trainee in sharing power, authority and responsibility within clear boundaries. Much of the dynamic is around confronting, defining, negotiating and clarifying the role of each person on the course in relation to one another as members of a learning community where there is assumed to be a high level of motivation towards change and growth. Three themes in relationships have been highlighted by Jacobs (1986): trust and dependency; authority and control; competition and rivalry. In psychodynamic theory these relate to early developmental stages and tasks (Erikson 1965). They provide a useful basis for exploring some of the dynamics in the training relationship.

Within this framework there are the human realities which can be experienced as vulnerabilities, fears and anxieties; power struggles; anger, conflicts and confrontations. These are connected with the demands made upon trainers and trainees as they engage together in the processes of learning, change and growth. Unconscious as well as conscious thoughts, feelings and behaviours come into play on the part of both trainer and trainee so that there may be projection, transference, countertransference, resistance (see Casement 1985; Thompson 1987). Training supervision is essential so that the trainer may understand more clearly the dynamics which are operating in training situations and be empowered to deal with difficult situations as quickly and as cleanly as possible and, where this is not possible, to be able to work with the messiness which is the very stuff of the learning and teaching experience.

Where there are difficulties in the trainer/trainee relationship they may arise because either the trainer or the trainee is confused, anxious, or fearful, uncertain and therefore vulnerable in some way. These feelings may produce dependency and counterdependency, envy and competition, anger, withdrawal, conflict or confrontation. Some examples of these feelings in trainers and trainees are given later in the chapter. The way in which they are expressed will largely depend on the presence of previous unresolved issues and material, on current levels of self-esteem and on the ability of both parties to engage in dialogue.

TRUST AND DEPENDENCY

Trainees need to trust their trainers to provide a safe place where learning can occur. This safety will be experienced if there is the experience of containment (Casement 1985) provided through the clear setting and holding of boundaries. Once the trainees are able to trust they will depend upon the trainer. This may cause difficulties if the trainer withdraws from them in any way or if the idealisation of the trainer leads to disappointment or splitting (Fairbairn 1952). This is particularly possible where there are a number of trainers. If the trainees' dependency needs are not met it may result in anger, guilt, anxiety or concern. Counterdependency is another possibility and this can produce ongoing conflicts and confrontations if it is not recognised and worked with. Let us consider some of the unconscious processes which may affect the trust and dependency dynamic between trainers and trainees. We will begin with transference and countertransference in the training relationship in which either or both trainer and trainee may make projections on to the other.

Projection

Oatley (1984: 132) states that in therapeutic terms projection is used to describe 'the expectations through which we both see the other and are blinded to who she is'. He notes that the projections which cause most difficulty are those which are connected to an image of the threatening or frustrating other and where we will have well developed patterns of response. Object-relations theory (Winnicott 1979) states that where there have been relationships with significant others in the past in which there has been threat or disappointment and where this has been internalised and not worked through, it will get acted out in later relationships. Oatley notes two aspects of response put forward by Fairbairn (1952). One is the 'split' which occurs when the mother is expected to be satisfying but is not and the image is then of her as seductive and frustrating. This causes disappointment leading to responses such as withdrawal. Another arises when the mother is experienced as punitive and the child begins to feel bad or unwanted, leading to responses such as rebelliousness. The training relationship may engender such responses as some of the above wishes and feelings from childhood re-emerge. This can happen for trainers and for trainees. Projection is an ego-defence mechanism in which we attribute to others our own unacceptable desires and impulses so that we do not have to deal with them ourselves.

Positive transference and countertransference

In the therapeutic transference relationship clients make projections on to the therapist. In the training relationship, transference and countertransference will occur without any conscious encouragement on the part of the trainer. Transference has been described as the unconscious shifting of feelings and fantasies, positive and negative, that are displacements from reactions to significant others in the client's past, with the client attributing to the therapist unfinished business from the past (Corey 1986). Countertransference occurs when the therapist's conflicts and unfinished business are triggered, causing the therapist perhaps to behave irrationally with the client. Corey notes that this is most likely to occur when the therapist relates to the client as if this person were mother, father or lover. A positive form of countertransference occurs in response to the transference of the client. In this situation the therapist notes how he or she is responding to the client and uses this information to gain insight into the client's transference – for example, when the client treats the therapist like a hostile parent the therapist can actually feel what that is like and how that must have been for the client in the past. Trainer and trainee will also experience the phenomena of transference and countertransference and if it occurs and is recognised, it can be viewed as a positive opportunity for the development of insight and for working through unresolved experiences in the past. However, when it happens unexpectedly it can be confusing and sometimes painful for trainer and trainee.

Positive transference and countertransference are present where there is liking for the other and it occurs, for example, when the trainer becomes a transference figure with whom the trainee 'has the opportunity to relive the type of parent–child relationship he might have wished for or to some extent had' (Jacobs 1989: 13). This is illustrated at work in the following example with a trainee whom I have called Stuart.

Stuart has worked hard to obtain a place on the counselling course and now that he is on the course he is investing a lot of personal energy and commitment in order to succeed. He feels that he walks a tightrope between success and failure and it would be easy to slip into failure. Lesley is the course leader and she realises how important success is to Stuart. She believes in him and takes time to give him positive and honest affirmation whenever she can. He is a very likeable trainee, full of wit and charm, spontaneity and openness, warmth and caring.

There is also a sadness about Stuart which lurks in the shadows and Lesley realises that she is drawn to his vulnerability as well as to the brighter part of his personality. She is also drawn to the courage and unassuming persistence which she experiences in him. She eventually realises that she sees these parts of herself in him. She praises the progress and effort that has been made and of course this affirmation produces further success. He starts at a low level of performance on the course and he finishes as one of the best students. This gives Lesley a great degree of satisfaction. She is honest with him, and challenging, but always in a supportive way. Whenever there is disagreement or conflict in the community meetings between Lesley and other members of the group, Stuart can be relied upon to remain objective and yet supportive. There appears to be a positive transference from each to the other.

Does Lesley in some way represent the good mother, the nurturing mother? Does Stuart represent to Lesley the son who needs her care and affirmation?

It is useful to explore some of the issues around such positive transference, either in the trainee or in the trainer. One of the obvious problems for Stuart is that he could become dependent on the person who represents a nurturing mother and if this were the case he would become over-reliant upon her presence on the course and might resent other course staff who did not fulfil his need for nurturing. Other course staff could feel confused by his resentment. He might also rely too heavily on the trainer's judgement and invest too much power in her, thus robbing himself of his own power. An example of this would be a reluctance to validate his own assessment of self when it is at variance with her judgement. He might need to invest a lot of energy in pleasing the trainer for fear of causing her displeasure which could in turn mean losing her support. He might feel he has to take on a role of rescuer on her behalf when the group is being critical and this in turn could lead to him being ostracised or marginalised by the group if he is perceived to be 'taking sides'. He might work too hard in his efforts to please and to maintain the level of affirmation he is receiving from the trainer. Finally, it is possible that she lets him down, turning out to be not a good mother, but a bad one, whom he perceives to be either disappointing, frustrating or punitive. After all she does have it within her power to pass or fail him at the end of this course. She is the trainer. What if she suddenly withdraws her support? What if he loses her? The relationship could feel very comfortable but he might not dare to take risks, for example challenging the trainer, in case this unsettles the relationship.

The issues for Lesley centre around becoming aware of and acknowledging the possibility of the positive transference and countertransference. There is a mutual dependency here – she is dependent upon him doing well and he is dependent on her being 'the good mother'. There are issues for the trainer herself, for the trainee, and for the trainer with the rest of the group.

A trainer in this situation would need to explore her own positive countertransference in relation to the trainee and she would need to ask herself in what ways this might be beneficial to him and in what ways harmful. It is beneficial because of the rapport between them and because the trainee is receiving affirmation and attention which is producing success on the course. It might be damaging because he could become dependent on the trainer which would cause problems for them both but would also prevent him from depending upon his own resources. As dependency develops he might start to transgress boundaries and this could cause tension between trainer and trainee as he begins to expect too much, for example, impinging upon time boundaries in tutorials or staying behind after group sessions to ask for extra help. The trainer may feel increasingly unable and unwilling to fulfil his expectations. He may gradually start encroaching on her time both inside and outside the course and this could create problems with other members of the group who notice that he gets more attention than they do.

So how does the trainer handle her positive countertransference towards him in a way that will be experienced as supportive but that will not produce inappropriate dependency? Having recognised and acknowledged her positive feelings towards him she needs to be aware that she may expect him to behave in a way which is reminiscent of a son, rather than appropriate for a trainee. She needs to be careful not to make demands on him which would be appropriate from a loving, supportive and loyal son but not from a trainee. She needs to be able to separate out her own positive feelings towards him, from his positive feelings towards her, and she needs to understand where his feelings are coming from and what she represents for him. This is not an easy process for the trainer to engage in and she may begin to feel confused, uncertain, fearful or even guilty as she gains insight into the dynamics of their relationship. Support from training supervision will be invaluable in helping her to accept the situation as it is, to accept and work with her feelings, to separate out the needs of each in the relationship and to work out strategies for remaining supportive whilst not encouraging dependency.

One of the main issues to be addressed would be whether the transference should be just acknowledged by her and not discussed with him because it might not be helpful at the time for such a discussion to take place. It would depend on his stage of development and his ability to handle such a discussion. If she decides that such a discussion should take place, then she would need to consider carefully the timing, the place, the setting and the objectives and hoped-for outcomes of the discussion. Such a discussion should not take place without adequate preparation on the part of the trainer, because the outcome is likely to be helpful or harmful, and probably not just neutral. There is an ethical obligation to safeguard the trainee in the same way that a counsellor will safeguard a client. Handling such a delicate issue as transference in a training relationship which is within the context of an assessment relationship requires sensitivity and sound judgement.

There is another important issue to be addressed and that is about the ending of the relationship. The trainer needs to be aware that Stuart will need to work through his dependency issues in some way so that the ending does not come as a shock or jolt. This could be done either implicitly or explicitly, depending on the judgement of the trainer. Even if the trainer decides not to discuss the transference issue directly, she can certainly spend time with Stuart talking about his future plans.

AUTHORITY AND CONTROL

The second theme which we will explore is that of authority and control in the training relationship. There are constant movements between trainers and trainees in relation to this dynamic and it can produce powerful exchanges and an opportunity for significant learning. One of the difficulties for counsellor trainers is that however much they try to move away from being seen to hold authority and power, trainees cannot perceive it to be this way. The course is the opportunity for trainees to develop their own authority and control and neither to deny it in themselves, nor to deny it in their trainers. Some trainees will be unable to own their own power, and some will be unable to accept the power of the trainer. We will look at this theme from different perspectives: transference and countertransference; resistance; loose holding; group dynamics and group process; archetypal roles; games and transactions.

Negative transference and countertransference

There are two types of negative transference and countertransference: that which is initiated and that which is responsive. That which is initiated occurs when a person brings previous unresolved conflicts or feelings of, for example, hostility, anxiety or resentment and attaches them in some way to the person in a current relationship. An example of this may be a hostile trainee who had rejecting parenting and who was told by his parents that he was stupid and useless. The trainee then projects this on to the trainer to make the trainer feel that she wants to be rude and hostile to him, which she then is. Responsive countertransference occurs in response to the transference initiated by the other as in the above example. It should be noted that not all negative feelings towards a trainer are transferential. They are only transferential if they arise as a result of previous negative experiences with a significant person which are now being projected on to the current relationship. Let us turn to an example of this in practice. Sally is a trainer who has experienced negative countertransference.

Sally is always well prepared and is usually very relaxed with trainees. She notices that whenever she has to talk through assessment arrangements she feels anxious and tense as she walks into the group. Normally she is calm but on these occasions, instead of the usual well humoured banter with the group, she likes to get down to the task straightaway. When the trainees start to ask the questions which they need in order to clarify the task, she starts to feel unsure of herself, as if her arrangements (and indeed herself) are going to be found to be inadequate. This produces in her a great feeling of insecurity and she even starts to feel threatened by the trainee who ferrets away for detail, the detail that would make that trainee feel less fearful of the assessment. She starts to feel irritable with the group and wonders why they are being so obtuse! The trainee becomes frustrated, angry and resentful.

Sally may become affected by the trainee in the same way that she has been affected in the past by a significant person who appeared to be undermining her, and such negative countertransference may lead her to be abrupt, dismissive or even confrontational with this trainee. On the other hand, Sally may unwittingly represent an authority figure who has been significant for the trainee in the past, and without realising it Sally becomes the object of negative transference with the trainee being confrontational in a rude and aggressive way. Sometimes Sally recognises what is going on and is able to separate out her own part in the discussion from the charged response of the trainee. If she can do this then there is every possibility that she will remain calm and manage the situation objectively. However, if Sally does not recognise that this trainee represents someone in her life who has been critical of her and who poses a threat to her self-esteem, argument and conflict may ensue. Sally notices that when she gets locked into this sort of confrontation she resorts to a misuse of her power and authority and can very effectively 'put down' the trainee. Once this has happened the trainee goes away feeling angry and resentful and may start to withdraw from contact with Sally, or engage indirectly in games and sabotage because of an inability to address the issue directly. Alternatively, the trainee may continue aggressively to challenge her authority whenever an opportunity arises.

It is worth noting that in this example the problems were interactive. Both trainer and trainee had vulnerabilities. Both were stimulating material from their pasts which was affecting their current encounter. Both parties needed insight in order to sort out their own processes and also needed courage and the skills of positive negotiation and confrontation if they were to sort anything out between them. It is possible that the trainee would talk to other course members about what had happened, and might also take the issue to the experiential group, to his or her own counsellor or even supervisor. The trainer has a responsibility to get help in training supervision so that the trainee does not suffer from an ongoing undercurrent of conflict. The trainer would probably need also to take the issue to her own therapy so that she could work on her own vulnerability and self-esteem. Trainer and trainee could then arrange to meet and to talk out what was happening between them with a view to understanding one another better. This is what would happen in an ideal world but we know that in practice problems like this can be slow to resolve because it takes time to reach an understanding of what has been going on, to develop the skills of self-disclosure, immediacy and negotiation and to muster the courage to enter into a dialogue.

Resistance

In psychoanalytic terms resistance is a defence against anxiety, an unconscious dynamic which prevents the client from bringing repressed material into awareness. It is those thoughts, feelings or actions which get in the way of change. Although it may be conscious or unconscious, it is often not in awareness. In analytic therapy it is the work of the therapist to make the unconscious conscious, and because the very nature of resistance means that the client is often unaware of it, it is the responsibility of the therapist to help the client to confront it. Resistances have an important part to play in defending the person from threat and anxiety and therefore have a positive function in keeping the person safe, as well as a disabling function in preventing change and growth.

As the training relationship is about learning growth and change, it is not surprising that resistance will be present as a defence against the anxieties and fears of engaging in difficult or challenging learning experiences. Helping trainees to understand their own resistances and to appreciate the way that they are supportive of the person or destructive of the person is an important activity. It is helpful for trainees to realise that everyone will have their own resistances, trainer and trainee alike, and in an intense learning situation such as a counselling course these will need to be understood, owned and worked with. Ekstein and Wallerstein (1972) distinguish between 'dumb-spots' and 'blind-spots' as a way of pinpointing the difference between resistance and stuckness. Some stuckness results in resistance, but not all. It only becomes resistance when the energy available for learning new things is being diverted into defensive routines. Dumb spots are gaps in knowledge, information or skill. Blind-spots are resisted information where perhaps transference or countertransference is not being properly addressed and is therefore leaking into the trainer/trainee relationship.

Examples of resistance can be very varied. Some of the more obvious ones in the training situation are: failing to hand in work on time; 'forgetting' assignments or course meetings; taking time off with no clear reason. John is a trainer from a psychodynamic background. He gives this example:

> The example that most stands out for me is of a trainee on a counselling course, Pat, who started to act out in a rather dramatic way. She appeared to be having an acute anorexic episode, probably triggered by being on the course. Pat would physically collapse, apparently fainting, at critical moments during course time and a number of participants got involved in looking after her. This became very disruptive of the work of the course.

> The intervention we made was to confront Pat and make clear that whilst we could sympathise with her difficulties and assist her to seek help, if she was to continue on the course we required her to fulfil her obligations as a trainee, which included being capable of undertaking the work of the course. Initially a

few course members were very hostile to myself and my co-trainer but this quickly died away. We took this to be their acting out Pat's aggression on her behalf. She quickly recovered physically and was able to complete the course reasonably successfully. Thus it appeared that our intervention, which was very much made from our role as trainers had a secondary therapeutic impact – presumably through providing a degree of containment and through challenging and defining the limits and boundary of her behaviour.

In my own training experience I have found that resistance comes in various guises. My own resistances as a trainer usually come into play when managing the whole course group. If I have spent much time and energy in developing a particular way of doing something and then the group decide that they do not agree with this I have on occasion found myself becoming defensive with them as a way of shielding myself from the anxiety which is being produced. If I were to try to accommodate their suggestions it would mean quite an amount of extra work which I am reluctant to take on, particularly when I convince myself that my experience of running the course tells me that my way has always worked well in the past! When I feel threatened in this way I become more fixed in my views, less able to listen to their ideas and there is an increased inability to be adaptable and flexible. I also start arguing the toss more vociferously as a defence against the perceived attack on my equilibrium. The ultimate negative response in this situation is a stubborn refusal to change.

Where does all this come from? What can I do about it? I recognise my own fears about losing control, my anxieties about being able to risk and let go, about what will happen if all the work on the course doesn't get done in time, about how I cope with conflicting demands. From somewhere much earlier in my life I need to work on the experiences that produced the anxieties, the fears and the strategies for coping which are now proving disabling and which need to be changed. I see a colleague with the group and she is able to hold her own ideas without having to cling to them. She appears to be very open and allowing with the group and she is genuinely more able to 'go with the flow'. Working with my resistances will help me as a trainer to do this more often.

I often encounter resistance in trainees and when it is obviously a result of their vulnerability I find it easy to understand the resistance and to help them to work with it. When the resistance is more complicated and results in competition, rivalry or envy either of the trainer or of other trainees then it becomes more difficult to manage. I sometimes wonder whether envy is at the root of the sort of resistance I experience whenever a group watch a video of an 'expert' counsellor. The discussion that follows the viewing almost always focuses upon the limitations and weaknesses of the so-called expert and there is a resistance to assimilate that which is good. Resistance will also occur in connection with fears of failure or of one's inadequacy being found out.

Jim was a trainer who started running a diploma course in counselling for the first time and tried to be very trainee-centred and to involve the group in all the major decisions about the course. One day they were discussing supervision arrangements and the possibilities for dialogue between the course and the supervisors. Two students were strongly arguing against any such communication on the grounds of confidentiality. They were completely resistant to the idea that course tutors might in certain circumstances need to talk with a supervisor about the progress of a trainee. Both these students were able to articulate their views ably and to influence others in the group who had less invested in this particular decision. As a result they swayed the argument and for that year of the course it was not possible for Jim to have any contact with supervisors. He had not had the experience which would have indicated to him that this could lead to problems.

In this example the cause of the resistance of these two students came to light as the course progressed. Each was different. Maggie worked in the health service and her supervisor was a colleague of some power and influence in the organisation, although not her line manager. Little wonder that she did not want the course to be communicating with him. She was terrified that if she was found wanting by the course then her supervisor would think she was not good at her job and the funding for her place on the course might be withdrawn by her employer. Her resistance to any dialogue between the course and its supervisors was keeping her safe. In Maggie's case Jim had few concerns. This was not the case with Brian, however.

Brian was working for a voluntary counselling service and supervision was to be arranged with an experienced person in the organisation. Jim noticed that although Brian appeared on the surface to be very able he showed resistance in several situations: getting started with his own client case-load; being absent from the course without prior notification; showing unwillingness to be supervised by a course tutor during videoed counselling skills training sessions. Jim was particularly concerned when Brian started avoiding individual contact with him and instead of following the course protocol, which was to inform the course staff about any absence, Brian would take group time to inform the group about where he had been, ignoring Jim's presence in the group whilst explaining. It was part way through the second term of the course that Jim happened to be speaking to Brian's supervisor about another matter. The supervisor suddenly said that he needed to inform Jim that Brian had not been turning up for supervision for some time and when he had turned up there was hardly any client work to discuss.

(The supervisor had obviously forgotten that it had been agreed that all such discussions should be via the trainee and in his concern he felt he had to report the problem.) Jim had not precipitated this discussion, but once he had been told about the situation he had to act. Brian's resistance to the dialogue between course and supervisors had been to protect himself from the problems he had in being able to work reliably with clients.

Jim was left with a serious problem. It is worth noting how it all started. It started because resistance by two members of a course group influenced a major course decision. The learning for Jim was that however trainee-centred he wished to be he now realised that the vulnerabilities of trainees could influence decisions in such a way that the welfare of clients was at stake. He decided to take a firm hold on this situation from the beginning of the second year of the course by explaining that in the future supervisors would be appointed by the course staff and that where necessary there would be dialogue between the course and the supervisor but always with the knowledge and preferably with the collaboration of the trainee. He explained that he had reflected during the past year on the arrangements and that he realised that they were not satisfactory. Because the trainees trusted his judgement and valued his earlier attempts to consult with them he overcame their initial resistance and change took place without any major difficulty in the group. By doing this he offered to Maggie and Brian a containment for their resistance that they might not have appreciated at the time and that they had been unable to provide for themselves.

Loose holding

I recall a client of mine once telling me that she had learned from her previous counsellor to try and keep a 'loose hold' on her relationships. It seems that is what we are trying to do in the training relationship. We need to offer the containment that provides a secure base and the space and flexibility that offers freedom to take risks, to experiment, to learn, to fail, and to succeed. Some interesting dynamics occur between trainers and trainees who have a mismatch of need or expectation in relation to space or containment. There will always be different needs within a course group and it is very difficult trying to meet all these needs.

One of the regular discussions that occurs on the course on which I teach, is between the members of the group who want more personal space for experiential work and those who are not prepared to sacrifice other activities in order to make this space. The issue usually comes to a head during the community group meeting. The meeting is often an uncomfortable experience at the beginning of a course when trainees are told that this is their space but the expectation is that it is not a therapy group, but a meeting of the course community, trainers and trainees together, to discuss on a regular weekly basis any matters arising. This happens in a very informal setting, sitting in a sort of circle on floor cushions. The trainers like to think that they offer a 'loose hold' with the 'hold' being the containment of a structure, which is the regular thirty-minute meeting and with the 'loose' being the freedom to do anything the trainees wish with the space within the thirty minutes.

Tim reflects in his learning journal on the dynamic between himself and other trainees in relation to the ongoing debate that takes place at the community meeting:

> S suggested that he felt there was little opportunity for personal growth and development. For me this seems out of place as I feel the course offers this in abundance and I stated that I felt the best opportunity 'for me' was in the experiential group. Although on reflection the whole course has the potential to aid in my own growth. I question myself then: Do I have further to go along the road of personal growth than I previously believed? Or am I able to spot a good opportunity when I see one?

Four weeks later the dynamic is hotting up and the course staff have either been asked not to be present at the meeting or have

decided that it would be best if they let the trainees work by themselves:

> There was no tutor present. It was a mess at first, discussions
> were on a superficial level. Discussion moved between this time
> being used in a structured almost agenda way or totally unstruc-
> tured and giving anyone the chance to bring issues they want to
> bring. We also talked about how and if at all this should be
> raised at the next meeting. I have no strong feelings yet lean
> toward some information giving with the bulk of the time being
> free, unstructured for anyone's business.

One week later and the tutors are present this time. Some trainees
are obviously inhibited by their presence and want space from the
'authority' of the course staff, and others like Tim are probably
relieved because the meeting will not be such a 'mess':

> Certain people skirted around issues as to what went on last
> week in this group. I didn't feel it was my responsibility to raise
> these issues as they don't belong to me, but I question my
> responsibility to myself to be congruent and behave in a way
> commensurate with my feeling. I felt angry with the bullshit and
> the avoidance, 'circling issues and not centring them', but
> remain unprepared to examine this further.

Two months later the same issue still rages but now it is also linked
with the whole issue of whether the group wants the course staff
to be present at the community meeting at all. Certain members of
the group are now taking up strong positions and Tim is getting
angrier:

> Again the subject of the use of time came up, again, again, again,
> again, again. Also how would the group look without the course
> tutors? Would it free the group up as some members obviously
> feel stuck and inhibited? For me I feel sick of playing with
> this issue around opportunity and self responsibility. I have said
> as much in previous meetings and will certainly remake this
> point if this theme continues. The course staff left early so that
> we could decide whether we wanted them in future and once
> they had gone certain members of the group 'started'. I listened
> for a while and then got up and walked out.

Such fragments from learning journals give insight into the ongoing
struggles in dynamics between trainees themselves and between

trainees and trainers. The flexibility offered by the trainers, to be present or not at the request of the group, is not working. For some, trainer presence is good, for others inhibiting, and for others a cause for anger and resentment.

Trainers have to live with this messiness week by week. In this example it rumbled around for months. Meanwhile the rest of the course continues and trainer and trainee have to relate to one another in many different groupings and situations during each session of a course. It is not easy to hold on to such uneasy group experiences even though they provide excellent learning opportunities for trainers and trainees alike. If we can stay with the mess my experience is that trainees will appreciate the efforts made, the ability to accept their uncertainties and the flexibility that will help them to arrive eventually at valuable decisions in the group despite the pain and upset along the way. This particular group took a year to work out their preferred *modus vivendi* but the result was a real sharing of responsibility and sharing of self, between themselves and with their trainers. It is useful to be aware of some of the theory on group dynamics and group process when trying to understand what is going on in the course group.

Group dynamics and group process

When considering group process it is important to recognise that there is a difference between group goals and individual goals (Agazarian and Peters 1989). A trainer is not only responsible for explicitly stating the goals of the group but must also listen for the implicit goals of the group with a sort of second or third ear. The trainer asks this question: what is it that the group wants by behaving as it does?

Whitaker (1987) presents a focal conflict model for working with groups and points out that individuals resonate within whatever group focal conflict is going on at the time, but group solutions may be different from individual solutions. However, core group conflicts are always associated with developmental issues in the group and if these are satisfactorily addressed the group becomes more capable of working effectively. This provides a strong argument for having regular experiential groups and community meetings on a counselling course to allow developmental issues to be aired and worked with regularly and frequently. Bion (1961) states that within a working group there may be 'assumption' groups where members behave 'as if' they all hold the same basic assumption.

Three types of assumption groups have been identified and each of these threatens to intrude upon the effective workings of the group. The first is concerned with dependency. In this assumption group members behave 'as if' there is leader who will give nourishment and protection. Bion suggests that this is like a magical solution in which all power and authority are invested in the leader and therefore the rest of the group is infantilised. Energy derives from this internal fantasy. The course group may be expecting too much of the trainer or they may 'set up' a significant member of the group to take over as leader in competition with the course staff. In either of these situations the group is not being fully participative. The second assumption group is concerned with pairing. These group members act 'as if' they are met to produce a new and better leader. Bion points out that this is connected with hope and in order to maintain hope the new leader must never be born. It may be that certain individuals in the group try to pair off with the trainer. Or it may be that they try to get rid of the trainer in favour of a new and better leader.

The third assumption group is fight/flight. These members act as if they are constantly under threat with only two options: to fight or to flee. They need the leader in order to help them to identify the enemy. Flight can take the form of absence from the course or absenting oneself from certain activities within the course. Fight usually means 'taking on' the trainer either in direct confrontation or through indirect criticism or scapegoating. Both reactions are responses to the fear of vulnerability. All these assumptions share the following characteristics: they are all regressive; they all serve as a protection against reality; they are closed systems rather than open systems; they cause the energy in the group to be devoted to protecting itself against fears and anxieties. However, Bion points out that these projections and the struggle to validate them precipitate the group into its necessary stages of development.

One way of looking at group development is through the four stages proposed by Tuckman (1965): forming, storming, norming and performing. An additional stage which completes the process, is mourning. This is the opportunity to work through the grief that surrounds the end of the life of the group and it is the opportunity to prepare for leaving it. At the forming stage there is usually high dependency on the trainer and hesitancy on the part of the trainees as they test out expectations and boundaries. There is great uncertainty at this stage as they find out about one another and start to assess themselves in relation to each other. At this stage the trainer lays the ground rules, offers structure and tries to provide orientation. Trainees will be asking themselves: Why am I here? What are we supposed to do? How are we going to get it? What will be asked of me? Will I be able to do it? Will it be safe here? Can I trust the others? Can I trust the trainer? Will I be accepted or rejected? Will I lose myself here? At this stage of group development there are major concerns about acceptance, inclusion and exclusion.

When the group moves into the storming stage trainees will start to question the trainer on the value or relevance of what they are doing and members may begin to display hostility, aggression, frustration and also risk-taking and experimentation. Tension and rivalry may ensue, with conflicts and confrontations. Some may become defensive or withdrawn. Storming can feel cold and painful. It can also feel exciting and exhilarating. The norming stage follows on from this as the group finds its feet and members start to respect differences and limitations and to express feelings constructively. This stage is characterised by warmth and closeness in the group. Roles are redefined and redistributed and there is a real opportunity for the group to take on responsibility and leadership now that they have worked through their major apprehensions and differences. Finally, the performing stage is the point at which the group becomes a powerful and effective working group and they may find it very difficult to end their work. If they have performed well they will experience considerable feelings of loss when the course ends.

Groups are not likely to go through these stages in predictable ways. They may get stuck in particular stages and trainers have the experience of groups which never seem to be able to move beyond the storming stage. Some groups will actually go through the stages in different sequences. They may for example start storming on day one if they are not satisfied with course arrangements, but then having got them sorted out they may have a hardly noticeable norming stage and appear to go straight into the performing phase. Groups revert back to old stages when people arrive or leave, when there is a change of leader, when the level of risk-taking heightens and causes regression. Because the life of a group is cyclically developmental the same issues are dealt with at ever deepening levels. The kind of course structure will affect developmental stages and processes and we would expect to see significant differences in a psychodynamic course, an integrative course and a person-centred course. Trainer style will also affect group process. If, for example, there is a trainer who is uncomfortable with conflict, confrontation and challenge he or she may seek consciously or unconsciously to avoid the possibility of 'storming'. We need, in seeking to conceptualise group process, to be aware of influences from both external realities and from internal processes operating from within the person of the trainer.

Archetypal roles

The relationship between trainer and trainees is a working relationship. It is also a complementary relationship in which there are various perceptions about what is expected of someone in the role of 'trainer' or 'trainee'. The trainer cannot get away from the fact that he or she has responsibility and power in the relationship. Proctor (1991), writing from her experience as a trainer, concludes that three dimensions converge in the power dimension of the training relationship: working agreements, experiential learning and archetypal roles. We have discussed the first two in earlier sections of the book when discussing the training model and when discussing the trainer as facilitator. At this point we will look at the idea of archetypal roles because they may help in understanding dynamics which occur through trainers and trainees being seen to operate from these archetypes. Jung (1968) talks about archetypal images arising from the collective unconscious, and therefore from the individual's unconscious, and which reflect universal meaning. 'Two of the most important archetypal images are those of anima and animus, the contrasexual images in man's and woman's psyche, thus recognising the equality of male and female values, of Logos and Eros' (Adler 1983). Another important archetypal image is that of the shadow side of the personality. Proctor sees the use of archetypal roles as exciting ways of sharing responsibilities and of channelling energy into power within the learning community.

One of my colleagues asked me what archetypes went into taking the trainer role; we immediately identified a number. There are the Guru, or Wise Woman, from whom wisdom is expected, and the Earth Mother – the all-provider, unconditional positive regarder. In contrast there is the Clown or Jester – enjoying performance, and cloaking his truth in riddles, without taking responsibility for how it is received. The Patriarch creates order and unselfconsciously wields power. The Actor/Director allocates roles and tasks and holds the Drama; the Bureaucrat demands compliance to the letter of the law. The Whore gives services for money, which can be indistinguishable from love, and re-engages with group after group. There is even the Warrior – valiant for truth; and of course the Judge – upholding standards and impartially assessing. The Shepherd/Sheepdog gently and firmly rounds up and pens; and if there is such an archetype, the Communicator talks openly and straightforwardly about 'what is'.

(Proctor 1991: 65)

Being aware of such archetypes can help to explain some of the dynamics that occur between trainers themselves and between trainers and trainees. We could add to the above list archetypes such as King, Queen, God, Guide, Father and Trickster as images which reflect some of the power in the trainer role. How can it be that a person can be both Earth Mother and Judge at the same time? Yet this is often what is expected of a facilitator who is also an assessor. I have had feedback from trainees that they see me as an Earth Mother and then they get a shock when I move into the assessment role and try to be as objective and impartial as I can be and am seen as the archetypal Judge, expecting and upholding high standards. How does that square with the accepting Earth Mother? Another dynamic occurs when there are two or more trainers, each representing different archetypes, some of which are perceived as 'good' and some 'bad'. When I am a co-trainer I can afford to be playful and I enjoy being a Clown or Jester. When I am in charge, however, and have to be a Patriarch or Actor/Director I find it difficult to accept that my co-tutor is being appreciated far more than I am because he can in that situation just be the kindly Shepherd or Sheepdog. There is a distinct possibility that splitting will occur in the group if one trainer is perceived consistently in a 'bad' archetypal role and the others are seen in 'good' archetypal roles. Some trainer roles are rewarding and satisfying and some are difficult and painful. They need to be shared. So trainers must hold a multiplicity of roles and they should be able to move flexibly between them. Some roles are seductive for a given individual and we need to be aware of the ones we may be seduced into maintaining, whilst at the same time developing the skill of adopting others.

Transactions and games

Another way of looking at the power relationship and group dynamics is through transactional analysis (Berne 1972). In TA terms the trainer is hoping to maintain an Adult–Adult relationship with members of the group but their perception may be that it is a Parent–Child relationship. The movements between these transactional states will vary according to particular course tasks and activities. However much the trainer wants the relationship to be Adult–Adult, when it comes to assessment trainees will perceive that the trainer has all the power and that the trainee has to comply to the expectations of the adult, and in this sense the transaction becomes Parent–Child. The trainer may be viewed as critical or nurturing and the trainee may become overly compliant in the desire to please, or rebellious because he or she feels put down. Using self and peer feedback and assessment really helps to move towards an experience which is more collaborative and therefore more Adult–Adult.

In transactional analysis there are some transactions which are called games and which finish with one of the players feeling bad.

A game is an ongoing series of complementary ulterior transactions progressing to a well-defined, predictable outcome. Descriptively it is a recurring set of transactions, often repetitious, superficially plausible, with a concealed motivation, or, more colloquially, a series of moves with a snare, or 'gimmick'.

(Berne 1987: 44)

Games are also explained by Goffman (1961) as specific forms of rule-governed interaction in which two considerations are paramount. The first is the rules and customs of the game and the second is the engagement and participation of the players. In TA terms games are a way of avoiding intimacy and of sustaining certain life-scripts such as: 'I'm not worthy'; 'I cannot succeed'; 'Poor me'; 'No one understands'. We live our lives according to our scripts which are messages internalised from significant others (Steiner 1974).

For example, assume that a person was given the message 'don't make it'. Also assume that she made the early decision not to succeed, for if she encountered any success, this would bring anxiety. As a child she may have engaged in games that were designed to help her fail. As time passes she may arrange her life in such a way that she continues to sabotage any chances of enjoying success. Thus games are a vital part of one's interactions with others, and they need to be understood if the person wants to decrease game-playing behaviour and live authentically.

(Corey 1986: 155)

In TA terms, games serve the purpose of maintaining or developing the script. What happens is that an exchange is made which appears to be bringing two people closer together but in fact it creates greater distance between them by the sort of transaction which provokes strokes and payoffs that lead to bad feeling. For example in the training situation a trainee may play the game of 'Yes, But' or 'Look What You Have Done To Me Now'. Either of these games could be played by a trainee wishing to defend him or her self from the challenging feedback of a trainer or in a group. The Karpman Triangle (1968) helps us to understand the dynamics of what is happening in some games in terms of a triangle of relationships between Persecutor, Victim and Rescuer. In the example just given, the trainee plays Victim with the trainer as Persecutor and possibly with other trainees as Rescuers called in by the Victim to support his or her position and to protect. The movement from one position in the triangle to another tends to be quite fast, so that Rescuer can quickly become Persecutor or Victim could become Persecutor. Trainers observe group members who are pulled into such games by trying to 'rescue' a floundering trainee who then turns on them and blames them for what is happening.

Phil was a trainer who encountered a difficult situation in which he had to make very quick decisions when a trainee became very angry during feedback in a counselling practice session. This was an incident in which the roles of Victim, Rescuer and Persecutor got played out between trainer and trainees in a small group.

This was a normal practice session in which there was a client, counsellor and observer. Phil went to supervise and his style of supervision is that of giving immediate feedback as the session is happening. He knew that the trainee, Gwen, who was in the client role for this session, had just had a bereavement. This was her first day back on the course and she had told him earlier that day that she was feeling very vulnerable. What Phil did not realise was that in the earlier session in this trio Mark had been in the client role and Sandi, who had been counselling Mark, had been trying to help him to work on some issues about his father whom he had experienced as very punitive. Mark, having just explored such difficult transferential material as a client, was now having to change role and become a counsellor for the next round in the group.

In the session which followed, Mark was the counsellor, Gwen was the client and Sandi was the observer. This is how Sandi, the trainee who had to play 'Rescuer', reflected upon the experience:

I had wondered whether Mark was up to counselling Gwen following our session. Phil was present as trainer and he was obviously unaware of the content of the earlier session. Mark was counselling Gwen and his aim was to allow her to talk about her recent bereavement. In the session Mark demonstrated some of his skills as a counsellor but he did seem to have some difficulty 'getting into' the story and in helping Gwen to get in touch with her feelings of grief. Phil interjected, which completely threw Mark. His comments were around the client–counsellor relationship and about Mark not being able to get in touch with Gwen's feelings. Mark became very angry; he could not accept the feedback and was unable to carry on. He was in a very distressed state, obviously very angry with the trainer who had given challenging feedback. Phil listened and then recapped on some of the positive aspects of the work so far and these were endorsed by myself and Gwen. Phil offered Mark the opportunity to express his anger towards him and he did this to some degree. Then Phil offered Mark two options: the first was that Mark could carry on counselling Gwen; the second was that Phil could counsel Gwen because Mark was too distressed to continue and if that was the case then Mark and myself could go off somewhere and I would counsel Mark about his anger and distress.

He selected the second option and by this time was very upset, obviously both distressed and angry. I had an agenda and that was to be able to get Mark to be able to leave the room intact. To this end I set up some physical work to rid Mark of his anger, and he certainly 'went for it'. It was not long before Mark had made the connection between the work we had been doing earlier, and his response to Phil, and gradually we worked towards Mark arranging to see Phil to talk things over.

Phil found that this situation tested all his resources as a trainer but, in retrospect, he was pleased with how he had handled it. These were his dilemmas. Mark was a trainee who appeared at one level to hear feedback, yet at another level he did not seem to learn from it. Phil felt that Mark's lack of ability to communicate empathy with this client who had recently been bereaved, was so important that he had a responsibility to give him honest feedback about this. In doing this Mark cast him in the role of Persecutor, with himself as Victim, and the distress and anger displayed towards Phil drew the other two trainees, Gwen and in particular Sandi, to being the Rescuers.

Once the anger and distress had erupted, Phil had to make a decision. Should he go and spend time alone with Mark leaving Gwen and Sandi to work together? This would have seemed the obvious thing to do. Yet Phil knew that Gwen, who had been mid-way into her client story, had just returned to the course and was finding life extremely difficult. It was possible that this outburst from her counsellor would now make her feel more unworthy and perhaps guilty that she had caused this to happen in some way. Phil felt a sense of needing to be a Rescuer for Gwen. Although Mark saw himself as the Victim in this situation, Gwen could also be feeling like a Victim. Phil's gut feeling was that it would have been unethical to leave Gwen in mid-story however angry and upset Mark was. Normally trainees were told that when in the client role they must take responsibility for their own material, and normally Phil would have allowed the group to support the 'client' whilst he dealt with the 'counsellor' who had messed up and was feeling vulnerable. But he had a hunch that this transaction was, in TA terms, a game and he did not want it to develop further at that stage. This is why he proposed the two options. In the event Sandi became Mark's Rescuer. This contained the situation so that Phil could ensure that Gwen was helped and then he was free to pick up the pieces with Mark.

In this example power and responsibility were shared between trainer and trainees, and Sandi's reflections, quoted above, indicate that it was an excellent opportunity for her to practise being a supportive, cathartic and creative counsellor who showed great presence of mind in an emergency. Another important point from this example is the negative transference from Mark to Phil which Phil had no way of understanding at the time he had to manage the crisis situation. Until Mark started, in therapy, to work through his past rejections, he maintained his anger with Phil who had definitely become a Bad Object (Winnicott 1979). This happens time and time again when working with groups. Proctor (1991: 69) talks about how long it took before she was able to tolerate being 'the Baddie' in practice even though she had known the theory about Good and Bad Objects for some time.

> Later I realised that some people learn best by finding and eliciting 'the bad' in their trainers. (In my experience they often go on to be successful using me as an anti-model Bad Object. Still later, I realized that that was what I myself had done with others, before I found Good Enough Objects to emulate.)

In the example given above Mark's reactions of distress and hostility engaged the group in a game of Persecutor, Victim and Rescuer. There are several possible reasons why trainees may play games: anxiety, vulnerability, fear, wanting to get the trainer on their side, deflecting as a means of self-protection or group protection, loyalty to a different trainer. It could be argued that most of the games played between trainers and trainees are difficulties around authority. The question must be asked: is the game being played for a payoff and if so what is the payoff? In order for the transaction to become a game the trainer has to play a complementary role. Forewarned is forearmed and so the trainer needs to be aware of the type of games he or she may get into. The trainer should also be responsive to the message which is being played out by the trainee in the transaction.

Games played by trainees could include: seduction by subversion in order to deflect from the group task; seduction by flattery with the hidden message 'be nice to me – I am nice to you'; 'evaluation should not happen between friends'; shifting the balance in the relationship from trainer/trainee to 'we're all equal round here'; name-dropping about other well-respected counsellors or trainers so that the trainer feels inadequate; 'so what do you know about what it feels like to be on this course' as a message that the trainer cannot possibly understand; the 'little list' which the trainee brings to a tutorial to stop the trainer from raising her or his issues; 'criticising myself first' so that the trainer can't hurt me during feedback sessions; 'I did what you told me but it didn't work' as a device to deflect failure, withholding information so that 'what the trainer doesn't know won't hurt me'.

As trainers we also play games to deal with our own vulnerabilities or in response to the games played by trainees. These may include: 'Poor me', I'm so pressured with work I can't possibly give you the time you need with me; 'I'm the nice guy, just one of the group' as a way of seeking approval or affection for personal qualities rather than competence as a trainer; 'I'm the one in the team who really cares about you', once more as a means of seeking approval by offering to transgress agreed course boundaries; 'I'm in charge' and have absolute power over you (and if you do not do what I want I can fail you); 'I'll tell on you' if you don't do it my way.

The basic question that the trainer needs to ask in relation to her or his own games, or those he or she plays with trainees is: What do I want to give in this transaction and what do I want to get from it? One response to games may be to refuse to play, which involves awareness of what is going on, acceptance of self as a trainer and confidence to be able to decline. Another response is to confront the game and focus upon the dynamics of the trainee's behaviour, drawing attention to the disadvantages of playing games because in the realm of transactions winning a game means losing an opportunity to become close and to change a life-script.

COMPETITION AND RIVALRY

The counsellor trainer is aware that trainees usually invest a great deal of energy and motivation, and compete against themselves and with one another, in an attempt to achieve a good standard of counselling and a good course result. This creates pressure which is usually experienced as productive pressure. Occasionally it becomes destructive or a source of great anxiety. Envy can also be present, particularly amongst adult learners who may see the trainers as possessing qualifications or having had educational or professional opportunities that they have not.

An example of this occurred recently when a trainer shared with a group a new approach to counselling which was shortly to be published. During the next twenty-four hours he noticed that a couple of members of the group were niggly and critical on several occasions. On reflection he concluded that envy was causing them to behave like this, because after all they were experienced counsellors, older than he was too, and why should he have the opportunity to publish and not they? He was sure that they were not acting deliberately from this motive but that was his interpretation.

Once he realised this he gave them some extra attention and affirmation which seemed to dispel some of the antagonism which was
probably really around 'Why doesn't someone notice us?' It is well
known in teaching circles that the cry for attention in a classroom
can be through negative behaviour and whenever such behaviour
gets attention, however punitive, the objective has been achieved.
Such attention-seeking behaviour is a symptom. Complaints are a
symptom also. They are symptoms of real distress at some level
and therefore as trainers we show care for our trainees if we
respond to complaints and criticisms with genuine concern.

An example of the effects of a sense of competition and rivalry in
a group is given by Hilary in her learning journal. She is in the
second year of the course and she has been asked by the course
leader if she will share her experiences of writing a journal with the
new first-year diploma group. She readily accepts the invitation
and goes along with her learning journal to the residential weekend
for the start of the new group. This is the entry in her learning
journal the following week:

> I have received feedback from both course tutors about my talk
> and it seems to have helped the group a lot. That makes me feel
> happy because that was my aim, to make journalling clearer so
> that they knew what was expected of them.
>
> It came out in the large group that I had been to talk to the first
> year group this weekend. It wasn't something I had purposely
> kept secret but didn't like to talk about it because it seemed like
> bragging. I felt really pleased to have been given the opportu-
> nity, yet find it hard to admit other than to myself why. I felt so
> embarrassed that the tutor had mentioned it in the group and
> now people were guessing as to why I had been! One theory was
> I had a lover in the other group!! Nothing so exciting!
>
> I explained to the tutor afterwards that I had felt embarrassed
> because it seemed like I was singled out and realised that it was
> strange for me to admit that people could learn from me rather
> than me just learning from others. I like to share my knowledge
> and have gladly shared my Journal and Practice File as I feel
> that this course is not competitive, rather it is about individuals
> developing their own unique qualities and skills alongside each
> other with support and encouragement (and challenge!) from
> each other.

On to the experiential group and with my aim in mind to 'let go' this week I shared how I'd felt in the large group and was able to do some work around why I'd felt embarrassed. My fears – alienation from the group and the need for positive strokes to reassure me. The other thing that struck me was that this had not been widely known in the group and I feel at this moment in time that 'secrecy' went against all that I believe in about being open and honest. Maybe that is why I feel uncomfortable. I found it hard when asked to say why I thought I'd been asked – I felt I could be enthusiastic and in my heart of hearts, I can accept it was because my Journal was good yet I felt it sounded 'boastful' to admit this – despite the fact that the group knew it already!! What games. Oh dear.

The learning for the trainer in this example is to be open and explicit with the group when asking for a volunteer to help in some way. Because Hilary had been 'invited', her values of openness and honesty had been compromised. If she had been confident she would have been able to tell the others, but because she thought that would be 'boasting' she could not. The result is acute embarrassment and fear of 'alienation' from the group. The trainer could never have guessed that such an invitation would have these effects on the trainee both personally and as a group member. Hilary is not uncompetitive in the sense of continuous striving for personal improvement but she would not want her own striving to impede that of anyone else.

The psychodynamic approach offers one interpretation of competition and Jacobs discusses the complexities of competitiveness and rivalry with particular reference to the genital stage in early development:

The inability to be competitive, sometimes manifested as depressed feelings of being unable to succeed and not being good enough, can cause problems in a society in which a certain amount of competition is inevitable – however regrettable that it should be so. ... The problem frequently lies not in any lack of ability (or personability in the case of relationships) but in the guilt which would be experienced were a person to be successful, in having 'defeated' others. Beneath the apparent unwillingness of some people to enter quasi-competitive situations, even those where it does not matter who wins or who does not win, we find not only people who have experienced some shame in the past at lack of success (a lack of confidence which is more indicative of anal stage problems), but also those in the genital stage who react against their wish to triumph over one another.

(Jacobs 1986: 114)

This chapter has explored the dynamics in the relationship between trainer and trainee and the next chapter focuses upon empowerment of the trainer through facilitation. An understanding of intrapersonal and interpersonal dynamics will help to explain some of the issues which arise for trainees in their role as facilitators of a learning community. Chapters Seven and Eight look at the trainer as educator and as assessor, and issues concerning skill development and the assessment of counsellor competence are raised. These aspects of counsellor training often highlight issues of power, control and authority and the insight from developmental and psychodynamic perspectives can be very helpful when trying to understand difficulties with individuals and groups, particularly at assessment times. In Chapter Nine there is a discussion of ethical and professional issues. Good training practice is examined in relation to three ethical values: integrity, impartiality and respect. An understanding of that which is going on beneath the surface in our training relationships may help us to be clearer about ourselves and our trainees. This insight needs to be aligned with ethical values which will both inform, and influence, our professional relationships.

Chapter 6

The trainer as facilitator

In this chapter two guiding principles for facilitation are proposed. The first focuses upon the trainee and the second focuses upon the task. The first guiding principle is that facilitators enable and empower trainees. This is discussed in relation to the core therapeutic conditions of genuine concern, respect and empathy. Characteristics of empowerment are given. The second guiding principle is that facilitators promote opportunities for learning and seek to remove obstacles to learning by being intentional, flexible and resourceful. Each of these aspects is discussed and some guiding principles for learning and development are suggested, in relation to both trainers and trainees.

The trainer is responsible for developing a climate and context within which learning may take place. A trainee-centred philosophy will emphasise learning processes as well as learning outcomes and will place the trainee at the heart of these processes.

Trainee feedback gives clues about the specific aspects of the facilitative trainer which have been appreciated. The following comments to a trainer at the end of a course illustrate those aspects of facilitation which trainees perceived as especially useful:

Greg	Supporting us with information that we could follow up ourselves.
Sarah	Empathy, concern, support and pushing although it felt painful at times.
Mary	Genuineness, listening, being there.
Paul	Understanding, help, support and humour.
Diana	Helping us to do things for ourselves.
Martin	Guidance, common-sense and support.
Angela	Showing an extensive grasp of the subject.

Anthony   Being astute and supportive.
Tim   Support and push in practice sessions.
Helen   Continued support and encouragement.

In this group of trainees the word mentioned most often is 'support'. The facilitative trainer offers support through the course structure and organisation as well as through his or her way of being. It is also noticeable that trainees do not see facilitation as support without challenge. They have valued the 'pushing' which has helped them to surpass their own expectations of themselves and which leads to a real sense of achievement.

PRINCIPLES OF FACILITATION

If it is accepted that a principle is a fundamental truth or a rule which guides behaviour then it will be apparent that principles of facilitation will relate back to beliefs about the person, about development and about learning. Trainers will vary in their beliefs and this will affect their style of facilitation. Facilitating the learning climate is about the balance between support and challenge. Support helps to develop an atmosphere of trust and safety and challenge offers the stimulus to change and growth.

> To be more specific, support for learning comes in several ways: first, the structured nature of the training experience, which tends to give people permission to try new behaviours; second, an atmosphere of empathy and trust in the group, where members feel genuinely understood and accepted; and finally, group cohesion or closeness, which seems to be a natural result of knowing and being known, of self-disclosing and giving feedback.

> The key challenge, of course, comes from the task itself: learning, using and integrating the helping skills. An atmosphere of challenge stems also from what might be called interpersonal courage: i.e. the willingness to involve oneself with others in the group and really see them, to self-disclose, to experiment with new behaviours, to challenge and be challenged. This kind of courage is important not only in group development, but also in helper effectiveness.

> (Bryer and Egan 1979: 9)

There will be those who favour being supportive and those who favour being confrontational in the interests of growth and learning. What we know is that the needs of each learner will differ and each will require differing degrees of support and challenge and these needs will vary during different activities and at different stages of counselling training. It is important that decisions about being supportive or confrontational are taken with respect to the needs of the trainee rather than with respect to what the trainer likes best.

TWO GUIDING PRINCIPLES

1 Trainee: *Facilitators enable and empower trainees.*
2 Task: *Facilitators promote opportunities for learning and seek to remove obstacles to learning by being intentional, flexible and resourceful.*

THE FIRST GUIDING PRINCIPLE: FACILITATORS ENABLE AND EMPOWER TRAINEES

The first guiding principle of facilitation is concerned with the trainees themselves. We need look no further than the work of Rogers (1957) on empowerment. Garfield and Bergin (1986) refer to Rogers' statement that the trainee therapist should learn in a facilitative environment similar to that which the therapist will provide for his or her client. The facilitative conditions have been found to enhance growth and learning. Moreover, the communication of empathy, acceptance and genuineness by the trainer give a powerful model for trainee counsellors. These authors cite Truax and Carkhuff:

> If the trainees could not experience high levels of warmth and regard, understanding and genuineness from the supervisor, then they could not be expected to function at high therapeutic levels themselves.
>
> (Truax and Carkhuff 1967: 262)

Studies which appear to validate this argument include Pagell, Carkhuff and Berenson (1967) who found that trainees given facilitative conditions were able to offer higher degrees of empathy to clients, and that volunteer counsellors: 'learned little and were more likely to drop out (over 50%) when assigned to a supervisor who provided low facilitative conditions' (Garfield and Bergin 1986: 828).

*

What constitutes the 'facilitative environment' (Rogers) and the 'facilitative conditions' (Truax and Carkhuff) which will enable trainee counsellors to learn, and will empower them to be effective counsellors?

At its simplest level, and at its most profound, it is the communication by the trainer of the core therapeutic conditions of genuineness, respect and empathy. If trainers live these core qualities then what we know about counselling effectiveness can be applied to training effectiveness and trainees will be enabled and empowered. Educational research, as well as counselling research, shows this to be the case (Flanders 1970; Burns 1982; Brandes and Ginnis 1986). Living these qualities as a trainer is no mean task, involving, for example, ongoing reflection on the learning task, supervision of training, learning how to manage conflict in learning groups and working towards a set of self-identified goals which enhance interpersonal relationships.

Communicating these qualities will free the trainee to learn about self and others, minimising defensiveness, maximising openness, moving from rigid forms of thinking, feeling and behaving to openness, flexibility and resourcefulness in both learning and counselling. Communicating these qualities will enhance self-esteem in trainees, thus making them into counsellors who are able to help their clients to develop greater self-esteem. At the end of counselling training one trainee said 'I now feel confident and competent.' She knew what she knew and what she still needed to know, accepted where she was, had the inner confidence and strength to keep learning and the wisdom to accept herself as a good enough, newly trained counsellor, engaged in the lifelong process of becoming.

Enabling trainees by communicating genuine concern

In counselling training the genuine concern for trainees cannot be separated from the genuine concern for their future clients – the *raison d'être* of training being client welfare. We care about trainees as persons and we care about them as counsellors. We care about their progress on the course, their counselling practice, their way of being with the group and with the trainers, their personal development and their personal circumstances. At times there is conflict between these elements and the trainer requires supervision in order to move forward. For example, Jack, a trainee, may be going through very difficult personal problems such as divorce, bereavement or financial difficulties. The trainer knows this, is concerned, and has spent time with Jack individually. Jack begins to miss sessions and hand in work late. He always has a reason.

The course has clear guidelines about attendance and about handing work in on time. Course members know about Jack's problems but they feel he sometimes uses them to extend boundaries when really he has procrastinated. Some of them resent this when they feel that they also have problems which nobody knows about and yet they have to stick to course deadlines. Alan, in the same group, starts to slip also. He cannot get his work in on time for very similar reasons, but his own feelings of inadequacy are so bad at the moment that he cannot bring himself to ask for leniency. He does not say anything to the trainer. Jack passes, with commendation for doing so well in the circumstances. Alan fails. This example raises a number of issues for the trainer. There are questions about congruence between caring for one trainee (Jack) and caring for the whole group; there is the issue of how to show caring when a trainee is unable to ask for help (Alan); and there is the issue about possible conflict between concern for trainees and concern to operate course regulations fairly. These are some of the issues that the trainer could usefully explore in training supervision. I refer the reader to Chapter Nine, on ethical and professional issues, where three values are explored: integrity, impartiality and respect. In the example outlined above, the trainer could be guided by these ethical values as he or she tries to balance conflicting or overlapping interests and concerns.

Authenticity

The authentic counsellor trainer is a real person and a real professional. Realness means being without front or façade, and is not just an image or stereotype. It means being unambiguous in our relationships, which involves taking risks. The authentic counsellor trainer does not let fear of the risks of being honest prevail. This honesty starts with self and is continually developed by the internal and external supervisor. Such transparent willingness to engage in developing authenticity can be an inspiration to trainees. It can also be daunting to them. It is the foundation for their developing sense of personal power. Trainers need to be honest about their own personal power so that trainees can learn to own theirs. There is a saying that nothing is so strong as gentleness and nothing is so gentle as real strength. It is the 'gentle strength' that we need to share with our trainees so that they come to appreciate that to be therapeutic is to be powerful, the sort of power that neither diminishes self nor other.

One of the most rewarding aspects of counsellor training is to honestly affirm. It is possible that affirmation is the most powerful aspect of both counselling and training in relation to deep and profound change, growth and development. Time and time again the honest affirmation given by a trainer to a trainee has allowed that trainee to affirm him or her self and then to develop the capacity to affirm others. The affirmation, however, has to be honest, specific and selective. In other words, trainees do not want to be told that their skills are excellent when they are good, or that their written assignments are distinction when they are above average. They want to know what terms like these really mean, and if they find that everyone is hearing that their work is marvellous they may well find such feedback at one level patronising and at another level dishonest.

The difficulties about authenticity are mainly in two areas: self-disclosure and the breaking of bad news. Counsellor trainers will vary in their views about the appropriateness of self-disclosure, just as counsellors from different schools of thought will differ on this issue. There are two kinds of self-disclosure here – the first about the way that the trainer experiences the trainee or the group, and the second about the trainer himself or herself. In the following example a trainer, John, is having his authority and power challenged by a trainee and he has a dilemma about when and how to disclose his thoughts and feelings about the issue. John had been teaching a certificate group for several months and had become increasingly concerned because one member of the group, Julia, appeared to be trying to 'take him on' at every available opportunity. This would usually be done by critical questioning and disagreement with whatever ideas were being presented. This group member had a debilitating effect on the group, and whilst on one level she seemed to be admired by several of the group, it was obvious that this admiration was more than a little tinged with fear. John reflected upon the situation and, when the other trainer reported the same experience with Julia, resolved to do something about it. John decided to disclose to the group his anxieties about the situation even though he realised that it would be very risky because the group might not agree with him and might wish to deny that there was a problem, because of their own fears. John explained to the group that he was concerned about the situation and their reaction was to deny that there was any problem and to rally to Julia's defence. John left the group feeling that he had achieved nothing and that all his hard-earned rapport with the group had gone.

This example is not uncommon and there are never clear remedies for such situations. John asked the training team for help during peer supervision. Some of the insights he gained were about transference and countertransference. Was Julia taking him on because he represented some unfinished business with authority figures, perhaps her father? Was John reacting in a frightened way to Julia's challenge because she represented a threat to his self-esteem, maybe in the way he had been threatened by significant others in his past? John also reflected upon the timing and appropriateness of his self-disclosure. He wondered whether he should have just seen Julia on her own and he wondered what stopped him from doing that. In hindsight, he felt that if he had talked it through with Julia first, they could then have taken the issue together to the group to decide on a way forward.

The other difficult area in relation to authenticity is the breaking of bad news, and with counsellor trainees who are highly motivated and conscientious it can be extremely difficult. Yet why shy away from this most important aspect of counsellor training? Isn't much counselling work about helping clients to deal with bad news? Bad news about a partner, a job, a marriage, a death? Surely, one of the most important aspects of a counsellor's training should be the experience of giving and receiving bad news. The bad news in counsellor training is often around failure in assessed areas of the course. It may also be about the way a trainee is relating to other trainees or to trainers on the course and it is a characteristic of a good course that issues such as these are tackled and not allowed to fester. If trainers genuinely care about trainees they will want to help them to develop and grow, particularly in the area of relationships. The trainer must risk not being liked, because the reaction of a trainee to honest negative feedback may be shock, anxiety or disquiet resulting in dislike or scapegoating of the trainer.

Mandy was a trainee who always liked to please those in authority, and who could be described as obsequious. However, there
was another part of Mandy which was manipulative and when
she received some negative feedback from the trainer about her
unwillingness to work collaboratively she (perhaps subconsciously)
turned the problem back on the trainer, suggesting that it was
the trainer who had the problem. Mandy then presented herself
to the group as a Victim, with the trainer as Persecutor. Several
group members then invested energy in becoming Mandy's
Rescuers. This all happened because Terry, the trainer, was
being authentic. The trainee needed the bad news that her lack
of willingness to collaborate was affecting the quality of the
work for the whole group. When she turned it back upon Terry,
however, he had to avoid getting hooked into a game (Berne 1987)
characterised on both sides by defensiveness, rigidity and covert
manoeuvres. The questions which arose for him were: How can
I remain congruent and caring whilst I feel that I am being
attacked? What can I do about the members of the group who have
been mobilised into rescuing?

By remaining authentic Terry resolved this potentially disas-
trous situation. He listened carefully to Mandy whilst she accused
him, and his internal supervisor (Casement 1985) went into top
gear. He realised that he did not have a problem but that Mandy
did, and he gently but firmly stated that. He affirmed Mandy in all
that was good about her and said that he believed that her lack
of collaboration was not intentional but that somehow it had
happened. Terry kept to the specific facts, the specific evidence.
He did not make generalised judgements or evaluations. Each
time Mandy tried to deny her problem and say that it was Terry's
problem he used immediacy to put it back where it belonged
– 'And do you hear yourself now, Mandy, doing to me exactly
what we have been talking about?' Such immediacy used empathically allowed Mandy to experience with her trainer the sort
of psychological holding and containment that she was unable to
provide for herself. She felt held, not rigidly as in a straitjacket,
but loosely and flexibly so that she could move around in the holding and feel her space. She broke down and cried. At last she was
able to give herself permission to be vulnerable and not to have
to be perfect in the eyes of her trainers. Terry had given this
permission by not diminishing the facts, by staying with them and
with her, and by remaining open and supportive to Mandy's

vulnerability. It is at times like this that the trainer/trainee relationship verges on the counsellor/client relationship and part of
the therapeutic holding involves holding those boundaries.

Mandy gained insight. Mandy, who had been running away from
her inner self suddenly realised that it was safe with this trainer to
face herself and that she was still accepted and prized. She could
now take the advice of her trainer and embark upon some regular
counselling for herself. She did this and the transformation
was under way. Mandy moved miles that day. Within a short time
group relationships were much better and course work had
improved dramatically. Terry took the opportunity to work with
group members on their feelings that he had victimised Mandy.
He took the problem to training supervision and realised some of
the things he could have handled better in the group. He disclosed
this to the group and they appreciated both his honesty and his
willingness to share his vulnerability with them. They appreciated
him being authentic.

Enabling trainees by communicating respect

When a trainee is selected for a counselling course he or she will
usually feel accepted and to some degree prized. Rogers stipulated
that the positive regard which is experienced as therapeutic needs
to be unconditional. The trainee is prized as a unique person.
Acceptance is free from judgement or evaluation. Respect does
not need to be earned, but exists of right in the relationship. All of
this is highly problematic in a training situation where there
are issues of power and equality, of judgement and assessment,
of evaluation and recommendation. So how do trainers pick their
way through such a minefield? First by recognising that there
is a problem; second by considering some of the attitudes which
inform the behaviours that communicate respect. Some of these
attitudes have been described (Egan 1986) as: being there for the
trainee; communicating that it is worthwhile to work with the
trainee; communicating a willingness to engage; having regard for
the individuality of the trainee and for the talents and abilities
of the trainee; accepting and trusting that the trainee knows
best about pacing himself or herself; assuming that the trainee
will want to do as well as possible; maintaining confidentiality
and holding boundaries with care and sensitivity.

Trainers are faced with the dilemma about whether it is possible to be perceived by trainees as having unconditional positive regard for them when there is an assessment relationship. I think it is possible, although fraught with difficulties. Unfortunately the perception of the trainee will often be very influenced by the assessment aspect, even though the trainer may be able to put this aside. When counselling trainees submit work for assessment they genuinely feel (and rightly) that it is more than the piece of work that is being assessed – it is themselves. By expressing unconditional positive regard for the person who has failed in their own eyes, the trainer can help the trainee to separate out their own worth from that of the assessed piece of work.

Sue was an example of this. Sue had a problem writing essays on a counselling diploma course even though she already had a degree in the humanities. She was determined to do well and saw the counselling course as the place where she might get the sort of distinction marks which seemed impossible on her previous academic courses. By the time she had done her second essay on the diploma course her grades were mediocre. When her trainer told her that she had not reached the level that she herself expected she was flooded with disappointment which soon turned to anger. Her anxiety reached such a point that she could not even hear the feedback the trainer was giving her and therefore she would not learn how to improve. She went away feeling very resentful and decided to return to say that she disagreed with the mark. Her trainer listened carefully and heard where this was really coming from. It was Sue's disappointment with herself and her unrealistic expectations of herself which, coupled with bad experiences of failure in academic work as much as eleven years earlier, had brought her to this point of complete blockage. Together they unravelled the story and tackled the blind-spots with support and sensitivity. Finally, the trainer said 'Sue, you may not have got a distinction on this essay but you can still be a distinction person'. There was silence. Sue did not allow herself to hear at first. The tutor repeated her sentiments.

This was the ultimate challenge: could Sue have unconditional positive regard for herself as a person, without having to attach her worth always to the academic success which appeared to elude her? The communication of that acceptance, respect and admiration for her as a person gave her permission to begin to free herself of her own blocks. She began to be able to hear feedback about essay technique. She was always creative in her work and her creativity was enhanced because now it was linked with academic requirements whereas before it had ended up in undisciplined ramblings. She started to get good grades and even got a distinction for her learning journal (the assignment which allows the quality of the person to really shine through). Most of all she let go and in letting go she became free from disabling anxiety.

Unconditional positive regard implies allowing trainees to become their own people. This can be hard when they begin to challenge dearly held beliefs, values and counselling approaches. The wise trainer and facilitator will know that this will occur, and will indeed encourage critical thinking in trainees right from the start. When trainees challenge it is then part of the learning process and not taken as a personal insult against the trainer. If the learning process is well structured there will be ample opportunities for the development of individuality on the course. Respect for trainees is communicated in many different ways: clear contracting, clear boundaries, negotiation, ongoing monitoring and evaluation, good quality feedback, realistic and high expectations, reliability and consistency, trustworthiness. Above all, the trainer shows respect by living and acting in the way that he or she expects trainees to live and act: with colleagues, trainees and clients.

Enabling trainees by communicating empathy

Some trainees experience empathy as understanding, others have appreciated the time that has been given in listening to them, and others have appreciated the trainer being there over and over again for them. What does the trainee want the trainer to understand?

Trainees sometimes want the trainer to understand things about themselves that even they don't understand! And isn't that what clients also want from counsellors? The trainee wants the trainer to understand that she or he is in the process of becoming and not to expect her or him to have everything properly 'together' right from the start. Trainees often want trainers to recognise their own defensive patterns as the necessary safeguards that they were in the past, protecting them from hostility. They want the trainer to realise that these patterns take time to change and that if the trainee experiences hostility or attack on the course she or he may well become defensive. They want the trainer to understand their vulnerability when being supervised, and not to expect too much. They want trainers to be with them in the truly Rogerian sense:

> Can I let myself enter fully into the world of his feelings and personal meanings and see these as he does. Can I enter it so sensitively that I can move about in it freely, without trampling on meanings which are precious to him? Can I sense it so accurately that I can catch not only the meanings of his experience which are obvious to him, but those meanings which are only implicit, which he sees only dimly or in confusion?
>
> (Rogers 1961: 63)

Rogers confesses that he found it much easier to feel this kind of understanding, and to communicate it, to individual clients rather than to a class of students. He found a stronger temptation to 'set students straight' or to point out errors. Trainer levels of empathic understanding will be affected by the amount of psychological space they have available at the time. I will be limited in my empathic understanding if I am tired, am under too much pressure at work, am rushing and have too little time to listen and observe. I will be limited in my empathic understanding if the trainee is overly demanding, is not assertive enough, is hostile, is devious, is unwilling or unable to be empathic with me. I will be limited in my empathic understanding if the course conditions are poor, if there are not sufficient hours allotted for tutorials, if the course group is too big, if the surroundings are noisy and with frequent interruption, if there is a culture or expectation that spending time with trainees is not efficient use of time.

Counselling training is intensive and it is searching. Trainees go through periods during their training when they feel confident and periods when they feel vulnerable, times when they feel competent and times when they feel incompetent, times when they feel skilled and times when they feel completely deskilled, times when they feel enabled and times when they feel disabled, times when they feel self-aware and times when they feel very lacking in awareness, times when they feel they are of value and times when they feel they have nothing to offer to clients. The trainer who can empathise with all of these feelings will help trainees to struggle through the difficult days of counsellor training and will share in the energy and excitement of those wonderful days when insight dawns, when a skill is mastered, when a book has spoken meaningfully, when a client says that he or she has been really helped. The more that the trainer understands and is able to face herself or himself (Jersild 1955) the more likely it is that he or she will be to be able truly to understand the trainee.

Some characteristics of empowerment

What would we expect to see in trainees as they become more empowered? The scale in Table 6.1 on p. 124 gives some character-istics of people who feel more or less empowered to take responsi-bility for their own learning. It is adapted from Hopson and Scally (1981). Trainers who are engaged in pursuing their own learning and awareness will hopefully be demonstrating movement along the scale towards qualities which are on the right-hand side. Trainees can be encouraged also to reflect at regular intervals upon the aspects of empowerment which are their current strengths and the aspects which need development.

Self-empowerment is the process of gradually taking charge of one's self and one's life. The spin-offs from the learning situation are observable as trainees are able to transfer their learning to other areas of their life. They become proactive rather than reac-tive, anticipating and initiating rather than just responding. Hopson and Scally (1981: 57) state that to operate in a self-empowered way entails being able to:

1 Look at oneself and to believe that one is open to change.
2 Have the skills to change some aspects of oneself and the world in which one lives.
3 Use one's feelings to recognise where there is a discrepancy between what one is and what one would like to be.
4 Specify desired outcomes and the action steps required to achieve them.
5 Act, to implement action plans.
6 Live each day aware of one's power to assess, reassess, influ-ence and self-direct.
7 Enable others to achieve the power to take charge of their lives and influence the different arenas of their lives.

The first guiding principle of facilitation relates to the trainees as persons and focuses upon the personal characteristics of both trainer and trainee as they become personally enabled and empowered. The next guiding principle, however, concerns the tasks involved in counsellor training as we ask ourselves the ques-tion: empowerment for what?

Table 6.1 Characteristics of empowerment

Less empowered		More empowered
Easily overwhelmed by new ideas	1 2 3 4 5	Relishes new ideas
Closed to change	1 2 3 4 5	Open to change
Outer directed	1 2 3 4 5	Inner directed
Reactive	1 2 3 4 5	Proactive
Easily prone to feelings of failure	1 2 3 4 5	Turns failure into a learning opportunity
Thinks that success is attributable to luck or chance	1 2 3 4 5	Thinks that success is achievable and in own control
Procrastinates	1 2 3 4 5	Gets started
Limited and narrow view	1 2 3 4 5	Sees alternatives
Blames others for own mistakes	1 2 3 4 5	Accepts and owns shortcomings
Negates self	1 2 3 4 5	Values self
Lacks initiative	1 2 3 4 5	Shows initiative
Lacks resourcefulness in learning	1 2 3 4 5	Is resourceful
Avoids difficulties	1 2 3 4 5	Confronts difficulties
Is aggressive or passive	1 2 3 4 5	Is assertive
Lacks determination	1 2 3 4 5	Is determined
Gives up easily	1 2 3 4 5	Perseveres
Does not ask others for help	1 2 3 4 5	Asks for help
Escapes into past or future	1 2 3 4 5	Gets on with the present
Blocked	1 2 3 4 5	Free from blocks
Cannot hold or be held within boundaries	1 2 3 4 5	Can move freely within boundaries

Source: adapted from Hopson and Scally (1981)

THE SECOND GUIDING PRINCIPLE: FACILITATORS PROMOTE OPPORTUNITIES FOR LEARNING AND SEEK TO REMOVE OBSTACLES TO LEARNING BY BEING INTENTIONAL, FLEXIBLE AND RESOURCEFUL

The trainer is responsible for providing an environment in which learning may take place. The task of facilitation relates to the structure and resources of the counselling course.

Facilitating through course structure

If the first guiding principle (to enable and empower trainees) is to inform the second, then the way that the tasks of the course are arranged and managed will reflect this. There will be an emphasis upon trainee participation, experiential learning, negotiation of the curriculum, self and peer as well as tutor assessment, learning contracts, course handbooks, clear and reliable information, trainee involvement in selection processes, resource-based learning, groupwork and teamwork. In a didactic teaching situation the communication is mainly between the trainer and the group. In an interactive learning situation trainees interact with each other as well as with the trainer and they all become resources for learning. Meanwhile, the trainer does not stay in one role, for example, that of instructor. The trainer in the interactive situation moves freely between different roles as the occasion demands, from provider to initiator to motivator to sustainer to moderator to critic to assessor to examiner to resourcer (Lea 1986; Steinaker and Bell 1979). The emphasis is on learning rather than teaching, on learners rather than trainers (see Chapter Seven). Within this framework the learner becomes empowered and accepts responsibility for his or her own learning, rather than leaving responsibility with the trainer. In the context of adults working together the roles become largely interchangeable. But let us be clear about where the buck stops! In the final analysis, who decides on pass or fail? That needs to be clear from the outset so that trainees know the parameters within which they accept responsibility and the boundaries of that responsibility. Good facilitation does not mean discharging all responsibility. It does mean being clear and honest about what is expected, what is given and fixed and what is negotiable and amenable to change.

Intentionality in counsellor training

There is much debate currently about the notion of quality in education and training and nowhere is this more needed than in the field of counselling training. One of the characteristics of quality in training, is intentionality. It is about clarity of purpose so that counselling training may be assessed against the quality yardstick of fitness for purpose. Whatever theoretical counselling approach is espoused by a training course, there is no excuse for lack of intentionality in how to make trainees on that course into the most effective counsellors in that particular field of counselling. The lack of good research into counselling effectiveness adversely affects training. If research cannot tell us with certainty what makes a good counsellor, then how can we be intentional in our training?

Despite the dearth of research which could inform counsellor trainers, there is enough evidence from educational and developmental psychology about the importance of intentionality as a facilitating factor in learning. Intentionality implies direction and focus, and that the trainer and trainee know where they are heading. Some would argue against this, saying that intentionality precludes flexibility. However, that is like saying that a walker who starts out with a map cannot move off the planned route! As long as the walker gets to the intended destination it probably does not matter which route he or she decides to take. Without a map as guide, time could be wasted, obstacles would not be avoided, the destination might never be reached and you might never know when you got there. To apply this analogy to counsellor training the implications become obvious. Since it is a professional training the destination cannot be left to chance. There has to be some broad agreement about where paths have to cross and on the general direction in which the group is headed. The facilitator gives permission for people to take their own pathways, as well as reaching agreement about the general direction for the group. The outcome of training is effective counselling and whatever our theoretical persuasion, and however supportive our facilitation, the training will fail if that intention of producing effective counsellors is not realised.

The trainee needs to be able to ask of the counsellor trainer: What do you, and what does this course, intend to do for me? – in much the same way as a person setting out on a voyage might ask the master mariner: What do I need to bring with me? Where will we be headed? What will you need from me? How will we get there? How will we know when we have arrived? In addition, clients and professional counselling bodies need the information so that ethical and professional standards may be monitored and safeguarded.

The answer to these questions lies in the communication of clear and specific information about course rationale, aims and objectives, processes and expected outcomes. The key to intentional facilitation is in the course processes. The issues are about keeping the balance between intentionality and negotiation, between direction and openness to alternatives, between process and outcome orientation. Here is a list of some examples of intentionality in practice:

1 Clear course objectives.
2 Clear course expectations, including attendance and participation.
3 Clear dates and deadlines for significant events such as assessments.
4 Clear codes of professional practice for both trainers and trainees.
5 Realistic and specific criteria for theoretical and practical assignments.
6 Consistent standards with regard to assessment.
7 Continuous reflection and monitoring of the work of trainees, trainers and course supervisors.
8 Ability to apply standards rigorously and always with concern for the safety and welfare of clients who are at the heart of the process.

Why is intentionality facilitative? It is facilitative for the professional development of the counsellor because it focuses the mind and heart of trainer and trainee upon the client. It is facilitative for the trainee because intentionality offers clarity of purpose, and a point of reference. It also gives the trainee the experience of psychological holding which is therapeutic in itself but which also models the way in which trainees will be able to offer this to their clients. At times during training when all the internal boundaries may be feeling blurred and when anxiety about progress can cause feelings of chaos and when the problems a client brings have disturbed the inner equilibrium, then it will be the security of clear external parameters and boundaries that will offer the trainee the opportunity to readjust, refocus and stay with the mess – in the security that this can all be held within a consistent structure of training. If intentionality is not present, then there is the possibility of harm and damage for trainees who may be left to flail and flounder in their own uncertainty whilst the so-called facilitators appear not to know how to help.

When is intentionality not facilitative? When it confines or is experienced as limiting, narrowing or controlling. When it prevents discussion, negotiation, adaptation and compromise. When it causes trainees to feel that they have been put into a straitjacket.

Flexibility in counselling training

The trainer is flexible in order to promote opportunities for learning and to seek to remove obstacles. Counselling training is essentially an active learning process and trainers need to be able not only to think on their feet, but also to have flexibility of feeling and action. Counselling training is a collaborative exercise which is constantly moving and growing. There is a stimulating and challenging dynamic at work. The more the trainees become empowered by the trainer, the more demands they are enabled to make. In a negotiated curriculum they may want resources which are not immediately available; they may request that the trainer shifts role to allow them more autonomy; they may wish to represent themselves on committees on which the trainer normally sits.

Flexibility involves, first and foremost, listening and then having the willingness, the courage and the resources to respond. It may mean having to let go of tried and tested ways of teaching and learning, it may mean being prepared to let go of strongly held beliefs about 'the right way to do things round here', or it may mean having to negotiate with other colleagues to provide extra time or equipment or books for a course group.

The issues concern balancing the needs of one trainee against those of others, balancing flexibility in one aspect of the course against a resulting constriction perhaps in another aspect of the course, balancing the desire to be flexible against the 'given' and fixed aspects of training. Willingness to be flexible does not always mean that there will be sufficient courage available on the day! It takes courage to listen when trainees are perhaps angry, hostile, resentful, apparently uncaring, demanding. It takes courage to remain open to their demands under such circumstances and to remain non-defensive during a heated argument in, for example, a community meeting or a course evaluation session. It is particularly difficult when the trainer knows that, having listened, he or she does not have the resources that would solve the problem.

What is always appreciated by trainees is the willingness to engage with them in their search for the answer to a problem. Such flexibility of attitude and mind is experienced as collaborative and supportive. Trainer and trainee then become engaged together as partners in trying to solve a problem and this is supportive of both parties.

It is most difficult to stay flexible when confronted by rigidity of thinking on the part of the trainee. At such times the opposite of facilitation can occur as both sides get locked in battle. All is not lost however, if such situations are taken to training supervision. Supervision gives the space for flexibility to return, for the trainer to try again, perhaps using immediacy with the trainee so that he or she also is able to be less rigid as they try to move forward together.

Resourcefulness in facilitation

If the task is to promote learning and remove obstacles within a context in which the learner is to become enabled and empowered, then the learner will need to know where and how to find information and develop skills. The trainer becomes not a teacher but a learning resource. If it is thought that such learning is less demanding than traditional styles of teaching, experience will soon reveal that this is completely untrue. Such a learning situation demands careful planning and management. Learners are encouraged to work actively with one another in a learning community where all ideas are shared. They work in groups of various sizes and structures according to particular tasks – for example: pairs for regular review; fours for skills training; eights for experiential groupwork; sixteens for workshops.

The resourcefulness of the trainer is evident in the structuring and groupings of various activities as well as in the provision of information about the content to be learned. The trainer may not deliver lectures for trainees to write copious notes, but would need to have all appropriate references available as well as up-to-date information about where to go to collect books, articles and journals. The resourcefulness of the trainer would also imply a good knowledge of local, national and global networks. If learners are to be encouraged to use a variety of learning strategies then the trainer will model these and trainees will become learning resources for one another.

It is the experience of those who are successful facilitators that the more they allow the learners to take responsibility for their own learning, the more resourceful they become. But this only happens where the learners have been fully supported with relevant information from well-stocked libraries which are easily accessible. It does not take long for learners to build up a considerable body of information between themselves. It is remarkable to note the amount of time which trainees will spend working on their own or in a group outside of course time as long as they know that their efforts will be recognised by their trainers.

Trainee-centred learning is facilitated by intentionality, flexibility and resourcefulness. In order that the facilitator may help trainees to participate actively and to learn from experience he or she needs to have a sound knowledge of the subject being learned; the ability to structure a variety of learning experiences; the ability to adapt quickly and flexibly to new and unexpected situations; the confidence to empower learners to work in ways which may not be familiar to them; and the sensitivity and understanding which are necessary to deal with any vulnerability or feeling of exposure in the learners. The facilitative trainer is managing both the subject and the learner and will need to keep a balance between the two.

This is a very demanding task which requires both skill and sound judgement – the skill required of the training methodologies, and wise judgement about the timing, pacing and appropriateness of the methods used.

In consultation with colleagues I have developed a set of guiding principles which are given to all trainees at the commencement of training. They provide the basis for an ongoing dialogue between trainer and trainee and they are used as review questions for trainers during training supervision. They may serve as a useful reminder about the aspects of facilitation which have been discussed in this chapter.

GUIDING PRINCIPLES FOR LEARNING AND DEVELOPMENT

We believe that learning and development is enhanced when:

TRAINERS/FACILITATORS

1 Know their subject and communicate it clearly, creatively and enthusiastically
2 Encourage enjoyment in the learning process
3 Communicate clear learning objectives and clarify expected learning outcomes
4 Respect and value the individuality of each learner
5 Collaborate with learners in the learning process

6 Are open to negotiate aspects of course content and methodology
7 Involve learners in the assessment process
8 Communicate honestly and openly
9 Continually listen to and try to understand the learner
10 Offer a balance of support and challenge
11 Help learners to find appropriate learning resources
12 Are available and accessible for ongoing consultation and support
13 Set up systems for continual two-way feedback in areas of strength and in areas for development
14 Structure the learning experience intentionally and flexibly
15 Set clear deadlines and keep to them
16 Respect the confidentiality and dignity of each learner
17 Are committed to ongoing personal and professional development through research, training, supervision, counselling and consultation.
18 Operate within ethical and professional boundaries
19 Act in accordance with being both professional and human
20 Are congruent in their way of being and working in relation to the core values and principles espoused by the course.

We believe that learning and development is enhanced when:

LEARNERS/TRAINEES

1 Are clear about what is, and what is not, offered by the course and its staff
2 Understand what is expected in order to fulfil academic, practical, participative and attendance requirements
3 Accept responsibility for their own learning
4 Commit themselves to participate fully in all aspects of the course
5 Share learning with others to create a learning community
6 Contribute to a climate of learning where risk-taking is encouraged
7 Take responsibility for communicating their needs to peers and staff
8 Manage time effectively and prioritise
9 Meet course and assessment deadlines
10 Take opportunities to consolidate learning outside the course
11 Are open to personal and professional development by giving and receiving feedback honestly and supportively

12 Use the staff for ongoing support by specifically requesting help

13 Respect and value the contribution of other learners and of staff

14 Are committed to ongoing personal and professional development through having personal counselling and supervision and through continuous personal reflection

15 Communicate the core qualities of genuineness, warmth and empathy to peers and staff as well as to those they counsel.

Chapter 7

The trainer as educator

The first part of this chapter focuses upon ways in which the trainer as educator can understand and accommodate the individuality of the learner. The question is posed: education or training? Discussion then follows on theories of learning; learning styles; personality, motivation and self-concept of the learner. The second part of the chapter focuses upon one aspect of educating counsellors: the development of counselling skills. The research literature is considered with particular reference to two approaches: the microcounselling approach and the problem management approach. The three major components of skills training are considered. These are: cognitive understanding through instruction and discussion, modelling, and supervised practice with feedback. Finally, trainee experiences of skill development in groups are shared.

It is useful to explore concepts such as education, training and competence and to see where they are distinctive and where they are interrelated. The word education comes from the Latin root 'educare', to lead forth. The concept of educating is therefore linked to processes of bringing out and developing. Such a concept assumes that there are within the learner abilities, skills and faculties which can be developed. The word training implies something further, namely learning activity which is action-oriented and which brings a person to a required standard. Training is therefore more focused upon specific learning outcomes or competencies. Competence implies successful performance against specific criteria and often leads to qualification or fitness for purpose within a specific subject area, field, occupation or profession.

The above definitions raise important questions for those responsible for developing the counsellors of the future. What is the relationship between teaching and learning? Should the emphasis be on learning process or learning outcome? Is competence-based learning narrow and restrictive and likely to produce mechanistic counsellors rather than integrated counsellors? Is the broader notion of professional development too woolly or is it more appropriate for counselling? Is training as well as education required for those who will be joining the counselling profession? Does the word 'professional' imply training and accountability to a specific standard and qualification? This chapter will seek to explore some of these questions.

EDUCATION OR TRAINING?

It has been suggested that the word education is susceptible to several interpretations, for example, the passing on of knowledge (Dewey 1916), initiation into culture (Durkheim 1956) and development of personal growth (Peters 1972). Tensions arise from these differing interpretations between those who see the educator as the focus, those who see the learner as the focus and those who view education as a collaborative process between the two (Bullock *et al.* 1988). Current thinking, particularly in the field of educating adults, emphasises that the learner is at the heart of the educational process and that learning is not limited to a particular course, but that it happens in both formal and informal situations. Learning occurs wherever learning takes place and learning is lifelong. It has been asserted that although the learner is an essential element in the educational process, the teacher is not. Teaching is dependent on learning, but learning is not dependent upon teaching (Jarvis 1985: 27).

LEARNING AND TEACHING

What then is the distinction between learning and teaching? Knowles (1984) distinguishes learning and teaching along five dimensions in relation to what he refers to as a pedagogical model of traditional teaching, and an andragogical model of adult learning. The dimensions are: concept of learner; role of the learner's experience; readiness to learn; orientation to learning; motivation to learn.

Knowles argues that when the focus is upon teaching (pedagogy) the learner is viewed as dependent and the teacher has full responsibility for making all the decisions about learning; the experience and knowledge of the teacher is the main resource; learners become ready to learn when they are told what to do; the focus is upon learning content and the motivation to learn is mainly from outside pressures, for example fear of failure. He argues that although this is a stereotyped picture many will recognise it from their own experience. He then characterises a learning-focused model: the learner is self-directing; learners become a learning community to which they all bring knowledge, skills and experience; readiness to learn occurs when they want to know something in order to live more effectively; their orientation is task-centred and problem-centred; motivation is intrinsic rather than extrinsic, with powerful motivators being around recognition and self-esteem (Knowles 1984: 8).

It has been said that learning takes place when learners know something that they did not know earlier, and can show it, or when they are able to do something that they were not able to do before (Honey and Mumford 1984). In the same vein, Hilgard and Atkinson (1967) assert that learning is a change in behaviour which is the result of experience. Such definitions emphasise the behavioural dimensions of learning, yet other writers note that learning can be simply the acquisition of knowledge even if there is no resulting behaviour change (Jarvis 1985). Egan (1993) states that learning takes place when options increase. This notion appears to bridge the divide between the acquisition of knowledge and the use of knowledge. Egan is drawing attention to the increased possibility of behaviour change as a result of learning, whilst recognising that behaviour change may be a step further along the line. His statement ties in with philosophical assumptions in education about freedom and empowerment (Freire 1974; Rogers 1983). Freire wrote about education as the practice of freedom, with an emphasis on education as a means of liberation from oppression – the oppression of poverty whether material, cultural or spiritual. Rogers is known for his emphasis on education as a means of developing the freedom to learn. He proposes that the facilitative conditions discussed in the previous chapter develop the internal freedom within the learner. This empowers by freeing the learner from anxiety, rigidity and narrow ways of thinking and acting so that in Egan's terms 'options increase'.

The values espoused in the model of training which has been put forward in this book are those which fit with a humanistic view of the learner at the centre of learning but in the context of training for a specific profession: counselling. This affects the educative process which would certainly be about leading forth, drawing out, developing and growing. In addition to a holistic, creative and reflective education the learner who would become a counsellor will need to be trained in counselling competencies. Education and training, therefore, go hand in hand. Training needs to be within the broader context of education so that skills and competencies are embedded within an integrative counselling style. Education needs to be grounded in specific practical training to ensure minimal levels of competence.

THE LEARNING CYCLE

If the learner is at the heart of education and training then we need to understand what will help and hinder individual learners during the learning process. Developmental psychology (Piaget 1952) helps us to understand the development of thinking processes and the developing ability to move from concrete operational thinking to abstract thinking. An example of this has particular relevance in counsellor training. Burns (1982) discusses Werner's (1961) orthogenetic principle which is that each stage of development brings increasing differentiation, articulation and integration. Thinking matures from the capacity to think concretely to the ability for abstract thinking. In the development of perception about people the developing ability to think in abstract terms results in greater use of constructs for understanding and describing both self and others. This has a positive effect on the capacity to be empathic.

Kolb and Fry (1975) translated the ideas from developmental and cognitive psychology into a theory of learning called experiential learning. They developed an experiential learning cycle which is most appropriate in counsellor training. The cycle begins with concrete experience, moves to the point of reflecting upon that experience, then to the formulation of hypotheses and then to the testing of these in new situations. Learning is therefore an active process on the part of the learner and it is rooted in the experience of the learner. However, it emphasises the fact that we do not learn from experience but from the reflection upon that experience. Behavioural psychology (Bandura 1969) helps us to understand more about motivation, incentive and reward and how these can be affected both negatively and positively in the process of learning. The contribution of the behaviourists is particularly useful when considering skill development, and this will be discussed later in the chapter. The behavioural approach also takes the experiential learning cycle into the action stage by stressing the importance of setting specific learning objectives which are realistic and rooted in action and outcome, and by always evaluating progress against specific criteria.

LEARNING STYLES

Within any group of learners there will be a variety of learning styles, and counsellor training programmes will need to be able to accommodate each of these. For this reason a varied training methodology is important. Honey and Mumford (1984) have developed a Learning Styles Inventory, known as the LSI. They have developed their ideas around the Kolb (1984) learning cycle but focused upon observable behaviours. They wanted to offer a self-development tool which could be used to increase awareness of those learning activities which would be most congruent with a preferred way of learning. By identifying a dominant learning style individuals are helped to understand why they find certain learning activities very difficult. Trainers also operate from preferred or dominant learning styles and it is valuable within a course team to have as many styles as possible represented.

The four categories of learning style which they identified are Activist, Reflector, Pragmatist and Theorist. Honey and Mumford recommend that trainers and learners assess learning opportunities in terms of preferred learning styles in order to find the match or mismatch between them and in order to identify individual learning needs. It is suggested that Activists learn best from activities when they can be involved with others; are involved in team tasks; can generate ideas freely; are given challenging tasks; and when they can become involved in short activities with immediate impact. Activists will learn least well when in a passive role such as a lecture situation or when the activity seems to be theoretical or academic rather than practical; when they have to pay a lot of attention to detail or when they are confined by instructions on how to perform the task. In counselling training, Activists will enjoy role-play activities, decision-making exercises, and active groupwork. Reflectors learn best when there is time to stand back from the activity and assess what is going on; when they can prepare by thinking before acting; when carefully thought-out detail is required and when there is the opportunity for review. They will not learn well in situations where they feel that not sufficient time or resources are allowed to do the task properly, where they are not given sufficient preparation time or when action is required without prior thought. In counsellor training the Reflectors will probably enjoy writing a learning journal and will learn from doing a research project or dissertation.

Theorists like structure, and the opportunity for question and analysis. They will enjoy the presentation of counselling theories and models and they will want ample time for discussion and debate. They will not learn well in an unstructured learning situation and they may find that groupwork which focuses upon feelings is uncomfortable. They will dislike courses which deal with concepts superficially and they will get frustrated if there is not time to cover theoretical ideas in sufficient depth. Finally, there are the Pragmatists. These are people who learn best from activities where there is an integration between theory and practice and where the learner can make obvious links between what is learned on the course and the real counselling situation. They will enjoy skills training activities, counselling practice and case discussion. They will not learn well from activities which they feel have no immediate relevance to their counselling work or when the theoretical ideas presented appear to be idealistic and not workable in practice. They may, therefore, resent some of the theoretical input on a course and they may also resent trainers who do not have credibility as counselling practitioners.

It is useful to apply the concept of learning styles to a particular aspect of counsellor training, namely skills training. Honey and Mumford point out that the Activist would be wanting to get on with the practice without the passive phase of attending to direct instruction. The Activist, therefore, may be moving ahead too quickly into the activity and the trainer will wonder why his or her clear instructions appear not to have been heard! The Reflector will want to be prepared before practising a skill and this would include not only instruction but also demonstration. If one of these elements is not provided by the trainer then the ability of the Reflector to learn from practice will be impaired. The Reflector will also require adequate debriefing and feedback after practice in order to learn best. The Theorist will need any skill to be grounded in a theoretical context and will require ample time for discussion about definitions and techniques, before embarking on practice. The Theorist will not take instruction at face value and will also want to have plenty of time to discuss and analyse the practice session after it has taken place. Theorists can be the learners who appear to be sabotaging practical sessions by asking too many questions when they are actually only preparing themselves intellectually for the activity. The Pragmatist is the learner who is most likely to enjoy and learn from the skills practice sessions as long as the sessions are well structured and have obvious relevance to 'real' counselling practice.

PERSONALITY AND MOTIVATION

Educators and trainers need to understand how internal factors such as personality, and external factors such as pressure from others, affect the motivation to learn. Much has been written in educational psychology about motivation and learning and it is not possible to deal in detail with the subject in this book. The reader would find it useful to refer to the work of Cattell *et al.* (1966) who developed the 16PF (Personality Factor) questionnaire and who discovered that school achievement was significantly affected by both personal factors and motivational variables. It would also be helpful to refer to the work of Maslow (1970) who pinpointed a hierarchy of needs which have to be satisfied in order that achievement and self-actualisation will occur. These needs in order of primacy are: physiological needs, safety needs, the need for love and acceptance, the need for self-esteem and the need for self-actualisation and self-expression. If these needs are considered in relation to personality and motivation it can be seen that they have a significant effect upon the ability to learn. A learner who is not sleeping well will not be able to concentrate, a learner who feels unsafe in the learning situation will be anxious and will feel under threat. A learner who has low self-esteem will lack the confidence to engage in new learning and is likely to be overly critical of self and others and therefore a problem not just to self but to the learning group. Maslow's ideas have provided a basis from which writers and researchers have been able to look more closely at the important relationship between perception of self, self-esteem and motivation.

SELF-CONCEPT AND SELF-ESTEEM

Burns (1982) has written extensively on the subject of self-concept development and education. He discusses developmental features and the discrepancy between the concept of self and the concept of ideal self; the effect of positive and negative feedback from significant others; the relationship of self-concept and achievement and the ways in which educators may enhance the self-concept in learners. He reminds us that self-concept comprises a descriptive and an evaluative element. The descriptive element is often referred to as the self-picture or self-image and the evaluative element is referred to as self-esteem, self-worth or self-acceptance. The significance of the beliefs and evaluations which comprise self-image and self-esteem is that they not only determine a sense of self and identity but they also determine what a person thinks he or she is able to do. There is a very important role for the counsellor trainer in relation to the development of the self-concept and it is twofold. First, there is the responsibility to provide a learning environment which enables the development of self-esteem and feelings of self-worth and self-acceptance so that the learner is able to function at a positive level unhampered by beliefs of inadequacy or inability. Second, there is the responsibility to foster self-esteem in learners because their own levels of self-esteem will have a direct impact upon their ability to work effectively with clients, who are also to a greater or lesser degree trying to work on self and concepts of self. It can be argued that the self-concept is learned and therefore it is amenable to change. Whatever learning takes place through the curriculum of a counsellor training course it should be focused upon the development of a positive and realistic concept of self-as-counsellor. With this in mind we now focus upon the educational aspects of a most significant part of the counselling curriculum: the development of counselling skills.

DEVELOPING COUNSELLING SKILLS

In earlier chapters a model was proposed for training competent and reflective counsellors. This section looks at the theoretical underpinnings for experiential learning in one important part of the model: counselling skills. Carkhuff (1969) was one of the first to isolate specific therapeutic skills and to discriminate between levels of effectiveness. Kagan (1967) introduced IPR, Interpersonal Process Recall, and this method was used widely to train counsellors to focus upon affect in counselling by recording sessions and debriefing immediately afterwards with the client. Gilmore (1973) emphasised the personal and skills development of the helper through what have become known as the Gilmore groups. Ivey and Authier (1971) used some of these ideas but went a stage further to develop an approach to skills training called microcounselling. These authors were not only influenced by Carkhuff but also by Bandura (1969) who contributed to the development of the microteaching format which is based upon behavioural principles. Ivey and Authier point out that in order to grasp the development and impact of microcounselling one needs to focus upon both academic and therapeutic arenas. They describe their microcounselling approach as a psychoeducator model of training which focuses upon normal coping with the environment, rather than dealing with abnormal psychology. This model therefore had much attraction in counsellor training when it became involved with training large numbers of helpers and counsellors who wished to work in non-acute situations dealing with the issues, problems and concerns of normal everyday existence.

MICROCOUNSELLING

The microcounselling approach was developed from microteaching, which is linked with social learning theory and which stresses the effects of social reinforcement applied externally, self-administered or experienced vicariously through the observation of models (Thompson 1976).

The task of microteaching is simple and direct, namely to learn one skill at a time and gradually develop a whole set of counselling competencies. The original model developed by Ivey and Authier consisted of three stages. The first was a baseline interview of five minutes recorded on videotape. The second was the training process based upon a written manual which described the skill to be practised, followed by a video model illustrating the specific skill, after which there was the opportunity for discussion. Then the trainee was allowed to view the original tape and compare performance with the modelled tape whilst the trainer maintained a warm supportive relationship with the trainee and focused all the time upon the skill being taught. The third stage in the microcounselling format was the re-interview, again videotaped, in which special emphasis was given to the skill being taught. This second tape was reviewed with the trainer.

This format has been adapted and there are many variations reported in the literature. However, there are fundamental similarities among them, namely the four stages of instruction for cognitive understanding, modelling to give what Egan has termed 'a behavioural feel', supervised practice with feedback, and generalisation of skills to helping situations.

Ivey (1971) lists some of the advantages of microteaching: it is more real than role play or case-study; the complexities of real-life situations are reduced so that one skill at a time may be taught and practised; because the training situation is specific and simplified there is a lower level of threat and fewer risks for trainees; the mystique surrounding counselling is removed by the focus upon specific behaviours which can be identified and learned; both trainer and trainee have greater control over the learning situation because it is clearly defined; overlearning can occur to promote the retention of skill; learners actively participate and take responsibility for their own learning; trainee needs can be met individually through the gradual development of skills and the gap is bridged between theory and practice.

Microcounselling is a method of teaching which divides complex human interactions into discrete observable behaviours. For this reason it is a form of training which has been frequently researched. Authier and Gustafson (1982) point out that many studies have been conducted which support the effectiveness of microtraining. Initial studies concentrated upon the basic attending skills (Ivey *et al.* 1968; Moreland *et al.* 1970) and whilst trainees did show significant improvements between pre-training and post-training tapes compared with a control group, they only retained 'minimal encouragement behaviour' at the one-year follow up. Reflection of feelings, use of open-ended questions and summarisation all declined.

Haase, DiMattia and Guttman (1972) also found that after a one-year follow up trainees had reverted to levels of functioning more like their baseline scores than their post-training scores. They concluded that the results support the theoretical underpinnings of the micro-counselling technique, that if a response is not followed by a re-inforcement, the probability of the occurrence of that response will decrease. The researchers raise two issues: is there a need for continuous reinforcement of behaviour, and are there parallels between the stimulus conditions under which trainees originally learn behavioural skills and the stimulus conditions in the environment in which they are expected to maintain those behavioural skills?

It is not simply a question of whether skill acquisition is retained and generalised, for there is also the question about which skills are more likely to be acquired through microtraining and which ones are more likely to be retained. In the Ivey *et al.* (1968) studies, 'minimal encouragement' was the skill which was retained over time. In the Haase *et al.* (1972) study, eye-contact skills were the only skills to remain consistent over time. Perhaps this indicates that non-verbal and paralingual behaviour is more likely to be reinforced by clients and therefore to be maintained.

Comparison studies show favourable results when microcounselling is compared with alternative skills training models. Toukmanian and Rennie (1975) used three groups to compare the effect of training upon the acquisition of listening skills. One group received microtraining, one group received human relations training, and one group were a no-training control group. Both the training groups showed improvements greater than the control group, but the microtraining group was also significantly better at empathic responses than the human relations group.

IS MICROCOUNSELLING AN EFFECTIVE FORM OF TRAINING?

Component research studies have indicated differences in the levels of difficulty of specific counselling skills and have also pinpointed the ways in which baseline knowledge and experience amongst trainees affect their ability to learn from supervised practice of skills. Personality factors and learning styles in trainees have also been found to affect significantly the outcomes of microskills training (Kasdorf and Gustafson 1978).

Thompson (1976) found that the superficial review of the literature on microcounselling, which demonstrates it to be an effective method of skill training, needs closer examination. He casts doubt upon the validity of some of the studies and comments that there is a general problem in interpreting the results of the studies arising from incomplete information about methodology and procedure. Four main types of investigation are noted:

1 Pre-test and post-test comparisons within one training group.
2 Comparison between a microtraining group and a no-treatment group.
3 Comparison between microcounselling and other forms of training.
4 Comparisons between different combinations of components.

Thompson reviewed 550 abstracts through ERIC in February, 1975. He also consulted several doctoral theses. He found that many of the studies used ratings on specific skills as the outcome criteria. He notes that this must favour microcounselling methods because the other forms of training are not so specific. Trainees in the microcounselling format would obviously have a greater awareness at the post-test stage, of the criterion measures used by the investigators.

This review of studies using the microcounselling format also noted that the reports did not include details of the pre-test and post-test instructions that were given. If the instruction differed between the treatment groups, then outcome must be affected. It was not apparent that there was parity in the obtrusiveness of the pre-test and post-test between treatment groups and control groups. Thompson remarks that for pre-test and post-test to be unobtrusive the experimental subjects should either not be aware that they are being studied or should be unaware that the recording of skill performance is related to the training study in question. It did not appear that any training studies included unobtrusive measures.

In the Ivey et al. studies (1968) previously mentioned, the pre-test instructions asked trainees to proceed in any way they liked when interviewing the client. In the practice and post-test sessions they were asked to reflect feelings, and therefore the significant change in score could have been a function of increased awareness of the criterion used. Also, in both pre-test and post-test situations, the client remained the same, and therefore greater familiarity with the content of the interview could have been the reason for improved performance, rather than skills learned through microcounselling.

In the study reported by Guttman (1973) defensive behaviours of counsellors appeared to be reduced significantly through supervision. However, Thompson notes once more that since the control group was unaware of the nature of the experimental treatment and therefore had little chance of knowing what was expected of them, this variable could have had a significant effect upon outcome.

Ivey and Authier (1971) admit that preliminary evidence concerning the generalisation and retention of microcounselling skills is mixed, but encouraging. They have found that training with specific criteria, follow-up and refresher training, and reinforcement in the work setting have an influence on skill retention.

There are several studies which show that short training programmes can increase basic listening and attending skills and increase levels of empathic responses (Kalisch 1971; LaMonica *et al.* 1976; Authier and Gustafson 1976; Hearn 1976). However, there is very little evidence in the microcounselling literature to suggest that the skills of confrontation, goal-setting and problem-solving have been adequately researched. Most research studies in the twelve-year review conducted by Kurtz *et al.* (1985) were of short courses of under thirty-five hours' duration and so it is not surprising that the training of paraprofessional helpers and counsellors was at the level of basic attending and listening.

More recently Baker and Daniels (1989), having done a meta-analysis of eighty-one studies of microcounselling, conclude that the microcounselling approach has made a significant contribution to counselling training, but that there was evidence that the dependent measures used in microcounselling research were limited and therefore research on teaching the more complex skills might be delayed:

> We believe it is time to focus on the effects of teaching higher order skills in more complex combinations. This will require concurrent efforts to improve and design valid and reliable dependent measures. To add to the complexity of this challenge, Hargie and Saunders (1983) pointed out the need to study the relation between individual differences and trainee outcomes, suggesting that training programs, rather than being standardised, may need modifications in response to individual differences.
>
> (Baker and Daniels 1989: 219)

THE PROBLEM MANAGEMENT APPROACH

The model for training competent and reflective counsellors, discussed in Chapters Three and Four, has been developed from several major influences. The development of skills in the model is based upon the microcounselling approach. However, the skills need to be located within a framework for the counselling process and the Egan model (1993) has been a major source of integration of skills within a process.

Egan advocates a systematic approach to helping which transcends the microcounselling approach. In his third edition of *The Skilled Helper* (1986) he reiterated his belief that there is a total process of helping within which certain skills may be appropriately used, but only at the service of other outcomes. He warned against the trend of training which focused mainly upon what he now refers

to as basic communication skills. He argues that these are fundamental to the counselling relationship, but they are not counselling.
He also isolates the skills of challenge in similar vein, stating that
they are needed throughout all the stages of the helping process
and not just in the intermediate and final stages of helping.

The skills required of effective helpers within a problem management perspective include establishing working relationships, basic
and advanced communication skills, helping clients to challenge
themselves, problem clarification, goal setting, action planning,
implementation and evaluation. Egan (1986: 11) emphasises the
importance of competency-based training in counselling and quotes
the report by Hatcher *et al.* (1978) who found that of 400 counsellor
education programmes surveyed in 1977, 71.6 per cent of those who
responded reported a commitment to competency-based training
and yet only 7 per cent had actually made the shift to a practical
implementation of that goal. Apart from the skills and the methods
required to make the helping model effective, Egan also emphasises
the need for working knowledge and skills in relation to developmental psychology, specific human problems, social settings and
the power of culture. For more detail about the way in which one
counselling course uses this model as a core theoretical model the
reader is referred to Chapter Four.

Stone (1982), evaluating the effectiveness of skills training programmes, presents some of the arguments which are now being put
forward against skills training approaches. He says that trainees
can be taught facilitative responses but they may have little impact
on other domains; an input–output model of specific behavioural
outcomes may ignore client needs, social benefits, conceptual and
professional development including personal beliefs and attitudes.
An over-emphasis on skills can lead to a training experience that is
stilted, mechanical and unrelated to personal development. It can
also lead to evaluation anxiety and a preoccupation with negative
feedback. The training situation may become unduly stressful and
focus upon avoiding errors rather than creatively learning from
them.

COMPONENTS OF SKILLS TRAINING 1: DEVELOPING SENSITIVITY AND FLEXIBILITY

In both the training approaches discussed above, the counselling
process and the counselling skills are presented through written

manuals and through a live lecture followed by discussion. The skill is clearly defined and the manuals give written examples of the skill in use. The *Skilled Helper* accompanying book of exercises, also provides lead statements from clients so that trainees practise discrimination of content and feeling in written exercises for group discussion. Pendleton and Furnham (1979) distinguish between sensitivity and flexibility in skill acquisition. The sensitivity is associated with a perceptual ability to discriminate fine differences in interpersonal interactions and this may be developed through methods which enhance cognitive understanding and cognitive clarity. The flexibility is associated with the development of behaviours which communicate that which has been perceived. Egan (1986) has a stage in training which lies between these two. He talks about gaining cognitive clarity and then developing a 'behavioural feel' for the skill, before being able to practise it. Having understood what it is, the behavioural feeling is the stage of understanding how it is practised. Having understood the 'what' and the 'how' the trainee may then move on to 'do'.

Campbell, Kagan and Krathwohl (1971) distinguish between the ability of an individual to identify accurately the feelings of another and the ability to use this knowledge or understanding effectively to promote positive client growth in a counselling relationship. They point out that a person may be highly sensitive but unable to use this aptitude. Arbeitman (1984) identified four components in the development of empathy and these were affective sensitivity (experiencing the experience of the other), role-taking (acts of imagination), emotional responsiveness and empathic communication. He noted the differences in the way trainees responded to the stages in the development of empathy. In the early cognitive stage they became preoccupied with the mechanics and often overlooked important verbal and non-verbal cues. In the intermediate or associative phase habitual patterns of responding began to fade and these were gradually replaced by new behaviours, and in the final, autonomous stage skills became natural and automatic, freeing the counsellor to focus entirely on the client. After reviewing several studies concerned with teaching skills through microcounselling, Arbeitman concluded that 'feeling reflection' was the only skill consistently and reliably taught by the microcounselling method. Studies by Kerrebrock (1971) and Moreland *et al.* (1973) support this theory.

COMPONENTS OF SKILLS TRAINING 2: MODELLING

There have been studies which examine the didactic component of training through modelling as well as through written and verbal instruction. Several sources are given by Ivey and Authier (1971) in support of the effectiveness of modelling for teaching new skills and strengthening previously learned ones. Modelling is particularly important as an aid to discrimination. There has been an assumption that only positive modelling should be used in counsellor training because of 'the hypothesis that negative models inevitably interfere with the acquisition of positive performance behaviours' (Newman and Fuqua 1988). However, Newman and Fuqua conducted a comparative study of positive and negative modelling in counsellor training and found no difference in training outcomes between the two groups. I am interested in this finding because I co-produced a set of video tapes called 'Listening and Responding' (Connor, Dexter and Wash 1984) and when I used both the negative and positive examples on the tapes I invariably found most interest in the negative models and the ensuing discussion about the negative example would be lively and stimulating.

Bandura (1977) stated that most human behaviour is learned through observation of models. He gave four aspects of skill learning: attention, retention, motor reproduction and motivation. Models may be live, as, for example, when the trainer demonstrates to the group with a co-trainer as client or with one of the group as client. My own experience has brought home to me that live demonstration is perhaps the most useful, but it is only of value if it demonstrates that which it was intended to demonstrate. For this reason I rarely use a trainee as client in a demonstration. There are too many unknown variables. It may be good, but it may not. With the limited amount of time available for modelling I prefer to ask a colleague to be 'client', not to tell me in advance what the content of the session will be, but for me to tell the colleague about the objectives of the demonstration. Models do not need to be live, but can be written (for example characters from literature) or filmed.

Bartlett (1983) reviewed a study by Robinson *et al.* (1979) which investigated the effect of written versus videotaped models and combined these with the effect of gender (male versus female model). There were five treatment groups for beginning counsellors: videotaped male model, videotaped female model, written model present, no written model present, control. No differences amongst the treatment groups was found. The quality of responses improved significantly for videotaped models over control, and written models over control. No difference between videotaped models and written models was indicated.

A study by Frankel (1971) is discussed by Thompson (1976) who also investigated the use of modelling in the microtraining format and found it to be effective. Frankel compared three methods of teaching psychology undergraduates the skill of reflecting feelings. One group had modelling followed by feedback on their own performance, another group had feedback first and then modelling of the skill, and the control group had neither modelling nor feedback. Those who were offered videotaped models with feedback on their own video performances were rated by clients as more effective. Control groups showed no improvement between sessions, showing that informed practice is not sufficient to increase the ability to reflect feelings. Both treatment groups which included modelling and feedback showed significant improvement in relation to the control group both after one exposure to modelling or feedback and at the end of the training sequence.

Ivey and Authier (1971) conclude that for the efficient imparting of complex skills, both instructions and modelling are essential. Perhaps the most challenging aspect of the theory surrounding the effectiveness of modelling concerns the function of the trainer as a model, not just on video tapes of specific skills but in the total process of training. This is an area which has not been mentioned in the research studies reviewed here. However, variations in the way in which the trainer is perceived by trainees could have a profound effect upon the outcomes of training in specific skills. It is surprising that in all the studies of the specific training component of modelling there is not the realisation that there is a 'macro' modelling effect as well as the 'micro' effect from the trainer. The total training process is a model which is more than the sum of the component parts of the training.

COMPONENTS OF SKILLS TRAINING 3: SUPERVISED PRACTICE WITH FEEDBACK

Skills practice in small groups is at the heart of training in both the microcounselling and problem management approaches. Many counselling courses use triads where each trainee alternates in the training roles of client, counsellor, and observer. Feedback in the groups is facilitated by the observer with the aid of audio or video recording of the interaction wherever possible. In addition, the supervisor or trainer will also be involved in the feedback process. In the training triads the trainees become models to one another and Robinson and Cabianca (1985) found that the accuracy of the trainees' reflection of feeling responses steadily improved from first counsellor in the triad to third counsellor in the triad. They suggest that if their initial findings become substantiated then trainers should expose trainees to one another's counselling behaviours in a more systematic fashion, ensuring that the strongest trainees are the first to act as counsellors in the triads.

THE TRAINEE EXPERIENCE

Extracts from a learning journal give some insight into the issues for trainees during skills training. On Hilary's course trainees are in training groups of four for counselling skills practice. Each trainee brings a video tape to each session to record their work. They view the tape between course sessions and they are invited to keep all the sessions on tape so that they can review their progress over a period of time. Two extracts are given from Hilary's journal. In the first one she tangles with the problems of learning from feedback:

Hilary

Most of the afternoon was spent in training groups. Feedback played a significant part in my learning this week both as a giver of feedback, and as a receiver of it. I feel in retrospect that the feelings around receiving feedback emphasised my own short-comings in observing and giving specific feedback and maybe that is one of the reasons behind my emotional reaction to my feedback. My objective today was to be relaxed enough to allow the client space and to be confident enough in my own ability not to have to prove I have the skills but to use them appropriately. I realised that I felt very tense initially, not because of the group, because I think I am settling into that, but wanting to prove to myself that I think I can do this. I had a counselling session with a young couple last week and really felt I had used my skills appropriately but allowed them space too, to be with them. This proved valuable and I was able to be quite challenging towards the end of the session as by empathic understanding we had achieved a trusting relationship.

Training groups is another setting and I suppose it is not just proving to me but to the others too that I have something to offer. This comes from a sneaking sense of inferiority in such a challenging group. Is this justified? And if it is, does it matter? Should I have chosen a more comfortable group? I think not – I need to feel stretched even if this produces discomfort along the way.

I was counselling M which proved useful in that she is a 'chatty' client and as I have already identified that I am finding this kind of client difficult to deal with, this enabled me, not only to gain more experience and have the opportunity to review this on video, but also to receive direct feedback from the client. I felt I managed to be relaxed enough to go at the client's pace and did use a variety of skills and was warm and empathic. I realised that we had not really dealt with the initial problem by the end of the session and felt disquiet about that, yet I feel we had explored M's feelings. M's feedback was really useful in terms of my interventions and the appropriateness and timing and I feel happier about that in relation to my other clients too.

The observer was A. She gave me feedback which was clear, specific and astute. I acknowledge the truth of it yet I felt hurt by the critical feedback. Why this reaction? Maybe initially I realised the difference between her clear and specific delivery and my rather woolly feedback. I think what upset me most was the reference to the latter part of the session becoming too relaxed and chatty. I felt angry at myself for letting M avoid her feelings and I see this now – it ties in with not following up a challenge. I see that I can remedy this by using immediacy and pointing out the choice to the client and asking what is around in that.

One of the recurring issues in skills training groups is the problem of defensiveness amongst trainees unable to accept feedback, and in the example above the trainee is dealing with some of her initial feelings of defensiveness through reflections in the learning journal.

The effect of audio and video feedback has been studied by Schwab and Harris (1984) who found no significant differences between the effectiveness of the two feedback modes when used with a group of thirty-seven counsellor trainees. Although they note that empirical studies in this area are very limited, their finding is in agreement with other studies – by English and Jelenevsky (1971), Markey *et al.* (1970) and Bailey *et al.* (1977). However they also quote Yenawine and Arbuckle (1971) who reported in favour of video recordings. They found that a greater degree of objectivity was achieved in evaluating videotaped interviews; that students were more comfortable in evaluating others' counselling performance and were more willing to review their own performance critically when video tape recordings were used, and that students were less dependent on the insight and leadership of the supervisor when video tapes were used.

In a study of the influence of supervisor feedback, Hayman (1977) made a significant discovery. Hayman found that the less experienced trainees in the study (sixty-four Masters degree graduates in a counsellor training programme) responded more positively to supervisor feedback and the more experienced students showed no improvement over the control group.

There were two treatment groups and a control group. One group had supervisor feedback after each target behaviour and one group had no supervisor feedback. The three skills taught were: open questions, paraphrasing, responding to feelings and emotions. There were three sessions of two hours each, over four weeks. The skill of responding was acquired most efficiently by those with other counselling course experience and not at all by inexperienced counsellors. Experienced students with no supervisor feedback were the group who learned most effectively. Several possible explanations are offered. Supervisor comment meant that trainees did not have to learn for themselves; anxiety about approval and disapproval of the supervisor could be detrimental to learning; there may be an assumption that supervision supplies the right answer and this prevents trainees from having to tease out and arrive at a consensus about assessment; the supervisor may have appeared to be didactic, and lack of experiential supervision may have limited the internalisation of concepts.

In another extract from her learning journal Hilary highlights the apprehension that can be felt by trainees when the trainer arrives in the group to offer feedback. This extract is a few weeks later than the one above and Hilary has decided to experiment in the training group with some gestalt dream work having recently been to a gestalt workshop.

Hilary

This week was spent mainly in training groups and I was looking forward to this as I felt very motivated to give the dream work a go. It is a good feeling that D is prepared to take the risk with me knowing that I have not done any gestalt dream work before. I had a few qualms when I realised that S (the trainer) would be observing too but in one sense I want to get that over with too! Of course I would like to be a wonderful, dynamic counsellor when the tutor is there but I feel that it is more important to fulfil D's request and for me to take the risk of trying something new out.

I went first in the group which was good and I did feel that it was a journey into the unknown together. I had read up about gestalt dream work but doing it is so completely different. I realise I was blinkered in some ways by my inexperience and not wanting other interventions to cloud the issue. However, I fulfilled my objectives of allowing the client choice and control, of not interpreting, of remaining in the present tense and of 'being there' for D, allowing him space. I surprised myself in some ways how comfortable I felt with the silence and space – a reflection perhaps on my slowly increasing confidence in my abilities. The client definitely reached a 'gestalt' and the space had proved very important for him rather than a series of experiments or interventions. In this sense it was totally client-centred and I feel I'd really appreciate the chance to do more dream work.

I felt anxious receiving the feedback especially from S (the trainer) and am interested in this dynamic of wanting to appear competent in their eyes when this is an arena to try out new approaches. Surely the feedback from the client is of vital importance particularly in such an experiential approach. In fact the feedback was really helpful and has motivated me to try out more new things. This week in my counselling at work I had used a gestalt technique quite naturally, it was the two chair technique and it worked well. It feels exciting that I will be able to use more and more techniques as my skill improves.

My turn to observe next and I tried to put into practice being more specific in my feedback. I was interested and relieved to see another member of the group having problems with a 'chatty' client. It isn't just me! I am appreciating the learning I am getting from being in this group with our often different perspectives and approaches yet a common desire to become effective counsellors. I find I learn so much from being one of two observers. Not only to emphasise what I do see but to realise that we also focus on very different aspects and how good it is to have such varied feedback. It broadens my ideas and allows me then to filter what I want to accept and what isn't for me.

Although I didn't focus on following up challenges today as my mind was totally occupied with gestalt techniques, I believe in fact it was very challenging for D in my counselling. However, I feel that an awareness of following up a challenge is helping me to allow the client the opportunity to see that they have maybe avoided a difficult area and the chance to look at why, rather than just letting it go. This hooks into my awareness of emotion and being open to allow the client intense emotion and not be afraid of that. It boils down to confidence – confidence in me as a counsellor and in the strength of the client as a human being.

In this extract Hilary gets anxious before the trainer arrives. Her anxiety is about being judged and not appearing as competent as she should: 'I would like to be a wonderful dynamic counsellor when the tutor is there.' She has a dilemma – should she play safe and do something that she knows she can do well 'for the tutor' or should she risk having a go at the dream work which her 'client' had asked her to do. Fortunately she decides to take the risk and finds that the feedback from the trainer is positive and that she is now feeling much more confident. As trainers, we need to be continually aware that trainees will feel apprehensive in our presence when we are there to give feedback and I find that asking the 'counsellor' to request what feedback he or she wants seems to take much of the threat out of the situation.

In my own training experience I have found that supervised practice with feedback is the most valued part of a counselling course for the trainees. For details about how it has developed on the course with which I am associated, I refer the reader to

Chapter Four. In my research (1986) I also found that it was the area of the course most appreciated by trainees. The trust which develops in the groups of four (counsellor, client, observer and facilitator) empowers the individuals in the group so that they offer to each other both support and challenge. They described this aspect of the course as the most difficult, the most enjoyable and the most useful part of the course. In other words, the work is not easy, but it is rewarding. Supervision of the work in these groups is a problematic area.

The research remains inconclusive with regard to the relative merits of self, video, peer and trainer feedback. In the research group mentioned, the most consistently favoured form of feedback was the peer group. The research by Hayman (1977) indicated that less experienced trainees benefited most from supervisor feedback and that the group which did best in that piece of research was the most experienced group with no supervisor feedback. The implication for us, as trainers, seems to be about empowering trainees to give valuable feedback to one another, and to accelerate the training process so that feedback skills are enhanced at an early stage in the course.

Trainees, in my experience, will give supportive feedback readily, but will be reluctant to give challenging feedback unless they have specifically contracted to do so.

The counsellor educator will be aware of the interrelationship of all aspects of training and particularly the way that attitudes, values and beliefs underpin the development of skills. Developing skills often involves a period of dissonance for the trainee who has to move through the stages of unconscious incompetence, conscious incompetence and conscious competence to the stage of unconscious competence when newly learned skills become internalised and integrated into a counselling style which is truly authentic.

Chapter 8

The trainer as assessor

The chapter is divided into two parts. The first part addresses assessment issues: the purpose of assessment; assessing skills and competence; validity and reliability; formative and summative assessment; self, peer and trainer assessment; the learning loop of objectives, criteria, process and outcome. The second part of the chapter deals with assessment at each stage of the training model: intrapersonal and interpersonal development; attitudes and values; knowledge and skills; reflection and evaluation. Trainer and trainee perspectives are included in this part of the chapter with examples from the experience of assessing learning journals, counselling skills and competence, and examples from supervised work with clients.

Perhaps the most unloved aspect of counsellor training is assessment. The whole notion of assessing implies judgement and therefore runs counter to much counselling philosophy. But there is also another facet which makes counsellors feel uneasy. Heron (1988) points out that assessment is a power issue and that the issue is a political one because it is about the way in which power is exercised:

> I have power over people if I make unilateral decisions to which they are subject. I share power with people if I make decisions on a bilateral basis in consultation with them.
>
> (Heron 1988: 77)

In an earlier chapter the notion of the trainer as facilitator was discussed and the first guiding principle of facilitation concerned the empowerment of trainees. In this chapter, assessment will be viewed from the perspective of empowerment: empowerment of the trainee, empowerment of the client and empowerment of the whole profession of counselling.

Before turning to particular areas of training which require assessment it may be useful to consider some of the current debates. These centre around such issues as whether to focus upon skills training or training for competence; whether to aim for competence or for excellence; how training programmes may be accredited; whether greater standardisation is possible by introducing National Vocational Qualifications (NVQs) in the area of counselling; whether the purpose of assessing counselling practice on a course is to assess performance or the capacity to evaluate performance; how far there should be self and peer assessment procedures; and whether there should be both formative and summative assessment on a course.

There are two main purposes of assessment. The first is to provide an opportunity for feedback to trainees about their performance and about their development. The second is to provide information about standards to clients, to the counselling profession, to training organisations, to validating bodies and to the wider community. Assessment cannot be divorced from accountability. Accountability is about ensuring basic levels of good practice. What constitutes 'good practice' arouses much debate. In any counsellor training course there will be a tension between that assessment which is perceived as valuable feedback for the developing trainee and assessment as an unwanted intrusion into the training course to provide information for outside moderators, examiners and accreditors. However, there will be one area in which all are in agreement and that is the welfare and safety of the client. With the client in the forefront of our attention the assessor has a serious responsibility. The assessor is not only an examiner, but is also a gatekeeper. Clients need to know that they will not be harmed when they enter into the field of counselling. Assessors control entry into that field and they should neither keep the gate firmly shut, nor allow the gate to remain open. It should only be opened to those who can clearly demonstrate that they fulfil the conditions for entry into the field.

ASSESSING COUNSELLING SKILLS OR ASSESSING COUNSELLING COMPETENCE?

Developments in microcounselling in the 1970s (Ivey and Authier 1971) helped counsellor trainers to isolate counselling skills and to develop specific criteria to assess performance in relation to these skills. This work developed from the earlier scales of counsellor facilitation produced by Carkhuff (1969) in which he had attempted to isolate the component parts of genuine concern, respect and empathy. Carkhuff asserted that these foundation qualities in counselling were only therapeutic if they were communicated to the client and if the client perceived them to be present in the relationship. (Refer back to Chapter Seven for a discussion of research into skills training.) Assessing counselling skills was, and is, a necessary way of assessing counsellor behaviour. Although it is necessary, however, it is not sufficient.

It has been said that competence involves not just behaviour but outcomes (Gilbert 1978; Egan 1990). If counsellor effectiveness is to be assessed then it must be assessed in terms of outcomes for the client, not just as satisfactory performance of behavioural skills. Research indicates that effectiveness depends on several factors both in counsellor and in client and these include not only the competence of the counsellor but the willingness of the client and the ability of the client to engage in a therapeutic relationship (Orlinsky and Howard 1986). It has been found that both personal and professional qualities in the counsellor affect the development of the therapeutic bond. McLeod makes a strong case for considering the assessment of counsellor competence, with counselling 'skill' as one component of competence. He defines competence as 'any qualities or abilities of the person which contribute to effective performance of a role or task' (McLeod 1992b: 360). The notion of competence links counsellor performance very definitely to client change or outcome.

COMPETENCE OR EXCELLENCE?

In 1993 a Lead Body was set up in the UK for the implementation of a National Vocational Qualification (NVQ) in Advice, Guidance and Counselling. This is part of a move towards greater standardisation in what to expect of counsellors and it may have a profound effect upon the accreditation and licensing of counsellors at a time when there is much discussion about setting up a professional register.

An NVQ might be seen as a measure of the ability to perform specific activities within an occupation or function to the standards of the relevant employer. As such, it necessitates much more clarity than we have at present. To achieve a non-vocational qualification, workers must demonstrate that they meet the set standards. The non-vocation qualification becomes a statement of competence of the range of tasks that the worker is able to perform to those agreed standards.

To reach this standard, the competence of the worker is evaluated in terms of outcomes to the client. One immediate spin off from this process is that it reminds workers of what it is that they are supposed to be doing and to what end. In other words, it reminds counsellors to know the key purpose of their work, and to be able to explain it to potential clients.

(Russell and Dexter 1993: 267)

These authors invited a small national sample of counsellors to provide material for their discussion paper to the advice, guidance and counselling Lead Body and they found an inability in experienced counsellors to state briefly the key purpose of their activity. They argue for a three-stage approach to competence: setting the key purpose of any counselling work through clear contracting with the client; having a series of elements of practice which can be evaluated; having performance criteria in relation to each element. They give examples of elements which could be viewed as outcomes in the counsellor's practice, for example, demonstration of respect for the client or empowerment of the client. The performance criteria would relate to each element and these could be assessed as, for example, accurate reflection and effective challenge as part of empowerment. What these authors do not do is to tackle the issue of assessment and evaluation causing possible intrusion into the counselling process and, at its worst, having a damaging effect on the therapeutic bond.

Some writers talk about a current obsession with standardisation and with a Credit Accumulation Transfer System (CATS):

To many educationalists, however, the competence movement represents a threat to the basis and fundamental principles of academic qualifications. They see the competence framework as a set of restrictive rules which must be obeyed, threatening their own erstwhile flexibility and autonomy.

(Johnston and Sampson 1993: 216)

The issue is about how far aims expressed as competence outcomes are compatible with educational objectives. Amongst the opponents of competence-based training there are those who feel

that once competencies have been defined they are reduced to
some form of naive simplicity which does not reflect the complex-
ity of human interaction. Competencies, such as skills, are integrated into a whole repertoire of helping where the whole is more
than the sum of the parts. There is a fear that if this is not properly understood 'we will have people with competencies rather
than competent people' (Callender 1992: 21).

> Is the term competence too imbued with the value judgement
> mere competence? Should we be thinking about a more sensitive
> terminology for assessment, mindful of the linguistic debate of
> competence versus excellence? There is an abiding suspicion
> that the whole competence movement could be substituting a
> baser quality, for excellence. . . . The fear is, perhaps, that stan-
> dards of competence are not sufficiently flexible (or enlightened)
> to assess individual excellence.
>
> (Johnston and Sampson 1993: 220)

This debate will continue and the answer must surely be that both
competence and excellence need to be assessed. NVQs may well
engender clarity and standardisation but other methods of assessment may also be needed for more complex and higher-order
competencies that are known by clients to be present in excellent,
rather than merely competent, counsellors.

THE VALIDITY AND RELIABILITY ISSUES IN
ASSESSMENT

Having discussed the function of assessment it will be apparent
that there are different views, and that assessment is for two purposes which may be in conflict with one another: developmental
feedback for the trainee and information about performance and
standards of competence for professional and validating bodies.
It is important for trainers and trainees to disentangle these two
purposes so that there is clarity about where they meet, where they
are in accord and where they differ.

Two aspects of assessment need to be considered in relation to
its purpose – validity and reliability. The introduction of NVQs is
an attempt at greater consistency or reliability in standards of
counselling, and this needs to be linked to the question of validity,
namely, does this measure of assessment and does this assessment
process tell us what it purports to tell us about the competence

of a counsellor? Questions of validity in counsellor assessment need to precede considerations about reliability. But questions of reliability are very important because we need to know if a trainee will be consistently competent with clients, rather than merely competent at assessment. McLeod (1993) notes that although there are plenty of ideas about how to assess counsellor competence there is little known about the validity and reliability of the techniques which are being used. He cites the example of the learning diary which can provide qualitative feedback to the trainee about her or his development during the course, but might be a very poor predictor of how effective the trainee will be when employed as a counsellor. Predictive validity is an important aspect of assessment and trainers should try to develop those assessment procedures which will provide evidence of what the trainee can, predictably, do in the real counselling situation.

Counsellor trainers need to look carefully at their existing assessment processes and procedures and to consider them in terms of validity and reliability. In terms of validity, does the sum total of assessment processes actually assess counsellor competence? Or does it assess idiosyncratic elements of training which it has been thought would be easy to assess? Or has it been included because the training institution or organisation has imposed certain 'traditional' forms of assessment which may be useful for certain academic courses but not for assessing counsellor competence? Are assessment measures being constantly reviewed in the light of recent research on the variables affecting client change and client progress? Sexton and Whiston (1991) conducted a review of the empirical basis for counselling with implications for practice and training. Their review supported findings by Lambert (1989) that the skilfulness of the counsellor may be an essential element leading to successful outcome in the client, despite technique, theoretical position or client predisposition towards counselling. In the light of this research they recommend that assessment procedures need to focus upon individual attributes and skills so that it is possible to identify those trainees who would have a negative effect on client outcome. This takes us back to the earlier point made about assessment as part of 'gatekeeping' for the counselling profession. Two other areas are highlighted for the attention of assessors. The first is the research which has shown that client factors influence the outcome of counselling. Research indicates that some counsellors may have negative attitudes towards certain groups such as women (Buczek 1981) or men (Robertson and Fitzgerald 1990), and this can lead the counsellor to be less than helpful.

The second area focused upon in the above research is that indicating that the counselling relationship is of major significance (Luborsky *et al.* 1988). Sexton and Whiston indicate that although much has been done in training people in specific skills there is still work to be done in researching the part played by specific skills within the total counselling process:

> Research in the area of helping skills may positively influence training curricula if we focus our attention on skills that seem to be supported by research (i.e. confrontational questioning) and focus less on those skills that do not seem to be effective (i.e. self exploration). Our review has suggested that the counseling relationship may be a mutually interactive process between the client and counselor rather than a simple demonstration of skills by the counselor. Martin (1990) argued that the field can now move beyond psychological skill training into a more comprehensive educational experience. We suggest that a comprehensive educational experience can occur if we focus on the elements of the interactional process between the client and counselor rather than exclusively on the counselor's implementation of helping skills.
>
> (Sexton and Whiston 1991: 347)

The value of the review of research quoted above is that it helps trainers to look at their assessment measures and procedures in terms of validity, that is in terms of what research shows that a competent counsellor is and does. The question then is: if this is what our trainees should be demonstrating, then do our assessment measures accurately assess these elements in the counsellor?

Once the question of validity had been addressed, the question of reliability must also be addressed. Assuming that a training course is clear about the outcomes of training to be assessed, then how can the trainer ensure that the measures, processes and procedures are reliable, that is, consistent? The assessment measures need to be consistently reliable across different trainee groups and if administered on different or separate occasions. The assessor must be consistent in the way in which judgements are made and specific criteria for assessment aid such consistency. Consistency must be evident across assessors and this should be tested continuously through the use of double marking, internal moderation and external moderation. There needs to be consistency between different training institutions and this is facilitated through external examining. Above all, the assessment must assess reliably whether this trainee is capable of demonstrating effectiveness not only in the assessment situation on a course, but also in the real situation with clients. The more reliable the assessment processes, the more real practitioner competence, rather than trainee competence, will be assured.

FORMATIVE OR SUMMATIVE ASSESSMENT? BY WHOM?

It would be impossible to separate out the question of formative and summative assessment from the question of who assesses in counsellor training. Formative assessment is that which occurs during the course and which is used as part of the development or formation of the trainee. Summative assessment is that which occurs at the end of a course and is often used to provide information about standards and performance not just for the trainee but also for validating bodies, professional organisations, clients and employers. There is, arguably, more use of formative assessment in counsellor training, such as the ongoing reflection which occurs in learning journals but which may only be assessed at the end of the course. Although there is a sense in which the final assessment of the journal is summative in that it happens at the end of the course, the process is formative. Another example of formative assessment is that which occurs when an assignment is marked or graded during a course but that mark or grade counts as part of the final assessment. Academic institutions have traditionally favoured summative assessment because it is believed that the assessment conditions can be controlled more easily, for example in a timed written examination, and this increases the reliability of the assessment. However, there has been a general move towards greater trainee participation in assessment and this in turn requires more creative approaches and reinforces the view that assessment is not an end in itself but part of a learning process, a part that can inform the ongoing learning process rather than merely being a final judgement upon it.

Once there has been a shift in perspective to view assessment as part of the learning process, it then becomes obvious that trainees need to be a significant part of that process and the power base shifts also, from exclusively trainer assessment to self and peer feedback and assessment. Then another shift occurs. There is a move away from content assessment only, to process assessment. 'Assessing how I learn and how I provide evidence of what I have learned is really more fundamental than assessing what I have learned' (Heron 1988: 85).

It has been suggested by Rowntree (1977) that if you want to discover the truth about an educational system then look at its assessment procedures. They will provide information about the sorts of qualities and achievements that are being rewarded and the extent to which the professed philosophy, aims and objectives are reflected in the assessed outcomes of the course. Purton (1991) makes an interesting observation about differences in approach to assessment on four counselling courses. The courses are the Facilitator Development Institute (FDI) course which is person-centred; the Master of Science (MSc) course at Goldsmiths College in London; the Psychosynthesis and Education Trust course; the Westminster Pastoral Foundation (WPF) course which is psychodynamic in orientation. He suggests that the differences arise from the kind of fear which predominates:

> In the case of the person-centred approach what is most feared, I think, is abuse of power and this is reflected in the emphasis placed in the FDI course on student self-responsibility and self assessment. In the MSc course I think the fear is that of bias.... Hence the maintenance of academic standards and values which have evolved precisely to guard against such dangers. In the psychosynthesis course I think the fear is that of a betrayal of spirit, a sacrificing of intuitive perception and the spiritual to the requirements of 'professionalism'.... Finally in the WPF course my guess is that the dominant fear is of unconscious pathology, the fear that apparently benign therapists may harbour pathological needs that will find expression in their work with clients.
>
> (Purton 1991: 48)

SELF, PEER AND TRAINER ASSESSMENT

The benefits of including self and peer assessment in counsellor training are obvious. It encourages self-responsibility and self-reflection as well as encouraging a feeling of responsibility to others in the learning community. Assessment becomes an on-going part of the learning process so that there is a learning loop which begins with the setting of personal learning objectives, followed by constant evaluation and assessment of self against these objectives which feeds in turn into the setting of new learning objectives. This development of autonomy in the learner has to match with the objectives of the course and therefore such an approach to learning involves initial contracting and ongoing negotiation of the course curriculum and of assessment processes and procedures.

Whilst most trainees willingly engage in self-assessment and experience great benefit from this, several trainees have difficulty with peer assessment. They may, like their trainers, have philosophical difficulties about making judgements on another person's work, particularly if they are asked to give a mark or grade. There needs to be clarity about peer assessment and where peer responsibility starts and ends. Counselling trainees will be encouraged throughout their training to give one another honest feedback, which has the characteristic balance of good counselling – that it is both supportive and challenging. If the term feedback is used, rather than the term assessment, this seems to help trainees to think and feel that they are involved in a collaborative process rather than a judgemental one. This can also clarify the distinction between the trainer's role, as ultimate assessor, and the peer assessor role which will usually fall short of the ultimate decision of pass or fail. It is recognised that in some person-centred counselling courses the trainee may in fact be the ultimate determiner of pass or fail and this would be in keeping with a person-centred philosophy. Purton (1991) noted that this was the case on the FDI (Facilitator Development Institute) course where the trainee makes the final decision about his or her theoretical and practical competence, but with the assistance of staff and other trainees. However, there is staff assessment which includes consulting with a trainee who is reluctant to receive negative feedback or to engage in self-assessment facilities provided by the course. The question that this raises is: is this mode of assessment trainee-centred at the expense of being client-centred? Is it possible, ultimately, to refuse to pass a trainee from that course who is not satisfactory, even though the trainee believes that he or she is? It is more usual that there is a mixture of self, peer and trainer

feedback but that the trainer takes the ultimate responsibility for
the assessment outcome. If a course uses a mixture of assessors,
there needs to be clarity about who in the last analysis is the final
arbiter when, for example, self and peers are in disagreement with
the trainer. Does the trainer's decision hold? If so, what is it that
is really being asked of self and peer assessment? Is it contributory
evidence or the power of the final decision?

Whoever the assessor is, there must be consideration about the
possibility of bias. It would be useful to have clients assess
the competence of their counsellor but is it fair to ask clients to
assess their counsellor with complete freedom from personal bias?
Is freedom from bias possible anyway for a client? The problem
of trainer bias is more pervasive because the trainer experiences
the trainee in so many different situations. Counsellor trainers
need constantly to reflect upon ways in which bias can enter into
assessment procedures. The more subjective the assessment, the
more likelihood there is of personal bias. The more vague the procedures the more likely it is that bias will play a part. The more
blurring of boundaries, the more chance that bias will creep in
along the ill-defined edges. Good assessment practice will try
to eliminate bias as far as possible and there will be awareness that
in an area with so many intangibles bias may be a very present
blind-spot. A powerful way of reducing bias is to be clear, open
and specific about assessment criteria.

THE LEARNING LOOP: OBJECTIVES, CRITERIA, PROCESS, OUTCOME

Assessment begins at the beginning. If assessment is being used as
an enabling and empowering part of the learning process it affects
the way that learning objectives are formulated and agreed.
Learning objectives need to be expressed as clear statements of outcome which can then be monitored and evaluated and these need
to be negotiated between trainer and trainee. Once clear behavioural objectives are set, then specific criteria can be agreed upon in
order to evaluate outcome. The learning process is then shaped in
such a way that it will enable the successful accomplishment of the
learning objectives. The implication of this for trainers is that training can not afford just to be expressed in vague terms. The intended
purpose and outcome must be clear to trainees so that they know
where they are headed. Assessment criteria need to be known from

the outset, so that trainees know exactly what is to be expected. Assessment criteria should be agreed and published in course documents, preferably in a course handbook. The quantitative (marks or grades) and qualitative (observations, statements and comments) assessment methods should be spelt out so that trainees understand fully the meanings behind these. Assessment procedures should also be published at the beginning of a course, together with the due dates for completing assessments. Trainers need to make clear the philosophy of the course with regard to deadlines. Is a deadline a deadline or a guideline? Equal opportunities issues are at stake here. Trainees have a right to know what the parameters are in which they operate so that all have an equal right to the time allowed for completion of a piece of work. Under what circumstances will it be possible, and not possible, to get an extension for a piece of work or to resubmit failed work for re-examination?

What is to be assessed and how?

The answer to this question relates back directly to the philosophy, values and beliefs that are translated into the learning objectives of a course. In relation to the model of training put forward in this book the major areas are intrapersonal and interpersonal development; attitudes and values; knowledge and skills; client work and supervision; reflection and evaluation. It will be noted that this is a mixture of learning content and learning process and that the assessment will cover both areas because they each inform the other. The methods of assessment need to be appropriate in relation to that which is being assessed and in some areas of counselling training there are great difficulties with regard to finding appropriate means of assessment, not least in the first area of intrapersonal and interpersonal development. At this point it will be useful to consider each area of the training model, but not without remembering the point made earlier in the chapter, that the total assessment process must be taken into account and that each part of the process must contribute to a total profile of what that course sees as an effective counsellor. Examiners of counselling courses are often amazed to find that this total profile has not been thought out. For example, trainees may be given so much choice in deciding upon their own assignment topics that it is possible to go through two years of a counselling training programme without ever having to demonstrate, for assessment, an understanding of a core theoretical model and how that model informs practice. It is also not unknown that a course will profess to be based upon a particular theory, but the practical assessment is based upon a completely different model. There is no coherence in such training programmes. Finally, there are courses in which the methods of assessment are not consonant with the course philosophy. For example, a course may be based upon a model which emphasises intentional counselling and yet the assessment processes are vague and not related to learning objectives, goals and outcomes.

ASSESSING THE CORE OF THE MODEL: INTRAPERSONAL AND INTERPERSONAL DEVELOPMENT

It is widely acknowledged that intrapersonal and interpersonal development is at the heart of effective counselling training and yet it is notoriously difficult to assess. It may be useful to consider the learning objectives which were given in the chapter in which the model for training was outlined. Learning objectives for intrapersonal development include: understanding and appreciation of self; awareness of and utilisation of personal strengths and assets; awareness of blind-spots, blocks and vulnerabilities; identification of areas to work on in personal counselling and experiential appreciation of the significance of developmental stages in personal development.

Learning objectives for interpersonal development include: understanding areas of strength and areas for development in a range of interactions; gaining confidence in appropriate self-sharing; developing the skills of giving and receiving feedback; facilitating growth in self and others through active participation in personal learning development groups; developing helping relationships with clients; continuously reflecting upon successes and setbacks; developing the internal supervisor.

Each of these objectives needs to be considered in relation to the questions: How will we know if this objective has been achieved? When will we know? Who will tell us? How reliable is their view? What is the evidence?

Assessing the learning journal

The first learning objective for intrapersonal development is: 'understanding and appreciation of self'. This sounds both vague and intangible. However, such a broad goal can be broken down into specific parts and evidence can indeed be provided by trainees, just as it was provided by a client recently, who was able to report on the number of occasions in the previous week when he had consciously managed to appreciate his own efforts and his own gifts and abilities. He had kept a daily journal with details of each occasion. Similarly, the trainee may keep a learning journal or portfolio with actual evidence of greater understanding of self (Pates and Knasel, 1989). Indeed, one of the criteria for assessing a learning journal would presumably be the inclusion of specific evidence of awareness of self and of movement arising out of that awareness through setting new learning objectives which have arisen out of reflection upon current evidence recorded in the journal. This becomes evidence which can be assessed. Vague statements and reflections, whilst having intrinsic worth, do not provide evidence against which an objective can be assessed. This example shows how the trainee is at the heart of the assessment process, with ongoing reflections upon development which are grounded in learning objectives which they have set for themselves. The trainer is involved at a second level by assessing the extent to which the learning journal has been used as a learning tool. The trainee thus assesses self against the objectives and the trainer assesses the way in which the trainee is providing evidence for that assessment. On the course which is discussed in Chapter Four, there are specific criteria for assessing learning journals which are based upon three core objectives:

1 That learning objectives have been regularly set and reflected upon;
2 That all aspects of learning on the counselling course, including unstructured learning and client work, are included;
3 That there is evidence of movement as a result of reflection upon learning.

Trainees are given eight specific assessment criteria and the reader will note that this includes practical guidance on, for example, how much is expected for minimum length of entries.

1 Regular weekly entries of a minimum of one side of A4 paper.
2 Ongoing learning objectives specified, evaluated and reflected upon.
3 Clear and legible presentation.

4 Links made with other course documents, e.g. essays, supervised counselling practice file, notes on reading.

5 Evidence of reflection on learning in all parts of the course: theory and workshop sessions, training group, group supervision, experiential group, review partner, practice in the work setting and individual supervision. Reflections, where appropriate, may also be included on learning from individual counselling or therapy and from significant life events and experiences.

6 Evidence of movement, learning and insight with regard to self and others.

7 Summary sheets at the end of each term.

8 Personal Development Profile of approximately 1,500 words at the end of each year.

(Counselling and Consultancy Unit 1993)

Rod is in his first year of the course and his summary sheet at the end of the second term indicates a theme of challenge. He has reflected upon the weekly entries and these are his learning points:

Rod

My first comment is that I have not focused sufficiently on areas outside the course: counselling in my work setting. This I will make as a firm objective for the next term. The journal continues to hold a theme of risk-taking and a high degree of reflection on feelings. An issue which arises with frequency is that again of transference and countertransference. My level of awareness on this dynamic is now much more in focus than previously, particularly being conscious of this during my counselling work. I feel that my skills are developing in a very general sense, such as my work in the supervision group. I feel more able to participate and offer helpful comments and ideas in the group supervision now. I also feel happier with the quality of feedback from other group members this term. It is more honestly supportive and therefore more challenging. The experiential group continues to be a place I go to work hard and I continue to do that. This group is beginning to grow in both strength and character. As a whole we are being encouraged to 'clean it up', deliver clear messages not wrapped in 'counselling each other' and being protective. I will in the next term attempt to give more direct feedback particularly in this group but in the course generally. My review partner continues to challenge me, doesn't let me waffle, moves me on and encourages me to engage more in divergent thinking and also focus more clearly on my own thoughts, feelings and perceptions. I continue to feel challenged, to challenge myself and although I feel stressed when I decide to take risks on the course I am finding that taking the risk pays off.

In terms of interpersonal development two areas of learning are that of being in the client role by having personal counselling during the course, and involvement in an experiential group for personal development. Both of these areas pose significant issues with regard to assessment. If it is a course objective (as it may well be on a person-centred or psychodynamic course) to be involved in personal therapy during the course, then how is the learning from this to be assessed? And by whom? Purton (1991) states that in a psychodynamic course (WPF: Westminster Pastoral Foundation) special attention is paid to the integration of psycho-dynamic theory both with trainees' experience with clients and with their experience of their own development. At the end of the second term in each year trainees write a self-assessment which is discussed with a supervisor and on the basis of this the supervisor writes a report which the trainee reads and initials if in agreement and comments if there are areas of disagreement. It is stated that although trainees are expected to engage in personal therapy, it is confidential and does not contribute to the assessment. Also, there is an experiential group which is led by a member of the course staff and which provides opportunities for informal assessment by self, peers and tutor, but does not contribute to the formal assess-ment process. It is worth noting that writers have called into ques-tion the whole notion of trainees engaging in personal therapy during training. Wheeler (1991) argues that personal therapy rather than being an essential aspect of counsellor training may actually distract trainees from the capacity to focus upon their clients because personal therapy may be stimulating material which negatively affects the equilibrium of the trainee in the short term.

The issue, about whether work in an experiential group should be assessed, has already been mentioned in Chapter Three in relation to the training model. If the objective is interpersonal development, and if fear that knowledge about the personal vulnerability of the trainee in the group would bias assessors to the detriment of the trainee, then formal assessment of the work in the group is counterproductive. However, if there is a learning objective which concerns the ability to learn in a developmental group, then there must be a way of providing evidence that this ability exists. One way to do this is to ask for a joint learning statement drawn up collaboratively between the group facilitator and the trainee and incorporating evidence from self, peer and facilitator. This distinguishes the capacity to learn and the ability to engage in the process from the content of the group sessions which can remain confidential. Themes can be highlighted, without reference to specific details.

STAGE 1 OF THE MODEL: ASSESSING ATTITUDES AND VALUES

If there is another area of training, or indeed of research in counselling generally, that is fraught with problems it is the assessment of attitudes and values. What attitudes should be assessed? What values should be assessed? Is there some standard that needs to be achieved in terms of attitudes and values that is consonant with the espoused philosophy of the training course and indeed of the profession of counselling? Is it right to expect any set standard in this aspect of training or is every trainee on a developmental continuum and it does not matter where each is on the continuum as long as there is evidence that they are moving in the right direction? And if so, what is the right direction? These are some of the questions that we will need to be asking in relation to the assessment of attitudes and values and the answers will vary according to course orientation.

In this book the learning objectives outlined for this stage of the training model (see Chapter Three) include: awareness of personal assumptions and beliefs; exploration and clarification of values and attitudes; development of core therapeutic qualities; awareness of ethical and professional issues and expectations in counselling; development of a personal code of ethics. The first two of these would presumably be evidenced in a learning journal. The awareness of ethical and professional issues can be assessed through written assignments: case-study, essay, counselling practice file, supervision records, research project. Development of a personal code of ethics will be evidenced in the learning journal and could be submitted as an argued piece of written work. The most difficult objective to assess, and the most important, is the development of core therapeutic qualities. It can be argued that the counselling course itself provides a myriad of opportunities for the development and ongoing assessment of therapeutic attitudes and values to be communicated amongst peers and between trainers and trainees. Instead of always looking outwards towards rating scales and questionnaires for evidence, courses would do well to build into their processes a contract for having an ongoing dialogue with trainees about the way their development of core qualities is manifest in the day-to-day experience of the course. The raw data is there to be worked with. In a collaborative learning community the dialogue would be two-way and therefore truly a dialogue, with trainers also receiving feedback from trainees.

STAGE 2 OF THE MODEL: ASSESSING KNOWLEDGE AND SKILLS

Assessing knowledge and skills is done through a mixture of written work and practical work. The learning objectives outlined in Chapter Three, for this stage of the model, include learning about major theories and approaches to counselling; the causes and manifestations of client problems; systems, settings and contexts; skills, strategies and interventions; and development of an integrated counselling style.

Assessing knowledge

Case-studies, essays and dissertations are traditional approaches to the assessment of knowledge and such approaches may benefit from self and peer assessment procedures which can greatly enhance the learning. On the course which was discussed in Chapter Four, there has been a movement towards self and peer assessment to supplement tutor assessment. Trainees are asked to help to draw up assessment criteria so that they become involved in the assessment process even before they start to prepare a piece of work. The staff have usually decided upon some core criteria but they do not prejudge what the trainees will suggest by giving this information before there has been an extended brainstorm with the group. If the group does not include criteria which the tutors think are important, such criteria would then be added. This collaboration helps trainees to take ownership of their own work. Once an essay or case-study has been written the trainee can invite one or two peers to assess it for her or him, in addition to the assessment of the course tutor. The policy of 'inviting' is important, because the work is precious to the trainee and the invitation is a mark of trust and respect towards the peer assessor, who will then usually respond with trust and respect when reading the piece of work and when giving feedback. This does not mean that the peer assessor will not be honest. Staff find that as they grow in experience of assessing they give more specific and challenging feedback.

Each trainee gets the opportunity to have peer as well as tutor feedback, but also to read the work of at least two other trainees. My experience of managing this process is that the practical arrangements need to be carefully thought through but the increase in standard of work after the experience of self and peer assessment is staggering. It is particularly helpful to weaker members of the group, because it not only opens their eyes when they see what other trainees are able to produce, but they also note different strategies for writing essays.

Some of the practical things which need to be considered are: How much time will it take for trainees to assess work? At what point does the tutor give feedback? How can the tutor manage to see each individual trainee on one day so that they all receive feedback as soon as possible? What happens when tutor and peer feedback is at variance? I would caution against setting up self and peer assessment procedures until this has been carefully considered. If trainees are led to believe that their assessment counts, they expect that it will really count, even at the point of a decision about pass or fail. If the course adopts a policy of trainees ultimately deciding whether they pass or fail (for the trainee experience of this see Battye 1991), then there is a clarity about the extent of self and peer assessment. But if the ultimate decisions rest with the course tutor then this needs to be clear to the trainees from the outset so that they know how much power and responsibility they have in practice. On the course on which I train, we stipulate that the ultimate decisions rest with the course tutor and that where there is disagreement between peer assessors and staff, or between self-assessment and tutor-assessment then this will be fully discussed and if a compromise cannot be reached then the disagreement will be recorded and discussed with a course moderator or external examiner. When these procedures fail, a complaints procedure is needed.

Assessing skills and competence

With regard to practical assessments of counselling skills and competencies the same policy of self and peer assessment applies. We usually find that this is the most stressful part of the whole course for trainees, who are asked to show specific skills or competencies on videotape recordings. With regard to practical assessment there is the issue about whether actual ability to perform specific skills or competencies at a specific moment in time is being assessed, or whether the ability to evaluate performance critically is being assessed. It is the dilemma about the developmental stage of the trainee. Some trainers argue that it is not fair to assess performance because assessment situations can only approximate to real counselling situations and therefore the assessment would not be a fair indication of what the trainee can do. Furthermore, some trainers argue that there is injustice in a situation where trainees are asked to perform in front of a video camera or live with a group and that this puts them under a pressure which is asking too much. There is also the problem of peer assessment of practical counselling where trainees are asked to assess others when they may not understand clearly what they are supposed to be demonstrating themselves.

Helen, a second-year diploma student writes about her final counselling practice assessment and about the debriefing session which followed in her group. This extract highlights some of the anxieties and difficulties of peer assessment for the assessors and for those who may resent the quality of feedback offered by their peers or by tutors. The arrangements for the assessment are that each trainee presents a video-recorded session which shows five elements. These are the elements for assessment: support, challenge, resourcefulness, immediacy, dynamics. On this course all trainees will have had to demonstrate fifteen specific counselling skills for their first-year assessment. The second year is intended to be qualitatively different. The assessment session is forty-five minutes and trainees are asked to set the agenda for their assessment session which will be in a group of four trainees and two tutors. To facilitate specific feedback, trainees are asked to produce an evaluative transcript of the session showing at what stage the five elements are demonstrated and with a self-evaluation of each. This takes a long time to prepare and it involves the trainee in editing video tape and in analysing it closely. It also means that in order to undertake the self-assessment the trainee must be quite clear about what these elements are in counselling and how they actually relate to them. The learning potential is tremendous, as is the potential for anxiety as Helen says in her learning journal:

Helen

I have spent a phenomenal amount of time preparing for this assessment; in reviewing, transcribing and eventually editing the tapes. Although I had put considerable effort into my preparation I felt a degree of anticipatory anxiety about the presentation and the fielding of possible questions. What I didn't expect was to find evaluating the work of other members of the group as difficult as it turned out. The speed of the presentations plus having to assess the skills demonstration and evaluation at the same time proved difficult, also making an attempt to grasp something of the content, process and dynamics. My feeling is that I sold the other group members short; and am much better at giving feedback than I displayed on this occasion.

My own performance. I was aware that as I heard and viewed the video I was conscious of the areas which I know I could have done better. I was also looking around the group for any non-verbals which may have given me a clue as to how the assessment was going: it seemed an interminable amount of time, although it was only about thirty minutes. I was delighted with the feedback I received. I celebrate my effort and I learn and acknowledge that my hard work pays off.

Learning for me with regard to my own assessment. Give clients more space, tone down the flow and eagerness of my own speech, offer less in the way of information-giving. I feel this may be to do with my own level of anxiety and enthusiasm.

Helen indicates the long hours taken in preparation, the difficulties of assessing her peers in a presentation session where there is so much to focus upon, the anxiety as she looks round the group hoping for some clues as to her progress during her own presentation. However, she is pleased with the feedback and can bask in the satisfaction that her hard work has been rewarded with success. However, one week later her group meet to debrief their assessment experiences. For one trainee it was not such a good outcome:

We contracted a time split, each of us to use the time as we chose. Anthony was feeling that he had given good feedback and that this was not paralleled by the group. I would echo this. I certainly feel that I am capable of giving better than I did, and I said so. Overall Anthony was happy with his assessment. Roz had put a lot of work into debriefing her assessment by reassessing her own tape against the backdrop of the comments which had been made on the day of the assessment. She seemed quite pleased with the comments which had been made. Jed was feeling bad about the whole thing. He had not done himself justice and was kicking himself because he wasn't able to say what he really thought to the tutors when they gave their feedback. The group felt that they had seen him work better and that the performance for assessment was well below his usual standard. We suggested that he go back to the tutors and ask for clarification about the areas he needs to work on because he said that he was so upset the first time he saw them that he didn't really hear what they were saying.

This extract helps us to understand how the assessment process will be used and experienced differently by each member of the course. Anthony does the work, gets a good result but is not satisfied with the quality of peer feedback. Helen says she felt the same but also realises that her own feedback was not up to her usual standard, and it would appear that the anxiety about being assessed oneself gets in the way of being able to be a peer assessor for someone else. Perhaps this group was moving between being assessed and assessing in one day. The tutors on that particular counselling training course have moved to a situation where trainees do not assess anyone else on the day that they are assessed themselves. Additionally, trainees do not do their presentation to their own group, to reduce possible collusion (however unconscious it may be). Each group is paired with another and they present to each other in turn. One week each member of group A, individually, presents to the whole of group B with two tutors present. The following week it is reversed and group B individually present to the whole of group A. Whilst one member of a group is being assessed the other members are given 'time out' for preparation or debriefing.

Roz makes the most of the learning opportunity presented by this assessment procedure. Not only does she prepare, present and self-evaluate. She also listens hard to the feedback and then goes away and works with it by reviewing her tape in the light of the assessment. However, Jed is left feeling bad because he knows he did not do his best, and because he got upset he couldn't use the session with tutors constructively. This extract reminds us how difficult it is for trainees to absorb feedback when they are feeling upset and how difficult it is for them to get their voice heard when they are in the sort of power relationship that is part of assessment.

The tutors on this course have a policy of giving immediate written and verbal feedback (within thirty minutes of the assessed presentation) to trainees as a mark of respect to them for all the hard work they have put in to the assessment, and also because the more immediate the feedback, the greater the potential for learning from it. A group discussion with peers and tutors follows the presentation and lasts for about twenty minutes. Then tutors go away and discuss the assessment amongst themselves and draw up a detailed joint feedback statement highlighting strengths and areas for development against the specific assessment criteria. The trainee then receives this written feedback and there is the opportunity to discuss the whole assessment. In the following week trainees are asked to collate all the feedback from self, peers and tutor and to write a short evaluative report which would pinpoint strengths and areas for development and which would help them to set future learning objectives.

STAGE 3 OF THE MODEL: ASSESSING CLIENT WORK AND SUPERVISION

The learning objectives at this stage of the model include the ability to distinguish between counselling and other helping activities and to be able to set up counselling contracts with real clients. Following on from this is the opportunity to practise counselling competencies in real counselling situations outside the course and to reflect regularly upon these experiences through the use of a learning journal, case-notes and counselling practice file. Regular supervision is required, both individual and group, and on the course as well as outside it. Two final learning objectives are to develop the internal supervisor (Casement 1985) and to develop confidence as a counsellor.

This is the part of the course where tutors can only have indirect access to the work of the trainee: through their own reflections, through what they bring to supervision on the course, what they

write in their case-notes, and what they take to individual supervision outside the course.

Two aspects of the assessment are worth discussion at this point.
One is the supervised practice file or log. The other is the report
from a supervisor. As my experience of being a trainer has increased
I have realised that this element of the course is probably the most
important. Nevertheless it is the one which can fall through the
assessment net because it is more difficult to assess, and because
counselling work cannot be subject to first-hand assessment for
ethical reasons to do with the client and the counselling agency.
We are not therefore assessing counselling itself at this stage, but we
are assessing the ability of the trainee to prepare for counselling
sessions; to reflect upon them; to have frameworks for reflection and
analysis; to be able to learn from supervision; to give evidence of the
developing ability to use the internal supervisor during counselling
sessions; to try out appropriate approaches, skills and strategies
and to work within professional and ethical codes. Additionally the
sort of evidence which trainers may wish to see includes a specified
number of counselling hours completed; a specified number of
supervision sessions attended; work with a variety of clients; confidentiality maintained through coding systems in written work;
brief excerpts of transcripts with process notes. Hilary tells what it
is like to keep such a supervised practice file:

Hilary

The discipline of writing up both counselling sessions in preparation for supervision, and the supervision itself adds significantly to my learning. It helps to clarify what I did or did not do,
what was really going on and where I need supervision. I thus
get the most out of supervision time and then can reflect on that
in writing it up. There is so much potential for learning and
growth in every counselling session, keeping the file taps into
that richness in a structured way. The negatives I feel are purely
time constraints where there seems to be so much to learn and
process.

It could be argued that supervision is a form of ongoing assessment,
providing an opportunity for self-assessment, peer assessment
if there is peer-group supervision on the course, and assessment of
an external supervisor if there is individual supervision. I believe

that all this valuable formative assessment must become part of the total assessment picture. If this is not included in the main course result, for reasons of safeguarding confidentiality between trainee and supervisor, then the most important part of the course is being left to chance and the qualification obtained by the trainee is of limited value. However, it is difficult to 'grade' the use made of something like supervision and so courses often have a joint supervisor/supervisee statement which has to be produced as a sign of satisfactory use of supervision but which does not receive a graded mark. If it is not possible to grade the joint learning statement, it is possible to grade a supervised practice file against specific criteria as outlined above.

This extract from the joint learning statement drawn up at the end of the first year of the course shows how Rod made good use of the interaction between the counselling practice file and supervision:

Rod: summary of supervision

Joint Supervision Statement Year 1

To start with, it may be worth reflecting upon the contract which was made with my supervisor at the outset and that the underpinning process for a contract should be that of consultation, integration and support.

Contract

1 To meet at least twice a term
2 To use audio taped material where possible
3 The use of transcripts
4 Time to discuss my general progress as a counsellor

Areas to consider

1 Impression of client
2 Client content
3 My content
4 The choice and delivery of intervention
5 Dynamics in the relationship
6 Theoretical underpinning of interventions

Supervision sessions followed a process in which I felt challenged to examine the various facets outlined in the contract. I feel that there has been a strong development in the intentionality of my counselling work. This I believe comes from a better theoretical foundation and perhaps more significantly a firmer grasp of the counselling process. I have found that the framework for writing up each counselling session allows for the examination of my own and the client's objectives, feelings and thoughts, also outlining the outcome of the session and any learning that has taken place. I feel that this has proved invaluable in enabling me to examine the dynamics within my counselling relationships. I have found a valuable aspect of supervision has been the constant challenge for me to examine my relationships with various clients, particularly those presenting from diverse backgrounds and with diverse problems.

Supervision has prompted me to ask myself if the client in any way reminds me of any significant other, thus bringing into the counselling arena anything which may enhance the therapeutic relationship in terms of empathic understanding or conversely hinder in the context of any unfinished business I may have. I am now much clearer about what is meant by transference and countertransference, having discussed them in relation to me and my clients.

I have found the use of taped extracts and transcripts useful as they demonstrate a representation of my attempts to develop skills within the counselling process. Significantly, they have served in enabling myself, along with the supervisor, to critically evaluate my skills within the process and also allowed the supervisor an access to 'the feel' of the client.

Supervision has enabled me to check out the development and skills within the counselling relationship, particularly skills which have been newly acquired and are in fact being 'tried out', viewing this in the context of the consequent impact upon the client and also for myself. For this I cite as an example the development of working with Gestalt techniques particularly in two-chair work. I also feel that the supervision allowed me to bridge the gap between techniques and client centredness in seeing certain techniques as intrinsic to the counselling process and the therapeutic relationship, and not something which is purely an addition.

I believe that by practising and constantly being able to monitor myself using the opportunity for supervision, that this has enhanced my confidence and I believe certainly improved my competence. I feel a significant area of improvement which is connected to the counselling process is my increased familiarity with Egan's model. Again in supervision this has been used as a cognitive map enabling both myself and the client to have an awareness of our sense of direction. Other key areas in supervision have been about ethical issues and in particular issues around the responsibility to divulge certain information. Also, setting up couple work.

Areas to continue to develop in future supervision

I feel it is of major importance to continue to monitor my feelings and to remain aware of the issue of transference. I wish to further develop my use of immediacy and also to balance the dialogue between myself and the client, with less wordiness on my part. I also wish to continue to develop my skills particularly in setting up experiments with certain strategies, thus enhancing my confidence and competence in their use, including refining my reflective skills and focusing more on the dynamics of the relationship.

This appears to be a very honest self-appraisal and it gives Rod's tutors some idea of the clients that have been seen, some of the presenting issues and some of Rod's issues and concerns as a counsellor. We also get an idea about how he has been using supervision and we get an impression of a supervisor who is both affirming and challenging, allowing Rod to feel safe enough to look at difficult areas, such as his own unfinished business and his attempts to experiment with new techniques. But how do we know whether the areas for development that Rod has put forward are the most important areas from the perspective of his supervisor? How do the tutors get to know about the weak areas that are perhaps blind-spots for the trainee and therefore not in his awareness? It seems to me that we cannot just rely on the perspective of the trainee. We are training professional counsellors and there must be professional accountability. This is where the supervisor's part of the joint learning statement comes in, and as it is 'joint' it means that it is read and agreed by the trainee before it is submitted to the course staff. 'Joint' can mean two separate but agreed statements or one statement jointly agreed. From experience, my preference is for the former because it allows for two perspectives, rather than what may become a diluted or colluded one. Rod's supervisor was Andy and this is an extract from his report at the end of the second year:

Andy: Rod's supervisor

Joint Supervision Statement Year 2

Themes which were memorably significant and commanded substantial time and consideration include:

1 The implications of entering a counselling relationship with a client who has been seen by several helping professionals in the past. The pros and cons of accessing previously recorded information on the client or 'going in cold'.
2 Gender of counsellor and client as a dynamic requiring constant consideration. This came to light with several clients, including one who asked for psychosexual counselling.
3 Contracting confidentiality. How important it is to get this right and the implications of having to change that contract at a later date. The moral and ethical issues involved in confidentiality and its limitations.
4 How clients experience Rod when he may have a dual role in their lives.
5 The recognition and management of countertransferential material which surfaces in counselling relationships.

Regarding the areas for development identified by Rod at the end of last year I would have the following observations. Rod's awareness of transferential and countertransferential issues arising in counselling interactions has increased substantially. He appears to have developed the appropriate antennae for listening out for relevant clues. Linked with this is Rod's use of immediacy which he had identified as an area for further development. Appropriate self-disclosure and challenging in the here-and-now are skills which Rod continues to work at. He does not back away from the discomfort which this may sometimes cause. Regarding the balance of dialogue between Rod and the client, there has been an improvement, but on occasions Rod's natural exuberance threatens to overwhelm some clients. The use of appropriate silence may be something he could profitably work on.

The implementation of previously unused therapeutic strategies and structures was a live issue for Rod at the end of last year but is now not so. He appears to have incorporated structured activities into his counselling without the clumsiness which he described last year. Reflective skills continue to develop, but perhaps this is a lifelong task which is at the heart of effective counselling and which we all have to continually strive to improve.

I have been particularly impressed with Rod's continued enthusiasm and dedication to the hard work of counselling and supervision. He has always prepared well for our sessions, invariably brought live and pertinent issues and been open to new perspectives whilst being able to substantiate his own point of view when he thought it justified. My perception is that he is a safe and effective practitioner who has demonstrated a combination of refined core conditions, developing interpersonal skills and a growing knowledge base. I have been stretched and challenged by the experience of supervising him.

This supervisor's report tells us more about Rod. It tells us that they have an excellent working relationship in which both are being 'stretched and challenged'. The tone of the report is supportive and yet honest, giving course staff an indication of areas where Rod may need more help and development. If this sort of information is fed back into the course then opportunities on the course for attending to weak areas can be maximised. For example, Rod's ebullience and possible verbosity can be monitored in group supervision on the course, and indeed in other areas of the course, such as community meetings, the experiential group, the larger group. He wants to develop skills of immediacy and self-disclosure and his supervisor thinks that he needs to. Once more the course can provide opportunities for this now that the course staff are aware of Rod's particular needs. If assessment is used in this way it is an ongoing aid to learning, giving valuable information which can be responded to and acted upon in the best interests of the trainee and of her or his clients.

STAGE 4 OF THE MODEL: ASSESSING REFLECTION AND EVALUATION

The first two learning objectives for this fourth stage of the model have already been discussed in this chapter. They are to reflect

continuously upon learning both in the course and in work with
real clients, and to engage in, and learn from, the process of assessment – self, peer and tutor assessment. In this sense, reflection and
evaluation continue throughout the course and the assessment of
these occurs at each stage, but is particularly focused in the learning journal. See the earlier part of this chapter (pp. 168–71) for a
more detailed discussion of the use of the learning journal as an
assessment device.

   The other learning objectives at this stage are concerned with
becoming familiar with research processes and becoming actively
involved in the field of research. I made the point, in Chapter
Three, that we are trying to encourage a 'research mentality' in
which questions are continually raised and explored. This can
permeate the learning journal and the counselling practice file.
Additionally trainees are often asked to engage in a small piece
of research for assignments such as a long essay, case-study or
dissertation. It seems important that trainees are given clear and
realistic objectives for such assignments, which would preferably
be in some way connected to their own counselling work. One
of the best research studies I have seen on a diploma course was
that of a trainee who researched her work with just two clients. But
the thoroughness with which this was done, made the results
meaningful to more than just herself and her clients. It did not give
definitive answers to research questions, but it allowed her to look
very carefully at her work, and to find out from her clients what
their experience of her was. As a result she discovered some blind-
spots in herself concerning one specific aspect of her counselling
and took action to implement the necessary change. It was only
something small, but it was significant and if she had not discovered this about herself it could have been a cause for continuing
irritation in her clients.

   At the other extreme we have the larger study, which may
involve statistical analysis and comparisons with different groups of
clients. This sort of study has obvious value, but only if it is done
properly, and if the research methods are really appropriate for the
design. Our assessment questions at this stage of the model are:
Are we assessing the ability to design a research project? If so, this
can be a paper exercise. Are we assessing the ability of the trainee
to demonstrate an understanding of existing counselling research
through a literature search and review? Are we asking them to
demonstrate the ability to use statistical analysis, or qualitative

analysis? If so, this can be done either through an actual project or through a theoretical exercise. Are we asking trainees to research their own counselling work in some way? We may wish for several of these, or we may think that only one of these is necessary. In the model presented in this book (that of training competent and reflective practitioners), the ability to engage, in some small clearly defined way, in researching one's own counselling work would be a must. See Watkins and Schneider (1991) for useful chapters on outcome research in counselling; single-case research in counselling; qualitative procedures for counselling research; and the ethics of researching counselling processes.

An ongoing issue for trainers engaged in assessment processes is to monitor and get feedback on our own competence as assessors. If a course has ongoing monitoring and evaluative processes and if the course is a collaborative learning community then trainees will be encouraged to give trainers feedback throughout the course. The final chapter of the book, on professional development of the trainer gives some ideas for maintaining adequate levels of competence. The chapters on the dynamics of the training relationship (Chapter Five) and on ethical and professional issues (Chapter Nine) give some practical examples of the struggles around assessment of both trainers and trainees.

Chapter 9

Ethical and professional issues in counsellor training

In this chapter five ethical principles are discussed: autonomy, fidelity, justice, beneficence and nonmaleficence. The three values of integrity, impartiality and respect are taken as the basis from which to explore training situations where there are ethical or professional issues. Issues related to integrity include: competence of the counsellor trainer; using informed consent; holding boundaries; handling conflicting interests. Issues related to impartiality include: bias; awareness training; disadvantage and discrimination. Issues related to respect include: confidentiality and vulnerability.

This chapter sets out to explore some issues in the training situation in relation to ethical principles. Codes of ethics and practice serve as guidelines to help us to know how to act. Each situation will, however, be idiosyncratic and trainers will need to be both knowledgeable and wise when negotiating ethical and professional dilemmas. As one trainer said to me recently: 'What appears to be the right thing to do is not always the wise thing to do.'

Having examined published codes of ethics and with my own training experience uppermost in my mind I have chosen to focus on ethical and professional issues in relation to three underpinning values: integrity, impartiality, and respect. These values are pinpointed in the BAC *Code of Ethics and Practice for Trainers* (1985) as values which inform ethical standards.

It may be useful to review some of the theory on ethical principles before looking at some of the issues which may arise in connection with these values in operation. Page and Wosket (1994), when considering this topic in relation to supervision, state that the theory which underpins ethical principles has its roots in moral philosophy. Principles help us to decide what is right action and, for that matter, what is wrong action. There has been debate about whether an act is of itself good or bad, with Kant (1886) putting forward the notion that one acts in certain ways regardless of consequences so long as promises are never broken or other persons never injured as a result of any action. Bentham (1970) argues that the morality of an act is to be judged by its consequences. Page and Wosket argue that both the 'morality of the act' and the 'anticipated consequences' are important in determining how to act. They take five guiding principles for counselling, adapted from earlier work by Ross (1930), Kitchener (1984), Thompson (1990) and most recently Bond (1993). Their five principles are: fidelity, justice, beneficence, nonmaleficence, autonomy.

Watkins and Schneider (1991), writing about ethics and counselling research, point out that relationships, such as counsellor–client or trainer–trainee, are professional relationships and therefore fiduciary relationships, that is relationships which are held or given in trust and which depend upon public confidence.

> The role of the professional (teacher, researcher or counselor) in such a relationship requires certain responsibilities that are not necessarily encountered in everyday life. Although one may argue that all relationships have ethical responsibilities, counselors and researchers need to be particularly attentive to their power, the potential for abusing that power, and the danger of creating dual relationships.
>
> (Watkins and Schneider 1991: 246)

The perspective they give on 'dual relationships' relates to situations where the trainer influences the trainee to behave in some way other than that expected of a trainee, as, for example, if trust is exploited in the relationship by asking favours or offering incentives for favours so that an unprofessional dependency is created between the two.

Fidelity assumes that we are faithful to promises made. Justice ensures that benefits are distributed fairly. Beneficence implies that we work for the good of the other. Nonmaleficence expects that we do no harm to the other. Autonomy encourages the exercise of maximum choice. When it comes to counsellor training I hear it said, 'The bottom line is this: will this trainee do any harm to clients?' In that sense it would seem that nonmaleficence is an overriding concern in counselling training, although it can also be argued that each of these guiding principles has equal significance. With these five guiding principles in mind we will turn to issues arising in the three areas of integrity, impartiality and respect as they affect trainers' policies, procedures and behaviours.

Ethical principles serve as a guide when we are faced with decisions. Difficult decisions are those where there are conflicting interests. Codes of ethics exist as a safeguard and tend to focus upon protecting the professional group and the client. They cannot encompass the complexities of specific situations in which trainers find themselves. One example of principles competing for precedence is: 'How should one decide between the principles of preventing harm or doing good when contrasted with infringing upon a person's autonomy?' (Watkins and Schneider 1991: 246). We will now consider how the basic values of integrity, impartiality and respect may be reflected in counselling training courses and we will reflect on some examples where there are conflicting interests.

INTEGRITY

In what ways do the policies, procedures and behaviours of counsellor trainers concur with, or deviate from, the values of integrity? A counselling course which is developed by trainers who have integrity would endeavour to provide the following:

1 Competent trainers who can honestly say that they have the necessary experience, knowledge and qualifications for training at the required level of the course. This would normally mean that the level of qualification of the trainer would be one which is more advanced than the course on which that person trains. There would be honesty about any limitations in the knowledge, skills or competence of the trainers or of the course.

2 Policies, procedures, regulations and expectations would be clearly communicated, both verbally and in writing, and they would be consistently followed.

3 The course would reflect the core theoretical approach in all aspects: aims, objectives, management, organisation and relationships. Trainers would model all those things which are expected of trainees: values, attitudes to self and others, standards of work and behaviour.

4 Consistency and reliability would be evident in all day-to-day aspects of course organisation and course assessment.

5 Regular opportunities for honest appraisal and evaluation of the course and its trainers would be in place for trainees, trainers, internal moderators, external examiners, assessors or consultants.

6 There would be honest and open communication between all those involved in the course: trainers, trainees, supervisors, the host organisation or institution, external liaising agencies.

7 Clear contracting and clear boundaries. Trainees would be given sufficient accurate information on which to make informed decisions about whether to embark upon the course, whether to stay on the course and whether to leave the course. Official appeals and complaints procedures would be published.

8 There would be evidence of a willingness of trainers to take immediate and necessary action in the event of incapability to train effectively, for whatever reason.

9 There would be explicit commitment of trainers to their own ongoing personal and professional development through counselling, supervision, further training and where appropriate through research.

10 Adherence to professional codes of ethics and practice for counsellor trainers would be maintained and monitored.

It can be seen from the above guidelines, which are by no means comprehensive, that the moral principles of autonomy, beneficence, fidelity, justice and nonmaleficence are all included in this view of integrity. Integrity involves honest, open communication in which necessary information is shared and not withheld and in this sense trainees who are accurately informed about course regulations, policies, procedures, expectations and opportunities are being given the chance to exercise choice over whether to apply, stay or leave. This aspect of integrity encourages autonomy. A course which has integrity will want the best for both trainees and their clients and will be structured and organised in such a way that least harm could be done to either. Thus the principles of beneficence and nonmaleficence apply. If course organisation runs reliably and consistently then the principle of fidelity is at work, and in order to be faithful to promises made there has to be a clear agreed contract of training in the first place which is open to on-going monitoring, evaluation and negotiation. Finally, justice is about fair dealings and that is largely about making explicit that which is implicit so that everyone engaged in the course has equal opportunity to understand what is on offer, what is not on offer and what is expected and not expected of all parties concerned.

Issues related to integrity

Competence of the counsellor trainer

In the UK there are as yet no standard routes of counsellor train-ing although there seems to be some agreement that the training normally implies doing a certificate and then possibly a graduate or postgraduate diploma. Some Masters level courses include professional training, but some are primarily academic. Voluntary agencies provide their own in-house training programmes and whilst some of these are now getting their training validated by the higher education sector, others remain in-house.

This can cause difficulties when a counsellor trainer is appointed to teach on a course without having the same level of qualification as the course on which that person will be training. Alex was an example of this. She was a counsellor and trainer with varied experience and she was invited to train on a course for counsellor supervisors. She had a diploma and Masters degree in counselling and she had significant experience in supervision. She had also done her special study on counselling supervision as part of her Masters degree. She had therefore, as have most counsellors at the time of writing, built up knowledge and experience without having done a specific qualification in supervision because there had not been any available. She was excited about the possibility of train-ing on this course and in her excitement she said she would be delighted to do it. Then she had a crisis of integrity. Should she train others for a qualification she did not have herself? Would this limitation affect what she was able to offer to those trainees and would they be better served by someone else (beneficence)? Would there be a danger that she could not deliver what the trainees had been told they would get (fidelity)? Would she actually cause harm to trainee supervisors and their counsellors

and their clients because she had not gone through this course herself as a trainee (nonmaleficence)?

This example is pertinent for two reasons. The first is that there
is no easy answer to such an issue. The second is that whilst
counselling training is in its early stages it will be necessary at
times that people enter into the training arena from alternative
and not completely orthodox routes. It would be ideal if there
were some standardisation in qualifications for counsellor trainers,
just as there is in the teaching profession, for example, but at the
current time this is far from the case. Alex is left with a crisis of
integrity. She may use the five ethical principles to guide her in a
decision. In terms of autonomy, she believes that trainees applying
for the course should know about her qualifications and experience so that they can choose whether to apply for the course. She
decides that she will only be prepared to co-tutor on the course if
she can be assured that the course leader has the relevant qualification and could plug any gaps left by her lack of qualification.
In terms of fidelity, Alex is confident that she can deliver what she
has been asked to do and arranges to observe sessions taught by
the course leader so that there is ample opportunity for her to
participate even when she is not actually teaching. This is part of
her development as a trainer. With regard to beneficence, Alex
thinks that she can do good on the course because she has long and
varied experience in training, in counselling and in supervision.
She also knows that in many ways her knowledge is greater than
that of the qualified course leader. She worries most about nonmaleficence because at the time of making the decision to join the
course staff she cannot really know how much harm she might do
by not having the appropriate qualification. She realises that
'harm' manifests itself in different degrees. For example, it might
be on the level of a trainee feeling a lack of confidence in Alex's
judgement and therefore lacking confidence himself when faced
with an anxious counsellor who has brought along to supervision
a client with severely disabling panic attacks. At the other
extreme, Alex might give bad or harmful advice to a trainee supervisor as a result of her own lack of training.

Alex reflected on these issues and decided to take the job. She
realised that although it was not an ideal situation she was still
probably the best person available at that time to train on the
course. She recognised that she did have much to offer and that
her knowledge, skills and experience would complement those of

the course leader. However, because she operated from the value of integrity she undertook to do a qualification in supervision at the earliest opportunity; she arranged for immediate and regular training supervision; she ensured that her own supervision work was frequent to keep herself up to date with the issues; and she decided to make arrangements for personal therapy in the event of any training issues arising which might trigger problems of confidence or self-esteem. These things were in addition to the normal course preparation and debriefing sessions with the other trainer.

Integrity is not just a given, but has to be worked at. However much we think we have done our best to operate honestly we need continually to question our motivations and our actions. At the same time, if like Alex we do operate from integrity as a value base, then flexibility is possible, given our limited resources.

Informed consent

Trainers make the assumption that when trainees accept a place on a course they have given informed consent. It has been said that informed consent is not enough (Bond 1993). It is only the bottom line. Hopefully we would encourage informed consent to be an active rather than a passive process. It has also been said that information is power. In order to empower there needs to be ample ongoing opportunity for questioning and negotiation about that information. Integrity demands that we give the trainee the opportunity to give informed consent and this is related to the principle of autonomy. Beauchamp and Childress (1989) give three conditions for informed consent: freedom to make the choice, relevant information, competence in making the decision.

Sometimes course complaints are about people. More often the complaints which can be upheld are about policies and procedures which have not been communicated clearly or carried out consistently, in which case it is a complaint about lack of information which affects the capacity of the trainee to give informed consent. On the other hand, it can be very reassuring, when confronted with an official complaint, to know that policies and procedures have been faithfully followed. When this standard is not operating as it should, trainees are likely to be confused, uncertain, anxious and then possibly panicky, resentful, angry and confrontational. They need to know what to expect: 'what happens if?', 'what happens when?', 'how?' Trainers will have heard these questions many times! I have come to realise that the spoken word is never good enough when it comes to policies and procedures. Everything needs to be written down, clearly and unambiguously. Trainees have the right to know. They need full information when they apply for the course. They need a course handbook at the start of the course with all the course regulations, aims and objectives, expectations, counselling and supervision arrangements, reading lists, curriculum, methodology, timetables, resource information, assessment processes, assessment criteria, dates and deadlines, examination procedures and complaints procedure.

Difficult issues will still arise even when a trainer thinks that course expectations have been made clear. A trainer may find, for example, that a trainee who speaks English as a second language may not understand fully the written instructions for the counselling practice assessment, and when the trainee submits a piece of work that obviously fails the criteria the trainer is left with the dilemma of how much the trainee actually understood about what was expected. I have used the example of practical assessment because this is the area where cultural norms and variations may cause difficulties anyway for the trainee, in addition to the language difficulty. In such a case it is essential to have had the written information, even though it may have been misinterpreted, because at least then there is some basis for discussion. If the trainer, or an appeals committee, were to rely on what the trainer thought he or she said, then there could be real difficulties for both trainer and trainee. We will return to the needs of trainees from different cultural backgrounds in the section on impartiality as an ethical value in training.

These issues can come to a head when a trainee leaves a course without completing or is failed against patently clear assessment criteria. The problem may be with the trainee, but it may be traced back to lack of informed consent in the first place. Take the case of Terry who leaves a counselling course, having completed three-quarters of it, and who says he is leaving because of pressure at work. The staff realise that he has been very reluctant to take on clients other than those patients he can see in his own work setting as a nurse. They have warned him repeatedly that he will not fulfil course requirements if he does not increase his client load of contracted counselling work, rather than situations in which he uses counselling skills with patients. In hindsight they remembered that he was the one in the group who was always bringing up the issue about not knowing the difference between counselling and using counselling skills during the first term of the course. Now he is leaving they are inclined to think that it was his own responsibility and he has knowingly failed to meet the course requirements. But was he able to give informed consent when he applied for the course? Was it made clear in course recruitment literature that counselling practice meant contracted work with clients? It was not until Terry had arrived on the course that these things were discussed and by that time he had committed himself to doing the course and had obtained funding from his employer. His job in a busy coronary care unit meant that he was fully occupied, and with both the job and the course he could not possibly find time also to start work with a voluntary counselling agency, as had been suggested by the course staff. Because he had not been given adequate information and explanations at the time of applying for the course, Terry not only failed to complete, but also experienced unnecessary anxiety, stress and confusion along the way. What appeared to the course staff to be lack of willingness to fulfil course requirements, was actually caused by lack of informed consent in the first place.

The integrity of a course can be called into question by trainees who wish to appeal against failure. What the course says is on offer may not be what is perceived to be on offer by the trainee. If a trainee appeals against a failure and the appeal is not upheld because all policies and procedures with regard to assessment have been clearly communicated and faithfully followed and documented, then it is not beyond the bounds of possibility that the trainee will look for another reason for the failure, particularly if the trainee has much invested in being a qualified counsellor. The integrity of the trainers themselves may then be called into question: their motivation, their attitude, their competence and their dealings with other trainees.

Holding the boundaries

An important issue with regard to integrity is that of maintaining clear boundaries between trainers and trainees. This can be a difficult area because the very act of holding the boundaries can be perceived by trainees to be lack of care and concern. If the trainer is not sufficiently attentive to the maintenance of boundaries it is possible to be seduced by the needy trainee. An example from Zita illustrates some of the dilemmas:

A man who had been a client of mine applied to come on a Certificate in Counselling, on which I was a course tutor. We had finished our counselling relationship six months before the course started and the ending had been mutually agreed at a point where the client's goals for counselling appeared to have been met. I did not interview him when he applied for the course. He had told me at the time we finished the counselling that he intended to apply for the course and I had clearly stated to him that if he gained a place this would preclude any further counselling involvement (not that he appeared likely to request this at the time).

Two months before the course started, when he had been offered and had accepted a place, he telephoned me to ask if I would see him for a 'one-off' session as something urgent had come up which he would like to discuss with me. I declined, telling him again that in view of his forthcoming presence on the course, any dual relationship as his counsellor and tutor would be unprofessional.

At the time he appeared to accept this, but once on the course I found myself continually trying to deter him from making what I now considered inappropriate self-disclosures to me. He would ask for a tutorial and then begin pouring out his personal problems instead of discussing his work. This situation was eventually resolved when, at my suggestion, he entered into counselling with an independent counsellor and saw my co-tutor for remaining tutorials. This experience left me with some uncomfortable questions, the most disquieting being: had I somehow mismanaged the termination of the counselling and had he applied for the course in order to try, in some fashion, to retain me as his counsellor?

In this example Zita had apparently been quite clear about the boundary between the counselling relationship and the training relationship. Sometimes it is possible for us to give mixed messages because although we want to be professional we also perhaps have enjoyed working with a client and subconsciously we are reluctant to finish. Zita seems to be asking herself this question at the end. However, it could just be that her client had dependency problems and unless Zita was able to hold the boundary firmly they would have been in muddy and unhelpful water together. In these cases it is not easy to hold the boundary when the trainee may interpret that as being uncaring and the very opposite of what to expect in a counsellor. In holding the boundary Zita was working from the principles of beneficence and nonmaleficence in that she knew that what the trainee wanted would not do good and would probably cause harm. Additionally, Zita was operating from the principles of fidelity and autonomy. She intended to be clear and consistent about what the trainee could and could not expect and by setting boundaries she was helping the trainee to become more autonomous instead of taking the easy way out and encouraging dependency.

Conflicting interests

Trainers are accountable to various parties and there will be occasions when their interests conflict. For example, there is the conflict between course staff and the organisation or institution which hosts the course when the professional judgement of the course team suggests a certain trainee/trainer ratio, and they are told that the norm for other courses is much higher and that the fees paid by the trainees do not allow for such generous staffing. It is obvious, on the one hand, that the employing organisation does not understand the professional requirements of this particular course, yet, on the other hand, the training team does not want to put pressure where it may be counterproductive. It has been known for well-established counselling courses to cease because of such pressure.

The trainers have a dilemma: should they compromise their professional standards, should they fight for more resources, should they increase the fees which will put the course out of reach of some of the trainees from more economically deprived backgrounds whom they had hoped to recruit, or should they suggest course closure? In this situation, if the course is to continue on a less well resourced basis the training team will need to be sure about what is the minimum level of staff contact required to deliver a course which will train safe practitioners. Applying the ethical principles the considerations would be: How can we ensure that the limitations of the course we are now offering are clearly understood by trainees and clients alike and how can we help trainees to find supplementary training elsewhere (autonomy)? How can we ensure that what we are promising at the start of the course will be delivered for the duration of the course without any further cutback in resources or staffing (fidelity)? How can we help trainees who find it difficult to pay increased fees, and should we look at providing an alternative mode of training with easier access and greater flexibility (justice)? What arrangements can we put in place to ensure that the decrease in resources for the course does no harm to trainees or to their clients (nonmaleficence)? Can we design new and creative ways of delivering the course to help trainees to get the most out of their training in what would otherwise be limited opportunities for learning (beneficence)?

The conflicting interests are not always within the organisation which holds the course. Sometimes they are between course staff or trainees and external agencies or supervisors. Let us consider the issue of trainee supervision. In Chapter Five, when discussing the dynamics of the training relationship, we considered a case of resistance in which trainees did not wish for any communication between their course and their supervisor. Eventually the trainer decided that such an arrangement, whilst appearing to align with the ethical principles of autonomy, fidelity and beneficence for the trainee, could actually contravene the ethical principle of nonmaleficence for clients. In this case the trainer decided that the needs of the client were more important. However, there are other situations where the need of the trainee is considered more important than the needs of, for example, agencies which offer to employ trainee counsellors. There are some agencies which insist on providing the supervision for the trainee who works there. They go further and insist that their arrangements are sufficient and they are not prepared to consider that the trainee has any supplementary supervision on the work within the agency by a course-appointed supervisor. In this case, the course would be approving the agency as a place for the trainee to counsel, but would not have control over the choice of supervisor. It is, perhaps, understandable for an agency to take this stance. They may feel that they are offering a service to the trainee, that their standards of supervision are high and that any further supervision would confuse the trainee, might damage the supervisory relationship at the agency and might put the client at risk, for example by extending the parameters of confidentiality. One agency director went further than this in stating that course supervisors have responsibility for training but do not have responsibility for the work taking place at a counselling agency (Wells 1993).

Page and Wosket (1994) note that where there is no direct relationship between the course and the supervisor there could be
serious problems: the supervision might not be appropriate for the
trainee; the supervisor might not be competent; there could be
no feedback mechanism when difficulties arose with the trainee and
there cannot be any kind of standardisation in the supervision
experience. Their view is that the training organisation has a responsibility to oversee the choice of supervisor and to create 'an effective line of communication within a clearly defined contract in which
all parties know what information will be passed to whom, by whom
and under what circumstances'. They pinpoint the central issue as
the dissemination of information. An extreme situation is offered
for consideration:

> The supervisor has substantial concern that the trainee is acting
> in a manner which is unethical and it has not been possible
> to rectify the situation through the supervisory process. We
> believe that the supervisor has a responsibility to communicate
> this to the course in some way. Not to do so risks the person
> being awarded a counselling qualification which could be tanta-
> mount to a licence to practise in an unethical manner. The
> supervisor has a responsibility to ensure their concern is
> addressed by the trainee and the course and that the trainee
> only receives a qualification if he or she is able to deal with the
> problematic area of their practice. This extreme situation can
> be formulated in terms of the supervisor and course sharing a
> mutual responsibility to the potential future clients of the
> trainee counsellor.
>
> (Page and Wosket 1994)

Although course staff need information about trainees in order to
make informed decisions about the award of a counselling qualification they are aware that if a trainee feels inhibited by a feedback
mechanism then the supervisory process may not get to grips with
the most significant counselling issues. Trainees may begin to
censor what they take to supervision. For this reason a course may
be loath to have feedback from supervisors. However, what Page
and Wosket highlight is that the interests of the client are of overriding concern, and if proper channels of communication are not
agreed upon then there may come a point where the principle of
fidelity is contravened, because if a trainee is working unethically
the course needs the information and may have to obtain it without

the knowledge of the trainee. This could have been avoided if clear guidelines were agreed from the beginning, guidelines which establish clear, open and collaborative lines of communication. There may, on occasion, still be tensions in this relationship but if the guidelines are clear, and are adhered to, these tensions can become a source of learning rather than a potential ethical pitfall.

IMPARTIALITY

If integrity is about clarity and honesty in setting out what the course has on offer and what is expected, then impartiality will ensure that all trainees can expect to be treated fairly and with justice. In what ways do the policies, procedures and behaviours of counsellor trainers and counselling courses concur with, or deviate from, the ideal of impartiality? A counselling course which is developed by trainers who work from the value of impartiality would endeavour to:

1 Encourage access to the course to be truly open to all those who qualify for it.
2 Treat all trainees fairly by respecting their inherent worth and dignity with regard to learning background, ability, gender, orientation, race, origin, status and beliefs, giving special consideration to those who are disabled or disadvantaged.
3 Celebrate differences.
4 Offer equal learning opportunities to all those who are on the course.
5 Ensure that policies, procedures, course organisation and assessment arrangements are free from bias.
6 Embed within the course awareness and sensitivity training with regard to: class, culture, ethnicity, gender, belief.
7 Provide opportunities for both trainers and trainees to be informed and updated on issues connected with oppression and injustice, particularly in relation to minority groups.
8 Show an awareness of and sensitivity to ways in which individuals or groups on the course may feel that they are not being treated impartially.
9 Monitor the course regularly with respect to discrimination and disadvantage.
10 Have a clearly understood complaints procedure.

Issues related to impartiality

Course access

With regard to the five ethical principles the value of impartiality is obviously mainly related to matters of justice in which we must ensure that benefits are distributed fairly. A counselling course is both a 'learning' benefit and a 'professional' benefit and success at the course can have significant benefits for the trainee, not only in personal growth terms but also in career and financial terms. In fact, one of the ethical issues which has now come to the fore for course selectors is to look carefully at the motivation of applicants because some are applying for counselling courses very much in business terms, as a way perhaps of escaping from their present employment and setting up their own counselling business. I use the term 'business' advisedly here because the issue I am raising concerns financial incentives for counselling rather than incentives which are about working with and helping people to change. I am not suggesting that there is anything wrong with setting up a counselling business – far from it. I am saying that there may be ethical reasons why certain applicants need to be carefully screened because it is already the case in this country that clients have too little information on which to make an informed decision about the professional standing of a counsellor. We have a responsibility at the point of access and at the point of exit from a course. In spite of the safeguards and controls which are in operation, it may still be possible for counsellors whose activity we would deem to be unscrupulous or unacceptable, to gain a counselling qualification unless courses have thorough selection and assessment procedures. The principle of justice is here linked to that of nonmaleficence and this raises difficult issues where what may be viewed as lack of impartiality (rejecting an applicant for training) may actually be upholding the value of integrity and the principle of nonmaleficence in relation to future clients.

At the other end of the spectrum we have the issues involved when trying to apply the principle of justice to disadvantaged groups, minority groups or groups which are under-represented on the course to the detriment of the course. There is a group of counsellors who have set themselves up as a counselling and psychotherapy centre in an inner city area. They want to make their training services available to the community and they see a great need within some of the more deprived, disadvantaged and marginalised groups in the city. However, these counsellors need to make a living and the sort of fees that they would need to charge would make their courses impossible for the very people that they wish to recruit. Would it be ethical for them to charge higher fees for other private work that they do with the better off in that city? How can anyone assess greatest need? It could be argued that although some people appear to earn a good wage, they have financial responsibilities which mean that they cannot afford high counselling fees and yet they may have an urgent problem which could be greatly helped by counselling. This group of trainers wants to work from a principle of justice but is finding that in doing something which would benefit one section of the community they may be contravening impartiality for another section of that city.

Let us turn now to another ethical dilemma. Many counselling courses have an under-representation of male trainees and trainees from ethnic minority groups. It can be argued that this affects learning opportunities, in particular the opportunity to learn from both the male and the transcultural perspective, and in turn this may be detrimental to clients who may get a counsellor with limited understanding of their issues. Should the trainer, operating from principles of beneficence and nonmaleficence, try to ensure that there is an adequate male and ethnic representation on the course, or should the trainer operate from the value of impartiality and make sure that places on the course are offered to those candidates who appear best qualified for the course, whatever their gender, class, race or ethnic group? Would the principle of impartiality be best served if a quota of places was reserved for those who might not appear to be best qualified but who had just reasons for not being best qualified, for example because they have had limited educational opportunity? It has been suggested by feminist writers that revisions be made to courses so that they take more account of women's issues, and the recommendations include employing significant proportions of both trainers and trainees from minority groups (Frazier and Cohen 1992).

These are issues in which several ethical principles may conflict with one another and where justice and impartiality need to be viewed in relation to the other principles of autonomy, fidelity, beneficence and nonmaleficence, and moreover with not just the trainees but also their future clients in mind. This issue can also be applied to the appointment of staff to a course when the interests served by employing someone from a minority perspective are not in accord with other criteria for what makes someone best qualified for the job.

Raising awareness with regard to discrimination and disadvantage

It has been noted (McLeod 1993) that traditional approaches to counselling can appear to discriminate against those who are 'disadvantaged or marginalised'. McLeod notes, however, that there have been many attempts to address this issue with women (Braude 1987; Chaplin 1992), those from the working class (Holland 1979; Bromley 1983) and those from ethnic minority groups (Gutierez 1992; Wade and Bernstein 1991) and a number of general strategies can be applied in order to help trainees to develop anti-discriminatory attitudes and behaviour.

> There are five distinctive forms which anti-discriminatory programmes have taken: constructing a critique of mainstream or 'majority' theory and practice; awareness training for counsellors; development of new counselling techniques; the adaptation of existing services and agencies to meet the needs of previously excluded client groups; and the creation of new, specialist agencies and services.
>
> (McLeod 1993: 121)

The reader is referred to McLeod's work for a stimulating and well referenced discussion of this area. What I realise from my own training experience is that awareness training on courses can actually provoke strong and sometimes destructive emotion. That is not to say it should not be done, but it is to caution about how it is done. There is a responsibility, with respect to the notion of justice, that trainees, particularly those representing minority views, cultures or beliefs will be respected and not exploited. Similarly, trainees who thought that they had no discriminatory ideas or stereotypes and find out painfully that they have, should not be punished for what they have expressed. I am reminded of a small incident which reverberated like an earthquake when, in good faith, a black trainee shared experiences of his culture and was told by another trainee 'but I don't see you as different'. The latter trainee was trying to be accepting, but the other perceived this as a denial of his black identity. They both ended up feeling exploited and needed much support from trainers before any sort of positive communication could be re-established between them. Yes, it was a good learning experience, but it was damaging along the way and the main problem had been lack of time for debriefing in the group. It could be argued that the principle of nonmaleficence had not been sufficiently applied by the trainers when planning this awareness session. If it had been considered then adequate time would have been allowed at the end of the session for supportive debriefing of all the group, which would have alleviated the tensions caused by the differences between the two.

Bias

Trainers can have difficulties with trainees who seem at every possible opportunity to wave the flag for their own 'crusade'. I use the word crusade because the experience has similarities with missionary zeal. It can be difficult to handle this in the group but it then becomes of even greater concern when the trainee who is given choice over assessment topics, always chooses an aspect of their 'crusade' to write about. The ethical dilemma for the trainer seems to be around trying to be accepting and encouraging of the trainee, and at the same time aware that any suggestion that the trainee appears to be too narrowly focused may be interpreted as bias on the part of the trainer. What ethical principles could be used in such a dilemma? With regard to autonomy, it would appear that the trainee is not being impartial by relying too heavily on one perspective. It would also appear that if the trainee is constantly using group time to focus on one perspective, this is infringing upon the other perspectives in the group and therefore reducing their autonomy. With regard to beneficence and nonmaleficence the trainer must ask herself or himself: 'Would I be doing good to this trainee if I address this issue, and what harm might I do?' Ultimately the question may be: 'Do I want to do something about this just because the trainee's crusade is not my crusade and just because I am resenting course time being used on this issue? Or do I want to address this issue out of justice to the trainee, the rest of the group and the welfare of the future clients of this trainee whom I perceive may be damaged by a counsellor with such limited perspectives?'

Bias can creep into training situations in several ways. There is the positive bias towards a core theoretical approach or model, which can become less than positive if it is experienced by trainees as limiting or prescriptive. The sort of bias which does not operate from the value of impartiality is that which singles trainees out in some way, either for favours or unjust treatment. Bias can also operate subconsciously as shown in the educational research (Delamont 1980) which found that teachers give more attention to boys than to girls in school classrooms – which could well happen with adults also. In that research boys gained more attention because they were more confident in asking questions and in giving answers, and because teachers expected them to do this. If a trainee is quiet and unassuming it is more possible that his or her needs will be overlooked, whether male or female. In this case bias is occurring almost by default and what is needed is an extra sensitivity to the needs of such trainees.

Nowhere in counsellor training is it more important to operate with freedom from bias as in course assessment procedures because justice does not simply need to be done, it needs to be seen to be done. This area has been explored in the earlier chapter on assessment and at this point we will briefly note one of the ethical dilemmas which may arise. It concerns practical counselling assessments where the trainee is asked to perform live, or on video, as a counsellor with another trainee who is the client, in order to demonstrate counselling competence. If trainees are grouped by the trainer and if a trainee is assigned a 'client' who is particularly difficult to counsel then justice will not be experienced by the trainee who had to counsel and who will feel that he or she has been disadvantaged by the course procedure. On the other hand, it is possible for two trainees working together to collude with one another either consciously or unconsciously. Deliberate collusion has occurred when trainees have scripted an interaction in advance and learned the scripts and then performed them. Whilst this indicates commitment and resourcefulness it does not fulfil the requirements for assessment which should be of a spontaneous counselling session. Unconscious collusion occurs where the trainee in the client role knows the aspects which are being assessed and unwittingly tries to help by offering material which will enable the appropriate responses. Trainers are left with the problem of needing some live evidence of counselling competence without harming real clients by involving them in an assessment process.

Complaints procedure

Currently there is an awareness that in addition to normal informal channels of communication for appeals and complaints, each counselling training course needs to express its commitment to the value of impartiality by having a written and formal complaints procedure. This is to encourage trainees to feel that their complaints will be heard fairly and will, if necessary, be acted upon. Some courses appoint an external ombudsman or mediator who knows the course, understands its objectives, knows about the staff but does not have any close link with the course or any of its staff. By close link it is sometimes specified that there would be no social or family relationship. If a trainee has a complaint he or she is normally advised to try to settle this internally. If this has proved impossible then the ombudsman or mediator would be approached and would work with both trainers and trainee in order to reach understanding and agreement.

RESPECT

In what ways do the policies, procedures and behaviours of counsellor trainers concur with, or deviate from, the value of respect? A counselling course which is developed with a high value placed upon respect will endeavour to:

1 Operate from a spirit of trust and collaboration.
2 Listen and respond to trainees.
3 Encourage individuality.
4 Be sensitive both to the robustness and to the vulnerability of trainers and trainees alike.
5 Avoid any exploitation or abuse of trainees: socially, psychologically, sexually or financially.
6 Be aware of the effect of course pressure upon trainers and trainees alike.
7 Be supportive to trainers and trainees whenever necessary.
8 Maintain confidentiality in respect of trainers, trainees and their clients.
9 Understand the needs and requirements of all those involved in the course and endeavour to meet their needs even where this involves negotiation and compromise: the host organisation, trainers, trainees, supervisors, counselling agencies, assessors, professional bodies.

10 Ensure that trainers are accessible and available to trainees on a regular basis for individual and group tutorials and consultations.

Issues related to respect

The communication of respect by trainers has already been discussed in the earlier chapter on the trainer as a facilitator where it has been examined as one of the three core conditions for effective therapeutic relationships as put forward by Rogers (1961). In this discussion we will focus upon the ethical dilemmas that can result from respect for the needs of different parties with confidentiality as the starting point.

Confidentiality

Trainers need to respect the confidentiality of trainees, other trainers, supervisors and the clients of trainees in order to provide a learning situation characterised by trust and safety. Bond (1992) points to the relationship between trust and confidentiality. As trainers we are held in trust by our trainees who will be asked to undertake difficult personal work on a counselling course as well as feeling vulnerable as they engage in a very demanding learning situation. Trainees need to feel that whatever trainers find out about them on a course will not be damaging to their future prospects or to their reputation. Bond argues for the ethical principle of autonomy to be applied to confidentiality and this implies that confidentiality is not thrust upon trainees but that it is a matter for negotiation with them. Additionally, he draws attention to the fact that such negotiations need to be in the context of competing ethical considerations which include contractual obligations to, for example, employers, funding or sponsoring authorities, supervisors, validating or award-giving bodies and counselling agencies within which trainees work. There are also legal considerations to take into account which follow from the maxim that private privilege ends where public peril begins (Bohart and Todd 1988). On training courses it is necessary, for two reasons, that information is shared between those involved in the course. The first is accountability, which includes both academic and professional accountability. The second is so that the trainer may obtain the necessary support and supervision. With a guiding principle of respect, the sharing of this information would only take place when necessary. It would preferably take place with the knowledge and collaboration of the trainee (autonomy), and it would be for the benefit of the trainee, the client or the public interest (beneficence). It would not be done with the intent of harming the trainee (nonmaleficence) and it would be a purposeful exchange and not one in which the trainee is demeaned in any way.

The starting point is to make a contract which spells out the extent and limits of confidentiality and the circumstances in which confidentiality may have to be broken. The BAC *Code of Ethics and Practice for Trainers* is currently under review but the existing guidelines state:

> Confidentiality does not preclude the disclosure of confidential information relating to trainees when relevant to the following:
>
> a. evaluation of the trainee by trainers or training committee.
> b. recommendations concerning trainees for professional purposes.
> c. pursuit of disciplinary action involving trainees in matters pertaining to ethical standards.
> d. selection procedures.
>
> (BAC 1985: 2.3)

There can be a dilemma when trainees working in a counselling agency are told that they cannot use material from their work with clients in the agency to take to their training course for supervision or case discussion. Cohen (1992), in an article about legal issues in counselling, highlights the issue of client material which has been given in confidence and used for training purposes:

> It seems plausible to say that the public interest in supporting literally total confidentiality between counsellor and client is outweighed here by the public interest in the proper training and supervision of counsellors, and in the development of a public body of knowledge about counselling.
>
> (Cohen 1992)

Whilst the public interest is being served by case discussion, the private interest must also be respected. Courses operating from such respect will ensure that clients are briefed about the fact that trainees have supervision; that where sessions are recorded in writing they are done so anonymously and without any details which could at a later date identify the client; that where sessions are recorded on audio or video tape the purposes of doing this are clarified with the client and the client is asked to sign an agreement proforma about the use of the material for discussion or assessment purposes. Working from the principle of autonomy, the client should be the person to decide what happens to the material once the express purpose for its use is over. For example, if it is an audio tape, does the client want it returned to herself or himself; or to have it destroyed by the counsellor?

Confidentiality issues can occur within a course, as well as in relations with those outside the course. An example is where the course operates some sort of 'closed' group for personal development work. In order that trainees feel uninhibited they need to feel protected in the knowledge that confidentiality will be contained within the group. What if the group facilitator finds out something about a trainee which would be a cause for professional concern, for example a disclosure which indicates that they may in the near future harm self or others? What, at a slightly less extreme level, if there is ongoing concern about the capacity and willingness of this trainee to engage in the group? In the first example it is usually taken for granted that confidentiality can be breached where there is concern about harm to self or others (BAC 1992). However, the second example is less clear and yet surely of significant concern to trainers who could award a qualification to this trainee without having access to this important information. The issue goes back to the importance of clear contracting. It could be argued that there is no aspect of training which is free from the possibility of disclosure of information where such information has significance for trainees' future work with clients, and that such disclosures would take place under clearly identified circumstances, within clearly identified procedures, and with information being used carefully, respectfully and with the explicit purpose of helping the trainee.

Vulnerability

Vulnerability is often associated with exposure and within counsellor training both trainers and trainees will experience exposure in relation to personal as well as professional development. Dissonance is often experienced by beginning trainees who find that their skills may not be as good as they had believed them to be.

They go through the stage from unconscious incompetence to conscious incompetence and this is where most vulnerability is felt, before moving on to the stage of conscious competence and finally to the confidence of unconscious competence. There are all sorts of reasons why they may feel vulnerable, and in Chapter Five we examined some of the dynamics which can occur as a result of this vulnerability. A course operating from a value of respect will be sensitive to vulnerability, and trainers will try to be empathic with trainees whose experience of the course seems to be at variance with that which the trainers intend. Listening to the validity of the trainee experience is a mark of respect. Responding to that experience is a sign of real collaboration. Ethical dilemmas have raised themselves when, in an attempt to assuage the anxieties and vulnerabilities of trainees, standards may be compromised. An example is the assessment of counselling competence. Is it most important to make assessment arrangements that meet the needs of the trainee or to make arrangements that meet required standards? An example of this dilemma occurred on the course discussed in Chapter Four. Trainers had assessed trainees on aspects of the counselling relationship in a video-recorded session, with another trainee from the same course group acting as client. This was easy to arrange and to implement.

In the first two years of operating this system the trainers became increasingly concerned about the fact that this was not evidence of counselling with a real client and they also realised the dangers of collusion between participating trainees. They therefore changed the regulation and stated that in future the session for the final assessment must be a recorded session with a real client, preferably recorded on video but, if that was not possible, an audio-recording. In trying to deal with one ethical issue, that relating to the integrity of an assessed counselling session, the trainers then raised other ethical issues. How ethical is it to expect that a trainee will be able to record a session with a client? Surely the circumstances under which the necessary arrangements would have to be made with the client would also alter the 'realnness' of the counselling session? Surely the client would collude when told that the session was for assessment because he or she would want the counsellor to do well (or possibly badly)? If the trainee could not obtain permission from any existing clients for all sorts of good reasons, how does that trainee find someone with whom to record the session? Is there a danger that the trainee might transgress boundaries and convince someone to 'act as a client' for the assessment? There are no easy answers to such dilemmas and it is hoped that practical assessments such as these will be supplemented with case-work from all other work with clients during the course and with a collaborative report jointly agreed by trainee and supervisor. In the example quoted above the course staff considered all the issues and still decided that their responsibility to both trainees and their future clients would be best served by assessing a session which most nearly would match that with a real client, whilst recognising all the limitations involved.

Another area where the vulnerability of the trainee needs to be recognised and respected is in setting the point at which trainees must start counselling on a course. Some courses specify that trainees must already be involved in counselling and have arrangements in place when the course begins. Other courses raise ethical issues with regard to untrained trainees beginning counselling before they are sufficiently equipped to deal with a range of client problems. As no counsellor ever knows exactly what sort of a problem will be brought by the client, we cannot be sure that the very first session undertaken by a trainee will not produce difficult material where the trainee feels out of his or her depth.

Trainers and trainees can feel constrained by requirements put forward by professional bodies that a requisite number of counselling hours be completed during training. Whereas this (100 hours is specified by the British Association for Counselling) may be easily undertaken by someone in, for example, community psychiatric nursing or in a busy counselling agency, it may not be very easy to meet the requirement of counselling hours for someone in an educational or small agency setting. The danger then is that trainees start too soon, or try to 'clock up' the requisite number of hours to satisfy requirements. Some courses are dealing with this issue by suggesting that a counselling qualification cannot be given unless the requisite number of hours is completed, but that hours can be completed after the end of the taught course. On some courses, trainees are not allowed to start counselling until they have passed a first course assessment to demonstrate basic proficiency, a few months into the course.

Training supervision is essential for providing the opportunity to discuss ethical and professional issues. Codes of ethics and practice serve to establish and maintain standards and to inform and protect trainees and their clients. However, they cannot provide answers to all our dilemmas. If we try to train in accordance with the values of integrity, impartiality and respect accepting that on occasion this will be extremely difficult and that at times our own vulnerability will prevent us from doing this as we would wish, particularly when faced with conflicting demands, we will offer to our trainees a powerful model of good practice.

Chapter 10

Professional development of the counsellor trainer

In this chapter twelve aspects of professional development are considered including: updating; active involvement in counselling and in supervision; training supervision; personal counselling or therapy; course audit meetings; co-training; work shadowing; active involvement in professional organisations; networking; collaborative partnerships; external moderation and examining; research; writing, publishing and disseminating. The chapter finishes with a trainee summarising the impact made on her life by the course which she has just completed.

That the development of the counsellor should be professional is not an option but an ethical responsibility. The ethical issue concerns the recognition of personal strengths and limitations and the requirement of competence. Professional competence needs to be continually monitored both by the individual trainer and by employing organisations and professional counselling bodies. Increasingly there is a demand for more than competence, namely for quality, in training and in counselling. Alongside the notion of responsibility is the requirement for accountability to ourselves, to our trainees, to their future clients, to the counselling profession and to the public.

Ongoing professional development is a source of continuous enrichment as well as a safeguard for the trainer, offering possibilities for affirmation and support as well as perspectives against which we can constantly monitor our performance. There are three main areas which together comprise professional development: personal development; counselling development; training development. We will consider these by looking at twelve aspects.

ASPECTS OF PROFESSIONAL DEVELOPMENT

1 Information and updating
2 Active involvement in counselling and in supervision
3 Training supervision
4 Ongoing personal counselling or therapy
5 Course review meetings
6 Co-training and work shadowing
7 Active involvement in professional organisations
8 Participation at workshops, conferences and courses
9 Networking and collaborative relationships
10 External moderation, examining or consultancy
11 Research
12 Writing, publishing and disseminating

INFORMATION AND UPDATING: POLICIES, REGULATIONS, RECOMMENDATIONS AND DEVELOPMENTS IN THE FIELDS OF BOTH COUNSELLING AND TRAINING

We are in a period of rapid growth in counselling training with the need to think flexibly about the way in which training is delivered, and by whom. Current issues include debates about distance learning packages; modular courses; and Credit Accumulation Transfer Schemes (CATS) which would enable trainees to move from one training organisation to another in a programme of training organised around modular courses. Such developments are of great concern to some counsellor trainers who emphasise the developmental nature of counselling training and the importance of membership of a developmental learning community over time. The notion of 'hopping' between modular courses at different institutions seems anathema. However, there is a body of opinion which supports CATS as a way of opening up opportunity, access and flexibility in counsellor training.

In the future this may be seen in the national context of an agreed and standardised counsellor training curriculum in which specific modules followed on one from another in several confederated institutions, or in a group of institutions that were recognised as providing the standardised curriculum. This could even extend on an international basis, with trainees able to complete certain modules in another country, either within Europe or further afield.

Linked with the discussion on CATS is the debate about APL, the Accreditation of Prior Learning. This is an important issue for counsellor trainers because it may loosen up traditional entry requirements for courses based in the higher education sector. It also has implications for professional counselling bodies, such as BAC, which currently gives recognition to courses. The implications of APL are such that, not only would learning prior to the start of a counselling course be considered for accreditation, but also those trainees who wish to change courses mid-stream could argue that their training so far be accredited in such a way as to allow them entry into another course part-way through. These examples are of debates which concern all counsellor trainers and on which we need to keep updated so that we offer the best training opportunities to our trainees.

These are examples of training issues. It will also be important to keep updated on counselling issues. A current example of this is the discussion about differences between what is meant by an 'eclectic' and what is meant by an 'integrative' counselling approach. Another current debate is about brief therapy, particularly in relation to that being offered increasingly in primary health care settings such as the fund-holding general practice or medical centre. There is also the ongoing debate about the counselling–psychotherapy spectrum and about the possible register of licensed counsellors. Another current issue concerns the relationship between national professional bodies for counsellors and for psychotherapists and whether organisations such as BAC (British Association for Counselling) and the UKCP (United Kingdom Council for Psychotherapy) wish to keep separate registers of accredited or licensed persons or whether there is some point of overlap and collaboration. As counsellor trainers we need to keep abreast of developments in these, and related, areas.

ACTIVE INVOLVEMENT IN COUNSELLING AND IN SUPERVISION

It is important that counsellor trainers remain in touch with what it means to be counselling and supervising so that their training is imbued with the reality of professional practice and professional issues. The problem is how to fit everything in to a busy schedule and how to make sure that we keep the balance between training work and counselling work. This is particularly an issue for those who are in full-time employment as trainers or lecturers and it is worthwhile at the point of entry into a post to ensure that the employer understands the importance of continuing some counselling and supervision work as a matter of professional integrity. The danger is that those who are engaged in training may only see private clients and may only see clients who are able to afford reasonable fees. The ideal would be to keep some involvement with the range of clients that would be seen by trainees, even if this means changing the arrangements for counselling from year to year to keep a breadth of experience. If a trainer is expecting trainees to go for supervision it is important to maintain the experience of supervising counsellors outside the course. It is important that we receive regular supervision on our own counselling and supervision work as this is the standard we expect from our trainees.

TRAINING SUPERVISION

Throughout the book there has been mention of the importance of training supervision and particularly in the previous two chapters which dealt with the dynamics of the training relationship and with ethical and professional issues. There are numerous situations in which the trainer needs to unload difficult material, or clarify what seemed to be going on in a group, or check out the appropriateness of decisions taken with regard to trainees, or to obtain support and affirmation, or to be helpfully challenged to confront blind-spots and develop different perspectives in situations where the trainer feels stuck or disabled, or to set goals or to engage in action planning.

Training supervision offers the trainer the possibility of sharing what can sometimes be a very emotionally demanding job. Regular opportunities for course staff to offer one another peer supervision in a group can help less confident trainers to realise that it is all right to admit difficulties and concerns and it is helpful for them to hear that the more experienced trainers in the team may have difficulties too. Such honest sharing and self-disclosure is cathartic, therapeutic and affirming. But the sharing also enhances the possibility of sensitivity and awareness during training sessions when a sort of internal training supervisor, similar to the internal supervisor which we use in counselling, develops and becomes more finely tuned. It is through hearing of the training experiences of others and listening to the ways they have managed situations that we begin to build up a more varied repertoire of training approaches and responses.

The main difficulties of such peer group supervision within a course team are boundary issues and confidentiality. It would not be ethical to harm trainees by disclosing information which damaged their reputation with other members of the training team and it would not be ethical to disclose information which had been given to a trainer in confidence. It may therefore be necessary for some members of the team not to be present for the discussion of a problem with a trainee known to them. It may also be necessary to have peer supervision amongst trainers who do not train on the same course. Each trainer would also, it is hoped, have someone they consulted on an individual basis for training supervision and this gives flexibility for decisions about which issue or concern to take to peer group supervision and which to take to individual supervision. Those courses which have partnership arrangements may wish to provide peer supervision on a termly basis across courses. An example of such courses are those which have achieved recognised status by the British Association for Counselling and where there is a requirement that a condition of recognition is partnership. Although peer supervision has not been suggested for such partnerships it seems to me to be a very good way of working with one another and sharing expertise.

ONGOING PERSONAL COUNSELLING OR THERAPY

Counselling training can trigger in the trainer issues which have been left unresolved from the past. It can expose in us ways of dealing with the world, and with people, which are not always helpful to ourselves or to our trainees. It can make us acutely aware of our shortcomings and limitations as well as giving us an opportunity to show our strengths. It can test our emotional resources to the full and leave us feeling tired or even drained. It may make us question our motivation and our values. We may even have some sort of identity crisis by attending personal development workshops in which we participate with trainees and then uncover issues which need to be examined. We may be at a developmental stage which has particular difficulties. Such growth and decision points in our lives may lead to changes in significant relationships, the need to move house or job, and there may be considerations about whether to change direction altogether. Additionally, heavy demands can be made by family or friends in need. This is particularly pertinent for the counsellor trainer who is likely to be approached to offer counselling to all sorts of people: colleagues, neighbours and friends of friends because he or she is seen to be willing and able.

Apart from the pressing needs that we may have, we will also have great moments of joy and exhilaration and excitement when the adrenalin really flows and the world seems full of opportunities. At these times we may wish to embark on interesting projects such as research, writing or travelling. At such times we may need to have some counselling in order to maximise the possibilities of turning dreams into reality, wishes into action.

A common problem I come across in myself and in other counsellor trainers is about how to prioritise and manage time in view of conflicting demands or interests. Often the problem is that there is so much that is interesting and fulfilling about counselling and training that we allow ourselves to become too heavily engaged with it all and indeed if we all engaged with everything I am outlining in this chapter as important professional development, we would be exhausted! Personal counselling can help us to examine what we are doing, to decide upon priorities and to develop the skills of assertiveness which will help us to achieve necessary change and to, at times, be able to say no to tempting opportunities which would stretch us beyond acceptable limits. Above all, we need continually to engage in our own personal growth if we are in the business of training others to work with growth and change in the counselling profession. My belief is that this is an ever-present need, not one that we 'grow out of'.

COURSE REVIEW MEETINGS

In addition to training supervision the professional development of the trainer includes attendance at more formal meetings which are set up to monitor and evaluate the quality of the course. Whereas the focus in supervision is upon the individual trainer, the focus in these meetings would be on the experience of the trainees. This is the opportunity to reflect upon whether the course is achieving its objectives and in what ways it could be enriched or improved. Such meetings are another opportunity to share training ideas, knowledge and experience and to open up new ways of doing things.

CO-TRAINING AND WORK SHADOWING

One of the most enriching training experiences I have found is to co-train. Co-training involves teamwork but the amount that can be gained from planning together and debriefing together is enormous. Obviously it is important to be able to choose your co-trainer because it needs to be a partnership if it is going to work well. We considered in Chapter Five the concept of archetypal roles. With a co-trainer it is possible to share out these roles and to change roles too. We can learn different approaches from a co-trainer and we can observe how he or she 'is' with the group and learn from his or her strategies with the group, as well as from counselling knowledge and skills. Co-training also increases learning opportunities for trainees who get a much richer experience from having two trainers' approaches rather than one. I have found that it works best when I and my co-trainer are different and can complement one another. One example is a co-trainer who has a gentle and very person-centred approach with a high capacity for just allowing things to happen. I need to have things organised. We work very well together because we can live with the marked differences between us and we each very much value what the other can offer.

Another person with whom I co-train has a similar training style. She, like me, is well prepared and needs things structured. However, we come from completely different counselling backgrounds. It works well because, once more, we respect and value the knowledge and experience of the other and we use the co-training situation for our own learning. I learn about the latest ideas in psychotherapy and she learns about the latest in my integrative approach. The trainees lap up the heated debate which can ensue! Where the trainees really benefit from the co-training arrangement, and where it makes for a much better arrangement for the trainer also, is in the modelling or demonstration of skills, approaches, techniques or strategies. I think that one of the most powerful learning experiences is when trainees are able to see a demonstration, live or recorded, of counselling approaches. The problem of the live demonstration is that the trainer can never be sure that what happens is what the trainer intended as part of the learning for that day. I have moved away from using volunteers from the group as clients in these situations because there are too many variables which cannot be controlled, and learning needs to have some focus. I now only demonstrate with another trainer or by using a video where I already know that the learning focus is actually demonstrated. Having a co-trainer means that one can be counsellor and one client; the one who is to be client does not necessarily tell the counsellor beforehand what the material will be, but is aware of the learning objectives and knows what the trainer is going to try to demonstrate. My ideal would be to have a co-training model on all counsellor training courses, for a large proportion of the activities.

Work shadowing is another way of learning about how other people train and this gives the opportunity, not only to observe how a trainer is with a group, but also how the trainer manages all the other aspects of the work, including managing staff, doing tutorials, administering the course, filing materials, developing resources, obtaining funding, participation on course committees, selection procedures, assessment and examination procedures.

ACTIVE INVOLVEMENT IN PROFESSIONAL ORGANISATIONS

One of the best ways of ensuring that we keep up to date with what is going on in the counselling profession is to be actively involved in professional groups or with a national body such as BAC. Sometimes, trainers have an excellent counselling background but limited knowledge and experience of training. Some will have no training qualification. Part of professional development may be to gain further qualifications in the field of counselling or of training or to join a professional network of counsellor trainers. In the UK some trainers gain support because they are from courses recognised by BAC and this means that representatives from the course can attend course recognition group meetings. I belong to another organisation called AMED, the Association for Management Education and Development. This may sound a far cry from counselling, but it opens up training and development ideas and issues. As I write I note that the current issue of the AMED publication (*Management Education and Development* 93 (24): 3) has articles on action learning, competence, mentoring, and development centres. Obviously the context in these articles is the management context but the ideas about training and development are more often than not applicable in the counselling field.

PARTICIPATION AT WORKSHOPS, CONFERENCES AND COURSES

We need to top up our batteries from time to time and to receive rather than always be the person who is giving out. This can be a problem for counsellors, as it can be for counsellor trainers. In addition to the obvious benefits of trying to increase our knowledge base and develop our competencies there is the useful learning experience of what it feels like to be in the position of the trainee. We suggest that trainees engage in personal counselling during their training and one of the reasons for this is so that they understand what it is like to be a client. Trainers need to know, experientially, what it is like to be a trainee. To experience feelings such as excitement, apprehension, enthusiasm, boredom, frustration, elation, achievement, failure, success.

I am currently doing a course in Personal Construct Psychology and I am learning as much about myself as a learner and group member as I am about the subject of PCP. I have found that I can easily disable myself and think that I cannot understand things unless they are very clearly explained. I have found that I learn best when examples are given and techniques demonstrated and where there is the opportunity to practise both in the large group as a whole, and in smaller groups or with a partner. I have found that I can get silly or even disruptive if I am bored or if I cannot understand what we have to do. I have found that I allow myself to get blocked by theories such as PCP if the language is difficult. My professional development on this course is both as a counsellor using PCP and as a trainer who will now be more sensitised to the experiences of my learners.

There is an annual conference in the UK called SCATS – the Standing Conference on Training and Supervision. It is a conference for those who learn well from a programme with plenty of optional workshops offered by trainers from varied training backgrounds and settings. The International Round Table for the Advancement of Counselling (IRTAC) organises an international conference each year and provides a useful international forum for sharing ideas in counselling on such themes as the family. There are also plenty of other conferences and summer schools organised by individuals or groups including the annual counselling Summer School at York which always has a programme for counsellor trainers and for supervisors. For updating from the major professional body for counsellors, there is the annual conference of the BAC.

NETWORKING AND COLLABORATIVE RELATIONSHIPS

People often go to courses and conferences with the main aim of networking. The fact that many counsellor trainers work part-time as trainers and part-time as counsellors means that there may be several networks represented in a training team. Another useful way of networking is through collaborative partnerships with other training organisations or courses. It has already been stated that this is a requirement for courses which have been recognised by BAC. It also happens where one organisation looks to another for validation of a counselling course and they enter into a relationship based on franchising. It is also worthwhile to develop such collaborative partnerships on an informal basis, perhaps with others in the same region, or training sector, or specialism.

EXTERNAL MODERATION, EXAMINING OR CONSULTANCY

Work which involves examining or consultancy may occur as a result of recommendation. There will be a growing need for trainers who are qualified to exercise these roles, as the number of courses increases. Such work provides a very good opportunity for becoming familiar with standards achieved in other institutions and organisations. In terms of professional development, it is a marvellous opportunity to work with other training teams, to learn different ways of delivering counselling training and to fine-tune skills of assessment and reporting.

RESEARCH

Research is not for everybody but there are many ways to do research, and at its most basic level it is something with which every trainer needs to engage. I am advocating an orientation to research which asks questions and which seeks to find answers by examining data and by reflecting upon the results thrown up by the data. It is to be hoped that we continually engage in monitoring and evaluation of our work. That can be a reactive approach, a way of checking on things as they are happening and after they have happened. Research is proactive, and is usually the result of reflection upon previous events or information which causes us to want more information, to draw up significant questions, to test these questions in real live training or counselling situations, to check the data obtained from the live situation with what is known through the counselling or training literature, to arrive at results or further questions and to make tentative interpretations about their meaning.

The counselling field lacks adequate research and for trainers the problem may be that we are so busy 'doing' that we have no time for researching. If this is important, then perhaps we need to be more active in finding ways in which we could find more time for reflection and research. I sometimes say that I need time and space in order to be able to engage in research and that it isn't just physical space, but psychological space that I need. In other words, I need to be freed from some of the everyday pressures and demands. Feeling that it is all right to ask for such space is difficult and some of us are hesitant to ask for something for ourselves. Being able to grasp the moment can also be difficult because deciding to do some research is one thing, but managing to get started is another hurdle. The development of the counselling profession will depend in some measure on good quality research and who better to engage in this than those who are training the next generation of counsellors.

WRITING, PUBLISHING AND DISSEMINATING

Some trainers are able to write and some may feel that they are not. However, there are many ways in which ideas can be disseminated, and offering to present a short paper at a conference, meeting or seminar can be a realistic amount of work for busy trainers who could not possibly embark on anything longer. It may also be possible to publish internally, within a training organisation, so that the expertise of trainers is disseminated in some way in the written form. As a first-time author there were many moments when the task seemed impossible and when I felt inadequate in the face of it. I was surprised to find out what I actually knew, in the process of writing it down, and the exercise of having to do this for other readers has clarified my own thinking about training on several fronts. In that sense it has been a powerful aid to my own professional development as a counsellor trainer.

Counselling training is a privilege, offering a unique opportunity to accompany trainee counsellors on their learning journey of growth and change. We will offer them most if we look after our own development so that we bring to the training situation energy, enthusiasm and excitement. Our hope will be that we are helping the next generation of counsellors to be reflective, competent and wise.

It seems fitting to finish this book with the story of one trainee, Joanna, whose learning journal I read in my role as external examiner. She willingly gave permission for this extract to be shared with others and it is a reminder to us as trainers, that we share with our trainees in what is often one of the most profound experiences of their lives.

JOANNA

My performing days are over . . .

I don't go through hoops anymore. The contortions have stopped. Even the rackets (racquets) are consigned to the bin. I have not left the circus, nor dropped out of a regime to attain physical fitness. Instead I have experienced more healthy development and growth than the most strenuous exercise programme could have provided. Like a demanding exercise programme, it has not been without pain and discomfort, but the rewards have far exceeeded anything I could have imagined. To mix metaphors still further, I have been on the most challenging and exciting journey of my life: the journey to myself and thence to others. There were times when I felt like the early explorers must have – any nearer the edge, and over I would fall into oblivion. But I never did, because almost from the beginning (specifically after the first residential weekend), when the risks were greatest, I had with me a group of people with whom I shared more trust and unconditional love than I have ever experienced collectively before. To someone outside the group I guess that might sound very twee – even nauseous – given today's cynicism. Although even I had clung grimly to the hope that that kind of caring did exist among my fellow human beings, the events of my life and those who had populated them had hardly reinforced my hopes.

How can I review the last two years in a few words when the demons and insecurities of the previous forty-two were (for the most part) successfully confronted and challenged – no longer afforded the power to influence me in the negative ways of my past? I have ceased to be the 'performer', either hiding for protection behind a thick self-built wall, or twisting and turning and trying to be all things to all people in the misconceived belief that that would gain me love and respect. Actually, I was very successful in my masquerade: Oscar material. The projected image was pretty convincing. In my previous life (!!) I have been described, variously, as confident, distant, tough and even fierce. I discovered after a gestalt exercise during the second residential that my 'power shoulders' had even caused a frisson of apprehension in Rik (my tutor), rekindling messages from students past. Pretty convincing stuff! Not so on the inside. During the 'difficult weeks' when the predictions and warnings that 'A Counselling Course Can Seriously Damage Your Relationship' were becoming disturbingly accurate and I was beginning to change as I found who I really was, my partner frequently reminded me I used to be a frightened little rabbit (and that maybe I was nicer that way) and that now I had become a 'self-opinionated man-hater' (I was researching an essay on misogyny at the time, and coming face to face with enormous sections of my past). The changes in me rocked lots of boats, some perilously near to capsize.

In doing so I probably learned the greatest lesson. Enforced change is frightening, but change creates change. Action initiates reaction. Although change had figured in my past, I had generally approached it from the wrong directions. I had tried desperately to change/rescue/influence individuals who did not conform to my rigid expectations and ideals that had been enforced during my early years by trying to be what 'they' wanted 'me' to be, in turn believing 'they' would then be what 'I' wanted them to be. I know now, and have proved, that the only person I can change is me, but through those changes (my choices, my wishes) inevitably those around me react and, on occasion, change too. Learning to stand firmly by my changes (because they feel right, because I have learned to trust and respect my own judgements, my own gut feelings, and not be intimidated into falling back into old compliant habits) has created tensions and difficulties – angry exchanges which previously I would have let lead me to back down through extreme discomfort at being in confrontational, sometimes aggressive situations.

But it does get easier. My relationships with all those close to me are clearer, and because of that, more valuable. I have become accepting of all sides of their natures. I would never have thought of myself as judgemental until exercises and experiences within the group gave me the opportunity to recognise, and more importantly deal with, prejudices and misconceptions of which I had been hitherto unaware. The general consensus, now that the process of change for us all has slowed after its initial shock and early momentum, is that I am now calmer and less inclined to become stressed by situations over which I have no control anyway! I 'go with the flow' and hence the racketing pattern which dogged my days has been identified and dealt with. I still have one significant demon to beat, but I know that I will. I have just begun to explore NLP, and I believe it could hold the key.

What has been so exciting about the course? Just when I thought, like Mr Punch, 'ah, that's the way to do it', another model, another theory is there to explore and each in its own way rings bells, works its way into secret corners, making me think 'yes, that's me, I've been there', and offers other avenues to explore in the process of self-discovery. This exploration was, and is, for me glorious. However, it is some twenty years since I trained as a teacher and in a position that required intensive academic study. I realised that I may be rusty and I definitely realised early on that the work required was very different in its approach: everything I had done before had to be very objectively written. At first I found the self-reflectivity required for written work very hard because it contradicted all the rules that had been drummed in at school and college (and home, 'self indulgence also damages your health!'). The books, however, were wonderful. I had forgotten the hunger I had for the written word. I voraciously devoured it all to the point where 'my' written words took a decidedly backward position. As I researched my first essay, one book's bibliography catapulted on to the next . . . and the next . . . and the next, until I realised that I had to put a limit on it, otherwise I would go on amassing material and never put pen to paper. As it was I found it impossible to abridge my essays as I developed my ideas and theories. It all became a great panic towards the end, to get everything finished because throughout there was always the nagging doubt that a few days hence something else which was highly relevant would appear. It is a hard decision to make.

The suggestion to keep a diary to facilitate this piece of work was an excellent theory. In practice, it has become a huge volume of jottings which I shall always retain because it encapsulates the mirror

I have held to myself along the way. The memories are many – among them, and probably most significantly, the two residential weekends when so much was shared, so many barriers dissolved, so much discovery occurred. I wish we could have had more opportunities to spend longer blocks of time together, for although our Thursday sessions provided wonderful opportunities to share, the strength, and love and courage that was generated when we were not governed as stringently by the clock, was inspiring. I remember the sense of loss as I drove away on both occasions, and especially the thought process as I drove to work on the Monday following the second weekend. I really wished I had been able to take the day off, because I didn't want to return to the 'real world'. Immediately, though, I realised that where I had been was in fact real (no pretence, no manipulation, no dilution or dismissal of feelings), and where I was going was back to a world populated by those whose behaviour, in the vast majority of cases, was dictated by the scars they carried with little hope of ever dealing with them and realising their true potential.

I remember the exercises we did as a group when exploring Psychodrama: lying head to head in a circle – embarrassed at first and uncomfortable – and then feeling the power of each individual and the group as a whole, as we reached inside for feelings and reactions to put into words. We had been together for nearly two years, and had shared many things, yet that evening drew me closer as memories and emotions were voiced. It also made me aware that in some ways, the parting was near. I know that several of us will stay close, but I recognise that realistically, some have to drift away. That makes me sad, and yet I know that the time spent together, albeit a very small part of a lifetime, has shaped my future.

It is a future I face now without fear, bitterness and resentment. I have taken responsibility for my own life. I know I am a valuable human being (I don't just kid myself – and others – that I am!). I know I now have the tools to deal with anything that life chooses to throw at me. I recognise that I may not always get it right, but that does not actually matter, as long as *I do something and the something is MINE*. The same philosophy applies in my relationships with others. I have already seen how much more positive the results can be when prejudice and imperatives are removed from the equation. Just as I have come to understand what has motivated (and undermined) me until now, I am also driven to understand the reasons why others behave as they do. As a result much hatred and bitterness and resentment have gone, taking with them a great weight. This ability to recognise how complex a script we all have to master enables me to try to 'love the sinner, hate the sin' (but it is not always easy!!).

I am full of enthusiasm for counselling but even if I never counselled again, the experiences and the skills, and the sheer adventure of the last two years would be enough. The friends I have, the support I have been given, the love I share, and the growth as a result cannot be quantified. I wish that such opportunities were mandatory, because I firmly believe that everyone would find their lives and their position in the overall scheme of things would have much greater meaning. It has truly been the most amazing two years of my life.

Bibliography

Adler, G. (1983) 'Jung, Carl Gustav', in A. Bullock and R. B. Woodings (eds), *The Fontana Dictionary of Modern Thinkers*, London: Fontana.

Agazarian, Y. and Peters, R. (1989) *The Visible and Invisible Group: Two Perspectives on Group Psychotherapy and Group Process*, London: International Library, Routledge.

Arbeitman, D. A. (1984) 'The interrelationship, measurement and teaching of affective sensitivity and empathic communication: an experimental study', unpublished doctoral dissertation, Cornell University.

Authier, J. and Gustafson, K. (1976) 'The application of supervised and non-supervised microcounselling paradigms in the training of registered and licensed practical nurses', *Journal of Consulting and Clinical Psychology* 44: 704–9.

—— and —— (1982) 'Microtraining: focusing on specific skills', in E. K. Marshall and P. D. Kurtz, *Interpersonal and Helping Skills*, San Francisco: Jossey-Bass.

BAC (British Association for Counselling) (1985) *Code of Ethics and Practice for Trainers*, Rugby: BAC.

—— (1988) *The Recognition of Counsellor Training Courses*, Rugby: BAC.

—— (1989) *Code of Ethics and Practice for Counselling Skills*, Rugby: BAC.

—— (1990) *The Recognition of Counsellor Training Courses* (2nd edn), Rugby: BAC.

—— (1993) *Code of Ethics and Practice for Counsellors*, Rugby: BAC.

Bailey, K. G., Deardoff, P. and Way, W. R. (1977) 'Students play therapists: relation effects of role playing videotape feedback and modeling in a simulated interview, *Journal of Counseling and Clinical Psychology* 45: 257–66.

Baker, S. and Daniels, T. (1989) 'Integrating research on the microcounseling program: a meta-analysis', *Journal of Counseling Psychology* 36: 213–22.

Bandura, A. (1969) *Principles of Behavior Modification*, New York: Holt, Rinehart & Winston.

—— (1971) *Psychological Modeling: Conflicting Theories*, Chicago: Aldine-Atherton.

—— (1977) *Social Learning Theory*, Englewood Cliffs, New Jersey: Prentice-Hall.

Bartlett, W. E. (1983) 'A multidimensional framework for the analysis of supervision in counseling', *The Counseling Psychologist* 11 (1): 9–18.

Battye, R. (1991) 'On being a trainee', in W. Dryden and B. Thorne (eds), *Training and Supervision for Counselling in Action*, London: Sage.

Beauchamp, T. L. and Childress, J. F. (1979) *Principles of Biomedical Ethics* (3rd edn), New York: Oxford University Press.

Beck, A. T. (1976) *Cognitive Therapy and the Emotional Disorders*, New York: New American Library.

Bentham, J. (1970) *The Collected Works of Jeremy Bentham. An Introduction to the Principles of Morals and Legislation* ed. J. H. Burns and L. A. Hart, London: Athlone Press.

Berne, E. (1972) *What Do You Say After You Say Hello?* New York: Grove Press.

—— (1987) *Games People Play: The Psychology of Human Relationships*, London: Penguin.

Bion, W. R. (1961) *Experiences in Groups*, London: Tavistock.

Bohart, A. C. and Todd, J. (1988) *Foundations of Clinical and Counselling Psychology*, New York: Harper & Row.

Bond, T. (1992) 'Confidentiality: counselling, ethics and the law', *Employee Counselling Today* 4 (4): 4–9.

—— (1993) *Standards and Ethics for Counselling in Action*, London: Sage.

Boud, D. (1988) *Developing Student Autonomy in Learning*, London: Kogan Page.

Brandes, D. and Ginnis, P. (1986) *A Guide to Student-Centred Learning*, Oxford: Blackwell.

Braude, M. (ed.) (1987) *Women, Power and Therapy*, New York: Haworth Press.

Bromley, E. (1983) 'Social class issues in psychotherapy', in D. Pilgrim (ed.), *Psychology and Psychotherapy: Current Issues and Trends*, London: Routledge.

Bryer, J. W. and Egan, G. (1979) *Training the Skilled Helper*, Monterey, California: Brooks Cole.

Buczek, T. A. (1981) 'Sex biases in counseling: counselor retention of the concerns of a female and male client', *Journal of Counseling Psychology* 28: 13–21.

Bullock, A. (1988) *The Fontana Dictionary of Modern Thought*, London: Fontana.

Burns, R. (1982) *Self Concept Development and Education*, London: Holt, Rinehart & Winston.

Callender, C. (1992) 'Will NVQ's work?', *Training Tomorrow*, November, 21.

Campbell, Kagan and Krathwohl (1971) in Arbeitman (1984).

Carkhuff, R. R. (1969) *Helping and Human Relations*, Vols I and II, New York: Holt, Rinehart & Winston.

Carkhuff, R. R. and Berenson B. R. (1967) *Beyond Counseling and Therapy*, New: York: Holt, Rinehart & Winston.

Casement, P. (1985) *On Learning from the Patient*, London: Tavistock.
Cattell, R. B., Sealy, A. P. and Sweeney, A. B. (1966) 'What can personality and motivation source trait measurement add to the prediction of school achievement?', *British Journal of Educational Psychology* 36: 280–95.
Chaplin, J. (1992) *Feminist Counselling in Action*, London: Sage.
Cicourel, A. V. and Kitsuse, J. I. (1963) *The Educational Decision Makers*, New York: Bobbs Merrill.
Cohen, K. (1992) 'Some Legal Issues in Counselling and Psychotherapy', *British Journal of Guidance and Counselling* 20 (1): 10–26.
Combs, A. W. and Soper, D. W. (1963) 'The relationship of child perceptions to achievement and behavior in the early school years', Cooperative Research Project 814, University of Florida.
Connor, M. (1986) 'Training in counselling', unpublished doctoral thesis, University of Keele.
Connor, M., Dexter, G. and Wash, M. (1984) *Listening and Responding: Communication Skills in Nursing Care*, York: College of Ripon and York St John.
Corey, G. (1986) *Theory and Practice of Counseling and Psychotherapy*, Monterey, California: Brooks Cole.
Corey, M. S. and Corey G. (1989) *Becoming a Helper*, Monterey, California: Brooks Cole.
Counselling and Consultancy Unit (1993) Unpublished Guidelines for the Advanced Diploma in Counselling, University College of Ripon and York St John.
Delamont, S. (1980) *Sex.Roles and the School*, London: Methuen.
Dewey, J. (1916) *Education and Democracy*, New York: The Free Press.
Doster, J. (1972) 'Effects of instructions, modeling and role rehearsal on interview verbal behaviour, *Journal of Consulting and Clinical Psychology* 39: 202–9.
Dryden, W., Charles-Edwards, D. and Woolfe, R. (eds) (1989) *Handbook of Counselling in Britain*, London: Tavistock Routledge.
Durkheim, E. (1956) *Education and Sociology*, New York: The Free Press.
Egan, G. (1975, 1986; 1st and 3rd edns) *The Skilled Helper*, Monterey California: Brooks Cole.
—— (1990, 1993; 4th and 5th edns) *The Skilled Helper*, Pacific Grove California: Brooks Cole.
Egan, G. and Cowan, M. (1979) *People in Systems: A Model for Development in the Human Service Professions and Education*, Monterey, California: Brooks Cole.
Ekstein, R. and Wallerstein, R .S. (1972) *The Teaching and Learning of Psychotherapy*, Madison Connecticut: International Universities Press.
Ellis, A. (1985) *Overcoming Resistance: Rational Emotive Therapy with Difficult Clients*, New York: Springer.
English, R. W. and Jelenevsky, S. (1971) 'Counselor behavior as judged under audio, visual and audiovisual communication conditions', *Journal of Counseling Psychology* 18: 509–13.
Erikson, E. H. (1965) *Childhood and Society*, Harmondsworth: Penguin.
—— (1982) *The Life Cycle Completed*, New York: Norton.

Fairbairn, W. R. D. (1952) *Psychoanalytic Studies of the Personality*, London: Routledge & Kegan Paul.

Flanders, N. A. (1970) *Analysing Teaching Behavior*, New York: Addison-Wesley.

Frankel, M. (1971) 'Effects of videotape modeling and self-confrontation techniques on microcounseling behaviour', *Journal of Counseling Psychology* 18: 465–71.

Frazier, P. A. and Cohen, B. B. (1992) 'Research on the sexual victimization of women: implications for counselor training', *The Counseling Psychologist* 20: 141–58.

Freire, P. (1974) *Education: The Practice of Freedom*, London: Sheed & Ward.

Freud, S. (1949) *An Outline of Psychoanalysis*, New York: Norton.

Gallagher, M. (1993) 'Evaluation of an integrative approach to training paraprofessionals in counselling using the problem solving inventory', *Counselling Psychology Quarterly* 6 (1): 27–38.

Garfield, S. L. and Bergin, A. E. (1986) *Handbook of Psychotherapy and Behavior Change*, New York: Wiley.

Gilbert, T. F. (1978) *Human Competence: Engineering Worthy Performance*, New York: McGraw-Hill.

Gilmore, S. (1973) *The Counselor in Training*, Englewood Cliffs, New Jersey: Prentice-Hall.

Goffman, E. (1961) *Encounters: Two Studies in the Sociology of Interaction*, Indianapolis: Bobbs-Merrill.

Goncalves, O. F., Ivey, A. E. and Langdell, S. (1988) 'The multilevel conception of intentionality: implications for counselor training', *Counselling Psychology Quarterly* 1 (4): 377–86.

Gustafson, K. and Authier, J. (1976) 'Marathon versus weekly enriching intimacy skills training for physician assistants', unpublished paper, University of Nebraska Medical Centre, Omaha.

Gutierrez, L. M. (1992) 'Empowering ethnic minorities in the twenty-first century: the role of human service organizations' in Y. Hasenfeld (ed.), *Human Services at Complex Organizations*, London: Sage.

Guttman, M. A. (1973) 'Reduction of the defensive behavior of counselor trainees during counseling supervision', *Counselor Education and Supervision*, 10: 16–22.

Haase, R., DiMattia, D. and Guttman, M. A. (1972) 'Training of support personnel in three human relations skills: a systematic one year follow-up', *Counselor Education and Supervision* 11: 194–9.

Halmos, P. (1982) 'The faith of the counsellors', in A. W. Bolger (ed.), *Counselling in Britain*, London: Batsford.

Hargie, O. D. W. (1988) 'From teaching to counselling: an evaluation of the role of microcounselling in the training of school counsellors', *Counselling Psychology Quarterly* 1: 377–86.

Hargie, O. D. W. and Saunders, C. Y. M. (1983) 'Individual differences and social skills training', in R. Ellis and D. Whittington (eds), *New Directions in Social Skills Training*, London: Croom Helm.

Hatcher, C., Brooks, B. and Associates (1978) *Innovations in Counseling Psychology*, San Francisco: Jossey Bass.

Hayman, M. J. (1977) 'The influence of supervisor feedback in the microcounseling format', unpublished doctoral dissertation, State Ball University.

Hearn, M. (1976) 'Three modes of training counselors: a comparative study', unpublished dissertation, University of Western Ontario.

Held, B. S. (1984) 'Towards a strategic eclecticism: a proposal', *Psychotherapy* 21: 232–41.

Heppner, P. P. and Roehlke, A. J. (1984) 'Differences among supervisees at different levels of training: implications for a developmental model of supervision', *Journal of Counseling Psychology* 31 (1): 76–90.

Heron, J (1988) 'Assessment revisited', in Boud (1988).

Herr, E. L. (1978) 'Does counselling work?', *International Journal for the Advancement of Counseling* 1 (2).

Hilgard, E. R. and Atkinson, R. C. (1967) *Introduction to Psychology*, New York: Harcourt, Brace & World.

Holland, S. (1979) 'The development of an action and counselling service in a deprived urban area', in M. Meacher (ed.), *New Methods of Mental Health Care*, London: Pergamon.

Honey, P. and Mumford, A. (1984) *A Manual of Learning Styles*, Maidenhead: McGraw Hill.

Hopson, B. and Scally, M. (1981) *Lifeskills Teaching*, London: McGraw Hill.

Hosford, R. E. (1980) 'Self as a model: a cognitive social learning technique', *The Counseling Psychologist* 9 (1): 45–62.

Ivey, A. E. (1971) *Microcounseling: Innovations in Interviewing Training*, Springfield, Illinois: Charles Thomas.

Ivey, A. E., Normington, C., Miller, C., Morrill, W. and Haase, R. (1968) 'Microcounseling and attending behavior: an approach to pre-practicum counselor training', *Journal of Counseling Psychology* 15 (2): 1–12.

Ivey, A. E. and Authier, J. (1971) *Microcounseling*, 2nd edn, Springfield, Illinois: Charles Thomas.

Ivey, A. E. and Simek-Downing, L. (1980) *Counseling and Psychotherapy: Skills, Theories and Practice*, Englewood Cliffs, New Jersey: Prentice-Hall

Jacobs, M. (1986) *The Presenting Past*, London: Harper & Row.

—— (1989) *Psychodynamic Counselling in Action*, London: Sage.

Jarvis, P. (1985) *Adult and Continuing Education*, Kent: Croom Helm.

Jersild, A. T. (1955) *When Teachers Face Themselves*, Columbia: Teachers College Press.

Johnston, R. and Sampson, M. (1993) 'The acceptable face of competence', *Management Education and Development* 24 (3): 216–24.

Jung, C. (1968) 'The archetypes and the collective unconscious', in *Collected Works*, 2nd edn, vol. 9, Part 1, London: Routledge & Kegan Paul.

Kagan, N. (1967) *Studies in Human Interaction: Interpersonal Process Recall Stimulated by Videotape*, Michigan: Education Publications.

Kalisch, B. J. (1971) 'An experiment in the development of empathy in nursing students', *Nursing Research* 20 (3): 202–9.

Kant, I. (1886) *The Metaphysic of Ethics*, trans. D. W. Semple, ed. H. Calderwood, Edinburgh: T. T. Clark.

Karpman, S. (1968) 'Fairy tales and script drama analysis', *Transactional Analysis Bulletin* 7 (26): 39–43.

Kasdorf, J. and Gustafson, K. (1978) 'Research related to microteaching', in Ivey and Authier (1971).

Kerrebrock, R. (1971) 'Application of the microcounseling method using videotape recordings, to the training of teachers in basic counseling techniques', unpublished doctoral thesis, University of Southern California.

Kitchener, K. S. (1984) 'Intuition, critical evaluation and ethical principles: the foundation for ethical decisions in counseling psychology', *The Counseling Psychologist*, 12: 43–55.

Knowles, M. S. (1984) *Andragogy in Action*, London: Jossey Bass.

Kolb, D. A. (1984) *Experiential Learning*, London: Prentice-Hall.

Kolb, D. A. and Fry, R. (1975) 'Towards an applied theory of experiential learning, in C. L. Cooper (ed.), *Theories of Group Processes*, London: Wiley.

Kurpius, D. J., Froehle, T. C. and Robinson, S .E. (1980) 'The effects of single and multiple models when teaching counseling interviewing behaviors', *Counselor Education and Supervision* 20: 29–36.

Kurtz, P. D., Marshall, E. K. and Banspach, S. W. (1985) 'Interpersonal skill training research: a twelve year review and analysis', *Counselor Education and Supervision*, March, 1985.

Lambert, M. J. (1989) 'The individual therapist's contribution to psychotherapy process and outcome', *Clinical Psychology Review* 9: 469–85.

LaMonica, E. L., Carew, K. and Winder, A. E. (1976) 'Empathy training as the major thrust of a staff development program', *Nursing Research* 25 (6): 447–51.

Layton, J. M. (1979) 'The use of modeling to teach empathy to nursing students', *Research in Nursing and Health* 2: 163–76.

Lea, C. (1986) 'From didactic to student-centred teaching', in Brandes and Ginnis (1986).

Luborsky, L., Crits-Christoph, P., Mintz, J. and Auerbach, A. (1988) *Who Will Benefit from Psychotherapy? Predicting Basic Outcomes*, New York: Basic Books.

McLeod, J. (1992a) 'Issues in the evaluation of counselling skills training courses', *Employee Counselling Today*, 4 (5): 14–19.

—— (1992b) 'What do we know about how best to assess counsellor competence?', *Counselling Psychology Quarterly* 5 (4): 359–72.

—— (1993) *An Introduction to Counselling*, Buckingham: Open University Press.

McLeod, J. and McLeod, J. (1993) 'The relationship between personal philosophy and effectiveness in counsellors', *Counselling Psychology*, 6 (2): 121–30.

Malikiosi-Loizos, M. and Gold, J. (1981) 'Differential supervision and cognitive structure effects on empathy and counseling effectiveness', *International Journal for the Advancement of Counseling* 4 (2): 119–29.

Markey, M. J., Frederickson, R. H., Johnson, R. W. and Julius, M. A.

(1970) 'Influence of playback techniques on counselor performance', *Counselor Education and Supervision* 9: 178–82.

Martin, J. (1990) 'Confusion in psychological skills training', *Journal of Counseling and Development* 68: 402–7.

Maslow, A. (1970) *Motivation and Personality*, rev. edn, New York: Harper & Row.

Masson, J. (1990) *Against Therapy*, London: Fontana.

Meichenbaum, D. (1977) *Cognitive Behavior Modification: An Integrative Approach*, New York: Plenum.

Minuchin, S. and Fishman, H. C. (1981) *Family Therapy Techniques*, Cambridge, Mass.: Harvard University Press.

Moreland, J., Phillips, J., Ivey, A. E. and Lockhart, J. (1970) 'A study of the microtraining paradigm with beginning clinical psychologists', unpublished paper, University of Massachusetts.

Moreland, J., Ivey, A. E. and Phillips, J. (1973) 'An evaluation of micro-counseling as an interviewer training tool', *Journal of Clinical and Counseling Psychology* 41: 294–300.

Newman, J. L. and Fuqua, D. R. (1988) 'A comparative study of positive and negative modeling in counsellor training', *Counselor Education and Supervision* 28: 121–9.

Oatley, K. (1984) *Selves in Relation*, London: Methuen.

Orlinsky, D. E. and Howard, K. I. (1986) 'Process and outcome in psychotherapy', in Garfield and Bergin (eds) (1986).

Page, S. and Wosket, V. (1994) *Supervising the Counsellor*, London: Routledge.

Pagell, W. A., Carkhuff, R. R. and Berenson, B. G. (1967) 'The predicted differential effects of the level of counselor functioning upon the level of functioning of outpatients', *Journal of Counseling Psychology* 23: 510–12.

Pates, A. and Knasel, E. (1989) 'Assessment of counselling skills development: the learning record', *British Journal of Guidance and Counselling* 17 (2): 121–32.

Patterson, C. H. (1985) *The Therapeutic Relationship: Foundations for an Eclectic Psychotherapy*, Pacific Grove, California: Brooks Cole.

Paul, G. L. (1967) 'Strategy of outcome research in psychotherapy', *Journal of Consulting Psychology* 31: 109–18.

Pendleton, D. and Furnham, A. (1979) 'A paradigm for applied social psychological research', in W. T. Singleton, P. Spurgeon and R. B. Stammers (eds), *The Analysis of Social Skill*, New York: Plenum.

Peters, R. S. (1972) 'Education and the educated man', in D. F. Dearden, P. H. Hirst and R. S. Peters, *A Critique of Current Educational Aims*, London: Routledge & Kegan Paul.

Piaget, J. (1952) *The Origins of Intelligence in Children*, New York: International Universities Press.

Proctor, B. (1978) *Counselling Shop*, London: Burnett Books/André Deutsch.

—— (1991) 'On being a trainer', in W. Dryden and B. Thorne (eds), *Training and Supervision for Counselling in Action*, London: Sage.

Purton, C. (1991) 'Selection and assessment in counsellor training courses', in W. Dryden and B. Thorne (eds), *Training and Supervision for Counselling in Action*, London: Sage.

Rachman, S. and Wilson, G. (1980) *The Effects of Psychological Therapy*, New York: Wiley.

Robertson, J. and Fitzgerald, I. F. (1990) 'The (mis)treatment of mini effects of client gender role and lifestyle on diagnosis and attribution of pathology', *Journal of Counseling Psychology*, 37: 3–9.

Robinson, S. E., Froehle, T. C. and Karpins, D. J. (1979) 'Effects of sex model and media of model presentation in skill development of counselor trainees', *Journal of Counseling Psychology*, 26: 74–80.

Robinson, S. E. and Cabianca, W. A. (1985) 'Effects of counselor's ordinal position when involved in role play practice in triads', *Counselor Education and Supervision* 25.

Rogers, C. R. (1957) 'The necessary and sufficient conditions of psychotherapeutic personality change', *Journal of Consulting Psychology* 21: 95–103.

—— (1961) *On Becoming a Person*, London: Constable.

—— (1983) *Freedom to Learn in the 80s*, Columbus, Ohio: Charles Merrill.

Ross, W. D. (1930) *The Right and The Good*, Oxford: Clarendon Press.

Rowntree, D. (1977) *Assessing Students: How Shall We Know Them?* London: Harper & Row.

Russell, J. (1993) *Out of Bounds*, London: Sage.

Russell, J. and Dexter, G. (1993) 'Ménage à trois; accreditation, NVQs and BAC', *Counselling* 4 (4): 266–9

Schwab, R. and Harris, T. L. (1984) 'Effects of audio and video recordings on evaluation of counselling interviews', *Educational and Psychological Research* 4 (2): 57–65.

Sexton, T. L. and Whiston, S. C. (1991) 'A review of the empirical basis for counseling: implications for practice and training', *Counselor Education and Supervision* 30: 330–54.

Small, J. J. and Manthei, R. J. (1988) 'Group work in counsellor training: research and development in one programme', *British Journal of Guidance and Counselling* 16 (1): 33–49.

Steinaker, N. W. and Bell, R. M. (1979) *The Experiential Taxonomy*, New York: Academic Press.

Steiner, C. (1974) *Scripts People Live: Transactional Analysis of Life Scripts*, New York: Grove Press.

Stone, G. (1982) 'Evaluating the effectiveness of skills training programs', in E. K. Marshall and P. B. Kurtz, *Interpersonal Helping Skills*, San Francisco: Jossey-Bass.

Strong, S. R. (1968) 'Counseling: an interpersonal influence process', *Journal of Counseling Psychology* 15: 215–24.

Strupp, H. H. (1980) 'Success and failure in time-limited psychotherapy. Further evidence: comparison 4', *Archives of General Psychiatry* 37: 947–54.

Thompson, A. (1990) *Guide to Ethical Practice in Psychotherapy*, New York: Wiley

Thompson, J. R. (1987) *The Process of Psychotherapy*, Lanham, Maryland: University Press of America.

Thompson, M. (1976) 'A study of the effect of having a trainee co-counsel with a live model during a microcounseling practice session', unpublished doctoral thesis, University of Minnesota.

Thorne, B. (1991) 'Key issues in the training of counsellors', in W. Dryden, *Dryden on Counselling* vol. 3, *Training and Supervision*, London: Whurr.

Toukmanian, S. and Rennie, D. (1975) 'Microcounseling versus human relations training: relative efffectiveness with undergraduate trainees', *Journal of Counseling Psychology* 22: 315–52.

Truax, C. B. and Carkhuff, R. R. (1967) *Towards Effective Counseling and Psychotherapy: Training and Practice*, New York: Aldine.

Tuckman, R. W. (1965) 'Developmental sequences in small groups', *Psychological Bulletin*, 63: 384–99.

Wade, P. and Bernstein, B. L. (1991) 'Cultural sensitivity training and counsellors' race: effects on black female clients' perceptions and attrition, *Journal of Counseling Psychology* 38: 9–15.

Watkins, C. E. and Schneider, L. J. (eds) (1991) *Research in Counseling*, Hove and London: Lawrence Erlbaum Associates.

Wells, P. (1993) Letter in *Counselling* 4 (4): 247.

Werner, H. (1961) *Comparative Psychology of Mental Development*, New York: Science Editions.

Wheeler, S. (1991) 'Personal therapy: an essential aspect of counsellor training, or a distraction from focussing on the client?', *International Journal for the Advancement of Counseling* 14: 193–202.

Whitaker, D. S. (1987) *Using Groups to Help People*, Individual Library of Group Psychotherapy and Group Process, London: Tavistock Routledge.

Whiteley, J. M., Sprinthall, N. A., Mosher, R. L. and Donaghy, R. T. (1967) 'Selection and evaluation of counselor effectiveness', *Journal of Counseling Psychology* 14: 226–34.

Winnicott, D. W. (1979) *The Maturational Processes and the Facilitating Environment: Studies in the Theory of Emotional Development*, London: Hogarth.

Wolfe, B. E. and Goldfried, M. R. (1988) 'Research on psychotherapy integration: recommendations and conclusions from an NIMH workshop', *Journal of Consulting and Clinical Psychology* 56: 448–51.

Woolfe, R. and Sugarman, L. (1989) 'Counselling and the life cycle', in Dryden *et al.* (1989).

Wosket, V. and Kennett, C. (1993) Course Guidelines for the Advanced Diploma in Counselling, University College of Ripon and York St John.

Yalom, I. D. (1980) *Existential Psychotherapy*, New York: Basic Books.

Yenawine, G. and Arbuckle, D. S. (1971) 'Study of the use of videotape and audiotape as techniques in counselor education', *Journal of Counseling Psychology* 18: 1–6.

Name index

Subject index

£12.99